# Social Theory in a Changing World

# Social Theory in a Changing World

*Conceptions of Modernity*

## Gerard Delanty

Polity Press

First published in 1999 by Polity Press
in association with Blackwell Publishers Ltd.

*Editorial office:*
Polity Press
65 Bridge Street
Cambridge CB2 1UR, UK

*Marketing and production:*
Blackwell Publishers Ltd
108 Cowley Road
Oxford OX4 1JF, UK

*Published in the USA by*
Blackwell Publishers Inc.
Commerce Place
350 Main Street
Malden, MA 02148, USA

ISBN 0-7456-1917-7
ISBN 0-7456-1918-5 (pbk)

A catalogue record for this book is available from the British Library and has been applied for from the Library of Congress.

Typeset in 10½ on 12 pt Palatino
by Ace Filmsetting Ltd, Frome, Somerset
Printed in Great Britain by MPG Books Ltd, Bodmin, Cornwall

This book is printed on acid-free paper.

# Contents

*Acknowledgements*                                                vii

**Introduction**                                                    1
   The Central Conflict of Modernity                                5
   Knowledge and Culture                                            9
   Towards a Cognitive Approach                                    13

**1  Defining Modernity: The Quest for Autonomy**                  17
   Introduction                                                    17
   Modernity's Three Logics of Development                         19
   Integration and Differentiation                                 27
   Conclusion: The Time-Consciousness of Modernity                 38

**2  The Limits of Modernity: From Autonomy to
   Fragmentation**                                                 42
   Introduction                                                    42
   Rethinking Modernity                                            45
   Autonomy versus Fragmentation: The Loss of Unity                50
   Beyond the Classical Tradition: Contemporary
      Theories of the Social                                       61
   Conclusion: Towards a New Time-Consciousness                    70

**3  Discourse and Democracy: Habermas's
   Theory of Modernity**                                           73
   Introduction                                                    73
   The Problem of Democracy                                        74

The Formation of Habermas's Social Theory 79
Rescuing Discourse: The Mediation of Democracy
    and Law 87
Discursive Democracy in the Global Public Sphere 93
The Question of Culture and Identity 95
Conclusion: Culture and Discourse 98

**4 Creativity and the Rise of Social Postmodernism:
Foucault, Lyotard and Bauman** 100
Introduction 100
From Deconstructionism to Constructivism 102
Bauman: Ethics and Postmodernity 115
Conclusion: Beyond Postmodernism 120

**5 The Return of Agency: Touraine and Melucci** 122
Introduction 122
Touraine: From Historicity to the End of the Social 123
Melucci: Culture, Identity and Change 140
Conclusion: Reflexivity and Democracy 146

**6 Reflexive Modernization: Beck and Giddens** 148
Introduction 148
Beck and the Risk Society 149
Giddens: Modernity, Reflexivity and Trust 160
Assessing Reflexive Modernization: The Question
    of Culture 170
Conclusion: Reflexivity and Discourse 177

**Conclusion: Knowledge, Democracy and Discursive
Institutionalization** 179

*Notes* 188
*Bibliography* 194
*Index* 209

# Acknowledgements

I wish to acknowledge the helpful comments of three referees consulted by Polity Press, Lynn Dunlop, Sarah Dancy and John Thompson of Polity Press and several graduate students at the University of Liverpool, in particular Rachel Cutler and Heidi Granger for reading an advanced draft. I am also grateful to Anthony Giddens for advice on the book at its initial stage and to Piet Strydom for reading and commenting on preliminary versions of the book. I would like to acknowledge exchanges with William Outhwaite and Peter Wagner, whose ESRC seminar series on social theory has been a useful forum for presenting some of the ideas in this book, and dialogues with John O'Neill, Engin Isen, Tom Wilson and Jos Lennards of York University, Toronto. Nobody but the author is responsible for the finished product.

# Introduction

This book explores the theory of modernity in the writings of key contemporary social theorists, in particular Habermas, Foucault, Lyotard, Bauman, Touraine, Beck and Giddens. Since the early 1980s the idea of modernity has become one of the central thematic concerns of a whole range of social and political scientists, constituting a framework for theorizing about society, culture and politics. This is of course not new for modernity has been one of the great dominating themes in social and political thought since the Enlightenment. In one way or another the idea of modernity has always provided an intellectual and historical frame of reference for many thinkers to reflect on the cultural specificity of their age and the direction of social change. It may be suggested that the motif of modernity encapsulated both a cultural idea – the project of the Enlightenment – and a particular civilizational complex, the European/western process of societal modernization. More specifically, we can say modernity entails a cultural project and a social project.

In recent times the idea of modernity in social theory has emerged from its position as a background notion into an explicitly defined concept challenging the hitherto dominant notions of industrial society and capitalism.[1] In general, mainstream liberal social science – with its functionalist and modernization bias – tended to favour the reduction of modernity to the institutional, or structural, processes of societal modernization, with Marxist social science favouring a similar emphasis on socio-economic processes, albeit from the perspective of class power. The idea of modernity as a cultural impulse was rarely related to the process of societal modernization,

and was frequently seen in conflict with it. Modernity, as a concept
in political philosophy and cultural theory, entailed a cultural process of self-renewal and transformation (Berman, 1982; Calinescu,
1987; Frisby, 1986; Rengger, 1995). Under the aegis of the avant-
garde, modernity as 'modernism' was in fact seen as revolting
against modern society (Bürger, 1984). With the break-up of the two
dominant models in modern sociology and the blurring of the disciplinary boundaries between cultural and aesthetic theory, political philosophy and social theory, we now can see more clearly that
modernity is both a cultural and philosophical idea as well as being
a statement about the nature of society more broadly. The notion of
modernity now seems to capture a certain sense of social transformation which is more than purely institutional or cultural but both
together.[2] Thus many authors stress the element of reflexivity in
modernity, or a certain propensity for cultural critique, moral learning and self-transformation (Bourdieu and Wacquant, 1992;
Calhoun, 1995; Szakloczai, 1998; Toulmin, 1992; Turner, S., 1996).
Despite the attempts of proponents of postmodernity to draw a
strict demarcation of a closed discourse of modernity from the open
horizon of postmodernity, modernity cannot be reduced to discourses of power and instrumentalism for it itself contains a reflexive moment, as William Outhwaite (1999) has argued. In this book I
will be emphasizing the discourses of reflexivity, creativity and
discursivity in order to capture the self-transformative impulse of
modernity.

What then is modernity? My central argument is that modernity, in the broadest sense of the term, can be seen as a tension
between autonomy and fragmentation – and since this conflict is
not over, we are still living in the age of modernity. On the one
side, modernity as a cultural project refers to the autonomy of the
Subject, the self-assertion of the self, or individual, and the progressive expansion of the discourses of creativity, reflexivity and
discursivity to all spheres of life. On the other side, modernity
entails the experience of fragmentation, the sense that modernity
as a social project destroys its own cultural foundations. Despite
this tension between the cultural and the social project of modernity, the self-understanding of modernity assumed a certain coherence in its dual nature. Even modernity's greatest critics, such
as Karl Marx, assumed that its cultural ideal (the belief in the
autonomy and emancipation of the Subject) could be reflected in
social reality in the overcoming of the discord between cultural
ideal and social reality. It was always Marx's contention that the
problem with bourgeois political and cultural modernity was that
its normative content was not realized in social relations. Today,

this tension in the two faces of modernity – the cultural impulse and its social project – is more pronounced than ever before. There is the suggestion that the social may be at an end, destroyed by endless fragmentations. If anything characterizes recent social theory it is the question of the possibilities for the autonomy of the subject under the conditions of the fragmentation of the social and the increasing loss of unity in modern society (Touraine, 1998a, 1998b). The social theory of modernity presupposed the unity and coherence of the social, whereas today the social is increasingly being seen as in crisis, if not at an end. Where this leaves the autonomy of the Subject is at best an open question, for one of the dominant traditions in the thought of the twentieth century – poststructuralism – has been the critique of the Subject and the very possibility of coherence (see Chapter 4). I am of the view that this movement is now at an end, having largely accomplished its objective – the relativization of identity and knowledge and the demonstration of the limits of the intellectual categories of the nineteenth century – and that we can therefore reopen the question of the Subject in the changed social and intellectual context of the twenty-first century: it is no longer a question of attacking false universalisms but of overcoming relativism and the fragmentation of the social.

To speak of modernity is thus to recognize the crisis of modernity. No sooner had the idea of modernity been born than the critique of modernity emerged. The early idea of critique, as in the critical philosophy of Immanuel Kant, referred simply to the critique of absolute knowledge and the belief of rationalistic philosophy that objective knowledge is possible. Critique for Kant entailed the demonstration of the limits of knowledge and as an Enlightenment construct it was mostly directed at the ancient authorities of Church and throne.[3] Modernity, as the self-consciousness of the Enlightenment, was self-evidently the emancipation of human beings from the prejudices of tradition. Modernity is thus defined by reference to the critique of tradition. In Kant's ([1784] 1995[4]) formulation modernity meant nothing less than the enlightenment of knowledge itself. The distinctive feature of modern knowledge for Kant was its autonomy; its ability to self-legislate and construct that which is to count as legitimate knowledge. The autonomy of knowledge reflected the autonomy of the Subject, who was self-reliant in matters of knowledge and morality. However, by the time of Hegel and Marx the critique of modernity emerges as a critique of the false promises of modernity, the growing discord between its cultural promise and its social reality. Yet, even in their writings modernity entails the promise of emancipation – the release of the historical subject from constraining structures. The political was to be the mediatory link between the cultural and the social project.[5]

In the *Philosophy of Right* [1821] Hegel demonstrated the incomplete realization of modern consciousness in civil society where an 'unhappy consciousness' prevails as a result of the fragmentation brought about by the relentless drive of capitalism and self-interest. In its quest for autonomy and recognition the modern consciousness seeks actuality in the higher domains of the state and is ultimately realizable, according to Hegel, in the domain of pure speculative thought. Hegel's disenchantment with the social was because he believed the condition of the social world to be fragmentation, which could only be an incomplete realization of the quest for autonomy. For this reason he abandoned his earlier ideas – as in *The System of Ethical Life* [1802/3] – on the inherently social nature of the modern project (Honneth, 1995a). With Hegel, the concept of fragmentation enters the discourses of modernity and the prospect of a political reconciliation is weakened, though not abandoned. Rejecting Hegel's political conservativeness and philosophical idealism, Marx proposed a critique of modernity that sought to realize autonomy in the social world itself, and thereby overcome the central conflict of modernity, the contradiction between ideal and reality. For Marx, autonomy entailed the political overcoming of alienation brought about by commodification as a result of capitalism and the release of human labour from the reified social relations of capitalism. Social actors, in the Marxian critique, must recover the autonomy of their action which is to be asserted in the political negation of the existing social structure. Modernity was seen as problematical by Marx and in need of a critique, which he termed the 'critique of political economy'. However, his critique of modernity was one that did not reject the basic cultural self-understanding of modernity – the autonomy of the Subject – but sought to realize it in a new social order.

Thus we may say that, by the time of Marx, modernity's critique of tradition began to be turned on to modernity itself, which was a project in need of completion. This position was of course a contrast to the reactionary conservatives of the age (de Maistre, de Bonald, Novalis, Burke, for instance) who advocated the rejection of cultural modernity and the retreat to the authority of tradition. Since Marx, the experience of modernity has been inseparable from a sense of crisis deriving from the loss of autonomy that has come with the fragmentation of the social. The social began to be seen not as realizing but as fragmenting the autonomy of the human Subject. But it was not until much later that the critique of modernity also targeted its critique at the Subject itself, calling into question the idea of autonomy and the belief that it could be realized with the aid of politics in a social order.

## The Central Conflict of Modernity

This sketch of the idea of modernity emphasizes its dual nature. Modernity expresses a deep ambivalence that lies at the core of modern society. This ambivalence can be said to be the sense that modernity entails a central conflict between two forces. I have emphasized the poles of autonomy and fragmentation as reflected in the discord between the cultural and social project of modernity. Others may emphasize the polarization of democracy and capitalism, the thesis of Johann Arnason (1997, p. 358), or the struggle of liberty and discipline, as Peter Wagner (1994) argues in his *Sociology of Modernity*. In my view, the concepts of autonomy and fragmentation express the wider experience of modernity and also allow us to theorize the continuities and discontinuities between modernity and postmodernity as a conflict between the social and the cultural projects of modernity, as I shall argue in subsequent chapters. Looking at modernity in this way enables us to reflect on the deep and ambivalent dualism that somehow sums up the modern project.

According to Cornelius Castoriadis, in his great work, the *Imaginary Institution of Society* ([1975] 1987), modernity entails a central conflict between the 'radical imagination' – which presents the image of a self-creating society of autonomous individuals – and the 'institutional imaginary' of capitalism with its penchant for rational and instrumental mastery of human being and objects. Similarly, Jürgen Habermas, in his *Theory of Communicative Action* ([1981] 1984, [1981] 1987a), sees the central conflict in modernity to be the struggle between instrumental rationality and communicative rationality, a conflict which is worked out in the encounter between life-world and system. Alain Touraine, too, in *Critique of Modernity* ([1992] 1995a), makes the revolt of the Subject from Reason the central theme and comes to the conclusion that today the domains of subjectivity (culture and social relations) and objectivity (economy and polity) have become utterly bifurcated; and, as a result, according to Touraine, the concept of the social, which presupposes a unifying principle, has been exhausted. According to Daniel Bell (1979) the culture of modernity is collapsing into a conflict between two cultural principles; the work ethic and the desire for leisure. More recently, Benjamin Barber (1996) has portrayed the current situation as one of a conflict between a globalized commercial culture and a religious fundamentalism. Finally, it may be remarked that Niklas Luhmann, in his *Observations on Modernity* ([1992] 1998), portrays modernity in terms of a paradoxical relationship between the observer and the world, a relationship which forces increasing contingency on the former, who retreats more and more into a constructivist world-view which is unable to bring about unity.

The classical figures of late nineteenth-century sociology saw modernity in much the same way. For Marx, as we have seen, the central conflict in modern society was between capital and labour, a conflict that existed alongside the broader conflict of cultural modernity versus the social reality of capitalist modernity. For Max Weber, modernity entailed a tension between instrumental rationalization (which is fashioning a uniform and bureaucratic world devoid of creativity and meaning) and cultural modernity, which though disenchanted retains a degree of autonomy. Like many cultural pessimists of his time, writing under the influence of Nietzsche and Schopenhauer, and who saw the *Zeitgeist* in terms of a conflict between culture and civilization, Weber believed modernity was in danger of becoming an 'iron cage'. In this spirit, Ferdinand Tönnies, too, saw modernity as a tension between the cohesive world of 'community', which is rooted in the authority of tradition, and the alienating and individualistic world of 'society', whose societal form is the contract and association. For Georg Simmel, modernity is expressed in the conflict between culture and society, the tendency for culture to become detached from the individual and become objectified in external societal forms, a tendency he called the 'tragedy of culture'. Emile Durkheim diagnosed the ills of modernity in terms of 'anomie', a theme epitomized in his great sociological treatise on suicide, and one which presaged the destruction the First World War was to bring. His sociology was an expression of a widely perceived malaise in European civic morality which he believed derived from the break-up of traditional forms of integration (which he termed mechanical solidarity) and the imperfect realization of genuinely modern forms of co-operative solidarity, which he called organic integration. For Freud the central conflict of modernity was represented by the struggle between the dark forces of the unconscious and the rule of the pleasure principle and, on the other side, the demands of the reality principle of civilization for repression. Finally, we may mention Norbert Elias's portrait of modernity as the imposition of the order of civilization on subjectivity: through state formation and the creation of the disciplined self, the forces of violence were progressively eradicated from the social. In general terms, then, by the early twentieth century modernity was the story of a central conflict between two principles, one signifying a cultural impulse deriving from the Enlightenment and the spirit of the American and French Revolutions and, the other, the sense of despair that the social reality of modern society may be making those lofty ideals impossible, or even undesirable. In a way this struggle was a reflection of the increasing recognition that the essentially liberal heritage of the Enlightenment – with its emphasis on the individual and autonomy – was not reflected in a social order in which intersubjectivity could thrive. The tension between these two tendencies can also be seen as the context for the shift from political theory (which was predominantly liberal) to social theory, which was born of the recognition that autonomy is essentially intersubjective, or social (Heilbron et al., 1998; Wagner, 1994). This shift was not direct: after the overly political conception of civil society in the early theories, a market-economistic conception of the social predominated, and when social theory eventually developed the social was already in decline.

Sociology and its concept of modernity were products of the 'great transformation' – to use Karl Polanyi's ([1944] 1980) famous term – of the late nineteenth century while having its origins in the European Enlightenment and its aftermath. It thus sought to reconcile the Enlightenment's sense of purpose with the feeling of crisis that had set in by the beginning of the twentieth century. This was the source of the dualism that the early sociologists bequeathed to subsequent generations and it is only today that we are emerging out of that epoch. Our world today is different from the *fin de siècle* of the founding fathers: as we enter the twenty-first century and a new millennium, the sense of change is less one of the ending of tradition than of the passing of the modern itself, or at least its fundamental questioning. The writings of the classics reveal a widespread sense of the crisis of modernity as having uprooted tradition with the uncertain, dynamic and instrumental world of modernity; yet, a modernity that, despite its ambivalences, was predominantly accepted as the carrier of autonomy. The sense of a discord between the cultural and the social project was one that did not require relinquishing the master theme of cultural modernity: the promise of emancipation through politics; in short the myth of progress or, in its Marxist variant, redemption through revolution. Yet, there is no doubt that as this discord grew, the belief that the central conflict of modernity could be overcome by a principle of unity – whether political or otherwise – became increasingly doubtful.

Nowhere was the fascination with the ambivalence of modernity more apparent than in the theme of the city in early sociology and modernist literature – as is testified by the works of Charles Baudelaire, Max Weber, Georg Simmel, James Joyce, Walter Benjamin and the early Chicago School. In their writings the culture of the city symbolized the emancipation of the modern individual and the emergence of new kinds of experience characterized by a certain fragmentation of form. However, it was never doubted that metropolitan subjects – the modern urban dweller, the socially up-rooted, the *flâneur*, the stranger – could impose their own form on the apparent fragmentation of experience, for consciousness could retain its synthetic powers. Today, that fascination with modernity and the city is more uncertain as a result of social change: the city has become a symbol of violence and cultural degeneration. For many, fragmentation has eaten into the heart of the city, under-mining the project of autonomy.

It is widely agreed that we are living in a global age and one no longer shaped by European modernity (Al-Azmeh, 1993; Eisenstadt, 1992; Turner, 1994). If modernity was the narrative of the Self – the assertion of the autonomy of the Subject – today, with the rise of a new politics of difference, it is a question of the Other. It may be suggested that the question of autonomy is being overtaken by the need for recognition.[6] In the context of multiculturalism a central conflict today is not just between the instrumentalism of capitalism or discipline versus a communicative or cultural life-world, but is one of intercultural understanding, which has pro-vided a new context for linking autonomy (the Self) to recognition (the Other) (Taylor, 1994). The identity of the Self is no longer that of the self-contained individual of nineteenth-century liberal theory or the intellectual of the *fin de siècle*, but an identity project constituted in discursive spaces and shaped by a whole range of social and cultural processes. The Self and its project of self-determination has also become inseparable from violence, which is all too often the attempt of the Self to determine the Other (de Vries and Weber, 1997). Max Weber's famous motif of the 'iron cage' of bureaucratic capitalism, which eliminated meaning and sensuality, is no longer an appropriate metaphor for an age that has witnessed the return of identity in many guises. With the rise of the new culture of inform-ation technology and the postmodern self, the 'iron cage' and the Protestant work ethic, which sustained an earlier capitalism, have collapsed, releasing, if we follow Daniel Bell (1979), a Self that is more defined by relations of consumption and information than of production and bureaucratic domination. What this all amounts to is that culture is no longer capable of providing a remedy against anarchy, as Matthew Arnold ([1869/1875] 1960) argued: culture has today become anarchic.

Contemporary societies are no longer defined by a dominant social actor or institution – churches, intellectuals, parties, movements – but by public discourse. Neither elites nor collective actors define 'the situation', which instead has become radically open. We are entering a period in which the specificity of 'the social' can no longer be defined in terms of a particular social actor which can impose its world-view on the rest of society. Previously, society was shaped by a central conflict between dominant actors who established themselves as elites – capitalists, nationalists, the political class, ideologists – and collective actors who opposed the power of elites in the name of a principle of opposition, be it solidarity, equality, justice, rights. Today, in the postmodern global age, there is no social actor in ascendancy; elites and radicals are no longer clearly distinguishable. The social movements of modernity have, to a degree, dissolved, their projects becoming partly diffused in new institutional contexts, and with the rise of new elites and radicals it is more appropriate to speak of a new anarchism of cultural forms. This also means that society cannot be defined by a particular institutional structure. We are living in a society that is not essentially 'capitalist', 'industrial', liberal democratic. As Piet Strydom (1999b) argues, the current situation can be characterized as a 'communication society' – that is, a society of competing counter-publics in which there is a high level of contingency. In sum, the notion of the autonomy of the Subject must be considered anew given the rise of different forms of social fragmentations, the anarchy of cultural models and the rise of new kinds of politics.

## Knowledge and Culture

I have argued that modernity entails a certain dualism, be it that between autonomy and fragmentation or a more elemental struggle between cultural and social modernity or, if one wished, democracy and capitalism, liberty and discipline. In the most general sense, this dualism is that of agency versus structure, the age-old debate in sociological theory between the priority of the individual and society. If this problem of dualism was fundamental to the experience of modernity, then it may be suggested that the problem of our time is one of mediation. In this book I shall be arguing that the reconceptualization of modernity in the works of the leading social theorists can be seen in terms of different attempts to find a solution to the essential problem of dualism in so far as this expresses the central conflict of modernity. This indeed has been the main task of Anthony Giddens's (1984) theory of structuration (see Chapter 6), the aim of which is to overcome the divide between agency and structure.

It is my contention – and in this I differ somewhat from Giddens – that the problem of mediation must be theorized in terms of a theory of culture. Agency and structure are mediated by culture, which is to be seen as a public system of communication. Thus, rather than see the problem of agency versus structure as one of a self-empowering agency versus a flexibly structured institution, it is a question of communicatively mediated competition. The notion of culture pre-supposed here is one that entails what I shall be calling cognitive (or discursive) practice (see Chapter 2 and Delanty, 1997c). A cognitive approach to culture is one that sees it as a form of knowledge, an interpretative framework which is also a form of action. Knowledge is not just a question of information, but is also a matter of experience and action. To that extent knowledge is highly discursive and conten-tious. One of my central arguments is that knowledge is becoming increasingly important as a medium through which the world is experienced and constitutes a form of mediation by which the dual-ism of modernity can be overcome. Culture is not just a system of values and norms, as an older sociology influenced by a conservative anthropology argued; nor is it reducible to ideology or false con-sciousness, as Marxists argued. In line with constructivist develop-ments in recent sociology, I am arguing that we can see culture as a communicatively structured form of social knowledge from which social actors draw and which is inseparable from their social prac-tices.[7] As such, culture is reflexive: it is shaped in the very process of communication through the discursive strategies of social actors. One of the most important dimensions to this is the contestability of knowledge claims.

Viewing culture as a form of mediation between agency and structure, we can make the further claim that it is transformative. Mediation – to draw from an idea of Adorno (1973, 1984) after Hegel and Marx – is a dialectical process of transformation. A basic idea of the dialectic is that in the movement and encounter of subject and object both terms are transformed. Relating this to culture we can say that cultural models provide the means of trans-formation; they are dynamic and always in tension with the social order, providing social actors with resources for their projects and transforming them at the same time. The idea of modernity as a process of perpetual social transformation cannot be separated from the question of culture and the question of social agency. Mod-ernity, it may be suggested, entails the political empowering of social actors who have the power of cultural self-reflection and are the bearers of knowledge.

Modernity, then, above all, refers to the encounter between the cultural model of society – the way in which society reflects and cognitively interprets itself – and the institutional order of social, economic and political structures. As a political project, modernity gains its impulse from the tension between the cultural and the institutional. In the most general sense, we may say modernity entails a political or transformative attitude to cultural interpretative models and to the social. The modern social actor is an interpreter who is both shaped by the prevailing cultural model and at the same time is enabled by virtue of his or her interpreting capacity to act in an autonomous manner. It is this autonomy, which we may also term, following Hans Joas (1996), the 'creativity of action', that gives social action a political dimension (see Chapter 2). It must also be stressed, however, that the autonomy of action implies a cognitive or 'epistemic' dimension: it is a question of the ability of the social actor to construct, or create, a model of knowledge. The autonomy of action is more than a mere question of cultural creativity in the narrow sense of aesthetic expressivism, but also entails a relationship to knowledge. In this sense the project of modernity is an expression of the great faith of the Enlightenment in the liberating power of knowledge. In so far as the social actor is an autonomous actor, capable of creatively interpreting cultural values and norms, the social world is never closed or determined, but is always open to transformation. Modernity is ultimately, then, a project of social constructivism. However, it is to be noted that in the Enlightenment model of modernity the role of knowledge was relatively limited, being confined to the cultural domain as an end in itself, whereas today knowledge pervades the entire fabric of the social order and has entered public discourse (Böhme, 1997; Castells, 1996; Delanty, 1998b). In short, knowledge cuts across the social and the cultural, which can no longer be separated in terms of a central conflict. Instead of a central conflict there is a plurality of conflicts, an anarchy of cultural forms.

In this book I am mainly concerned with the political or transformative implications of the relationship between the two orders of modernity: on the one side, the question of the cultural model of society and, on the other, the question of the constitution of the social itself. This relationship is something that can be seen only in terms of a tension or an ambivalence, for the two domains never fully coincide: the cultural capacity of a society is always more than its specific institutional or structural form. In other words, culture and structure are always in tension. The cultural ideas in any period always contain more potential than is concretely realized in the social order. In his famous work, *Ideology and Utopia*

([1929] 1936), Karl Mannheim analysed this tension in terms of the relationship within the cultural model between ideologies and utopias. Ideology, he argued, is a belief system which serves to legitimate the prevailing social and political order, while utopias are those ideas that transcend the status quo. The theory of culture I am tacitly drawing on here is one that takes for granted the internal inconsistency and even contradictory nature of cultural value systems, which never entirely serve merely to reproduce the prevailing social order: cultural ideas are always potentially in tension with social reality. More importantly, however, is the tendency of culture to contain what Cornelius Castoriadis ([1975] 1987) called a 'radical imaginary signification' which transcends the institutional order. By this he meant the existence within the cultural model of society of a creative potential which cannot be reduced to the existing social order. By virtue of the radical imaginary every society contains the image of an alternative order. This tension between culture and the social order is reflected in the autonomy of agency. Precisely because the cultural capacity of a society for reflection and interpretation is always more than its specific institutional form, we can speak of the autonomy of agency. The very notion of the autonomy of agency implies a notion of a political, or transformative, project.

Fundamental to the idea of modernity, then, is a particular relationship, characterized by tensions, contradictions and ambivalences, between culture, structure and agency. On the one side, society can be understood from the perspective of its cultural models and its social structures. On the other side, it can also be seen from the perspective of social actors who are never fully determined by their environment and always have the capacity for political action.[8] Political action is possible because social actors are creative actors and have the cognitive capacity for social learning (see Chapter 2). We cannot reduce modernity to one of its dimensions: modernity as a dynamic process entails complex interrelations between the cultural, the social and the political. Thus, modernity is more than modernism, which is a specifically cultural idea in the narrow aesthetic sense; it refers to the wider cultural model of society and includes the normative and the cognitive, as well as the political and the societal. As a cultural idea, modernity refers to the capacity of a society to interpret itself and to act on the basis of knowledge; as a social concept, modernity refers to the domain of social institutions in which social relations are structured; and as a political notion, modernity refers to the dynamic movement of society by which social actors bring about social change by bringing their creative and learning powers to bear on the concrete situation in which they find themselves.

## Towards a Cognitive Approach

I would like to conclude this introductory sketch by characterizing a little further what is meant by a cognitive approach to culture, since this is crucial to my argument.[9] A cognitive approach to culture entails a constructivist view of the relationship between agency and culture, a relationship which is reflexively and discursively constructed. It has been a basic tenet of the sociology of knowledge that cognitive systems – knowledge as a social category – construct social reality: reality is a social construction (Berger and Luckmann, [1966] 1984). Social actors are competent bearers of knowledge that is available as cultural forms, models or codes, and the interweaving through communicatively mediated competition and conflict of their respective cognitive practice is constitutive of society. In other words, their competences relate to culturally available tools, images, models, codes or knowledge upon which they draw in order to engage in constructive activity. This view of knowledge and culture assumes a certain reflexivity on the part of social actors, but it is one that presupposes a certain anarchy in the relation between culture and action. Knowledge and culture have in common the fact that both are means by which the world is experienced. A central thesis of this book is that the question of knowledge is becoming more and more central to our experience of society: our society is a knowledge society (Böhme, 1997; Böhme and Stehr, 1986; Stehr, 1992). Moreover, this conceptualization of knowledge and culture assumes that social actors have learning capacities – that is, they have the cognitive means to learn. It is the ability to learn, which is an essentially social activity and one inseparable from the development of moral consciousness, that distinguishes human beings from the world of things.[10]

Finally, it is to be noted that knowledge and culture are characterized by discursivity: they are expressed in communicative forms. Indeed, it might be suggested that social reality is increasingly being defined less by the structures of economy, polity or cultural values systems than by the cognitive structures of communication. In so far as knowledge and culture are discursively mediated they are open to contestation. One of the hallmarks of the current situation is precisely this contestability in knowledge and culture, which is evident in virtually the whole sphere of human experience: in social identity, science, food, health, gender, politics, citizenship. A number of authors have chosen to characterize this discursivity as 'reflexivity', by which is meant the tendency towards a more intensified mediation of agency and structure, and one that has a high degree of contingency. Strydom (1999b) argues for the recognition of contemporary societies as 'communication societies', for communication as a publicly mediated cultural form constitutes a new form of contingency. Reflexivity thus suggests a growth of autonomous thinking and individualistic creativity, but one that is related to an awareness of different cultural forms, models or codes which give individuals and groups the problem of having to make a choice in their use of cultural tools when engaging in constructive activity and thus of articulating their differences with others.

The concept of cognitive practice I am tacitly drawing upon is one that stresses the reflexive component in culture and which is also present in knowledge. With the growing tendency towards the cognitive codification of culture – the rise of the information age, as outlined by Manuel Castells in his three-volume opus, *The Information Age* (1996, 1997, 1998) – this discursive space and the role of knowledge within it is becoming more and more central to the constitution of the social. In my view the challenge today is to see how this space can be captured in order to enhance the project of human autonomy and democracy.[11] This concern is central to the authors discussed in this book, who have all made the question of defending human autonomy and democracy central to their work.

Chapter 1 aims to give a working definition of the idea of modernity. I look at the classic understanding of modernity from the Enlightenment onwards as a discourse centrally expressed around the idea of autonomy (the autonomy of the political Subject, the autonomy of culture and of knowledge, and the autonomy of the social) which is articulated through the radical discourses of creativity, reflexivity and discursivity. The chapter offers a comprehensive view of how this idea of modernity can be related to the central organizing principles (integration and differentiation) of modern society and its zones of tension.

Chapter 2 takes up this older definition of modernity, demonstrating that, as a result of recent developments in the key areas of contemporary society, the classic conception has been rendered problematic. It is argued that the concern with autonomy is being seriously undermined by processes of fragmentation. Rather than dismissing the idea of modernity, however, I show how we can reconceptualize it and its project of autonomy around the radical discourses of creativity, reflexivity and discursivity, which are no longer contained by the two central organizing principles of integration and differentiation. To this end I discuss some recent theoretical work which in my view offers a conceptual basis for a new theory of modernity.

Having clarified some of the theoretical issues that are at stake and the historical and sociological background to modernity, Chapter 3 looks at the work of Habermas. In this chapter I document the shift in Habermas's thinking from a position of dualism to one of mediation. My thesis is that his recent work, which stresses less the dualism of instrumental versus communicative rationality (or the conflict between life-world and system) than the mediation of democracy and law in discourse, offers social theory with a very important contribution to understanding social change today. However, Habermas's particular rendering of discourse is problematic, since it excludes the crucial question of culture and identity, thereby sacrificing creativity to a decontextualized notion of discursivity.

Chapter 4 provides a discussion of theories which provide exactly what is missing in Habermas, namely a concern with the creativity of action. In this chapter I focus on the postmodern critique and document the shift in postmodernism away from the post-structuralist approaches of Foucault and Lyotard – for whom the question of discourse and knowledge break with any concern with agency and autonomy – to a view of culture that seeks to recover the relevance of the social under the conditions of postmodernity. In this context I look at the work of Zygmunt Bauman, who brings a normative or moral approach to bear on postmodernism.

Chapter 5 looks at the social theory of Alain Touraine, whose work, I argue, is explicitly addressed to the question of the interlinkages between culture, knowledge and social action. The importance of Touraine is that his notion of social action is much more finely developed than that of other theorists considered here. The shift in his thinking, from one that gains its impetus from social movements to a new theory of the Subject under the conditions of what he calls 'demodernization', is documented. Drawing in particular from the recent work of Alberto Melucci, this chapter introduces the centrality of the concept of reflexivity and discusses its relation to collective identity.

Chapter 6 deals with the social theory of Ulrich Beck and Anthony Giddens. The focus here is on the concept of reflexive modernization. After outlining their respective positions, I argue that these authors have made the notion of reflexivity central to the reconceptualization of modernity and that this pertains centrally to the question of knowledge. The critical position that I advocate is that neither Beck nor Giddens develops an adequate theory of culture as a cognitive system, seeing knowledge in a too narrowly delimited way. My argument, developed with a critical appraisal of the theory of culture of Scott Lash and Jeffrey Alexander, is that the mediation of culture and agency must be conceived of as being articulated through cultural models. In this context, the question of social knowledge as reflexively and discursively constructed takes on a new significance (but in a way that departs from the approaches of Lash and Alexander), since what now becomes of central importance is the role of the public in the construction of cultural models.

# 1

# *Defining Modernity: The Quest for Autonomy*

## Introduction

My way of defining the central thematic of modernity is to take the problem of autonomy as a starting point. Modernity can be seen as the pursuit of autonomy in many different areas of life, of which three projects can be highlighted: the autonomy of the political Subject, the autonomy of culture and the autonomy of the social. Today, the quest for autonomy is frequently seen as collapsing into a variety of fragmentations. But for the era of 'high modernity' – the Renaissance through the Reformation and Enlightenment to nineteenth-century reform and radical movements such as liberalism and socialism – the central conflict was less the spectre of fragmentation than the tension between cultural ideal and social reality, a conflict which was to be overcome by means of the political. In other words, the problem of modernity was one of realizing the project of autonomy by means of the reconciling power of the political.

In the next chapter I shall explore more fully how modernity as the quest for autonomy is being undermined in the climate of fragmentation that characterizes the current situation. In this chapter my aim is to provide a more complete definition of the original impulse of European modernity in order that we can see exactly how the tension been autonomy and fragmentation has increased today and how it has undermined the coherence of the project of modernity.[1]

In the introduction I argued that modernity has always been seen as articulated around a central conflict – be it democracy versus capitalism, liberty versus discipline, the individual versus society, differentiation versus integration or cultural ideal versus social reality – and argued, moreover, that in the most general sense this conflict was related to the problem of reconciling the autonomy of the political Subject, who is essentially free and self-legislating, to the demands of the social order. For the classical tradition, despite the discord of the central conflict of modernity (between civil society and capitalism), there was an assumption of a certain coherence in the relationship between, on the one side, the social project of institution-building and wealth-creation, however imperfect, and, on the other, the cultural model of a discursively centred civil society. In this chapter I will be focusing on the principles of differentiation and integration as a conceptual and more flexible means of analysing the central conflict of modernity, which in its most elemental form was a conflict between social reality and normative or cultural ideal. The tension between integration and differentiation can be formulated as follows: modernity imposed a logic of unity on the world – largely by means of the nation-state which set limits on politics – but it was also articulated through a logic of differentiation which provided the foundations for the project of autonomy and its radical discourses.

Modernity was the background to the classical tradition in sociology. The three founders of the discipline – Marx, Durkheim and Weber – expressed in different ways the rise of the social under the conditions of modernity. The modernization tradition, with its strong emphasis on functionalism, stressed the idea of *differentiation* as the distinguishing feature of modernity – the progressive differentiation of social functions into specialized spheres. The idea of differentiation was central to the writings of Comte, Spencer, Durkheim and Parsons, for all of whom it was tied to an evolutionary theory of society and signalled a future based on co-operative community in the liberal polity. The fundamental concept in the sociology of Weber was the idea of *rationalization*. Modernity entailed the unfolding of processes of rationalization in the spheres of religion, economy, law and bureaucracy. While the evolutionary-functionalist tradition emphasized the societal dimension to social change, Weber strongly emphasized the cultural: the quest for meaning in a rationalized and intellectualized age. For Marx, the distinctive feature of modernity was neither differentiation nor rationalization, but *commodification* – the penetration of capitalist social relations into all spheres of life. The essential problem that Marx was concerned to resolve was the relationship between structure (the laws of capital) and agency (the emancipation of labour from class relations). Despite these differences, all three founders believed that politics could provide a solution to the crisis of modernity: for Durkheim it was a civic and co-operative polity, for Weber a plebicitarian democracy and for Marx a communist revolution. For all three, politics was capable of redeeming modernity and reconciling it with its contradictions, though there is some evidence to suggest that Weber grew pessimistic about this prospect.[2] In short, modernity entails a self-constructing dynamic. What we need to understand are the developmental logics of this project of the self-construction of modern society.

In this chapter I shall, first, outline three central developmental logics to modernity – in the domains of politics, culture and society – as it has been conceived historically around the project that began with the Renaissance, and continued with the Reformation and the Enlightenment. These are the discourses of creativity, reflexivity and discursivity. In my conceptualization, these developmental logics – which can be seen as radical discourses of constructivism – pertain respectively to the three main communicative domains of autonomy central to modernity – namely, the autonomy of the political Subject, the autonomy of culture and knowledge, the autonomy of the social. Modernity can be seen as the progressive extension of these radical discourses to all areas of life.

In the second section in this chapter I shall outline in detail the central conflict of modernity – namely, between differentiation and integration, for modernity existed within a societal framework which established, by means of a central organizing principle of unity, limits to the constructivist logic of development inherent in the project of modernity. Creativity, reflexivity and discursivity were not unbounded but were constrained within the spatial and temporal horizons of modern society, which struggled to impose a unity on diversity. In the next chapter the collapse of this framework and the release of the radical discourses of modernity will be discussed. Finally, I draw some conclusions about the time-consciousness of modernity.

## Modernity's Three Logics of Development

Modernity can be seen in terms of three developmental logics, which relate to its political, cultural and social dimensions and which can be theorized as radical forms of autonomy. First, as already argued, it entails the autonomy of the political Subject in the sense of a creative agency. Second, modernity concerns the autonomy of culture and knowledge, which is inherently reflexive in its cognitive structures. Third, modernity involves the autonomy of the social, central to which is discursively structured public communication. Thus we have three radical discourses: creativity, reflexivity and discursivity whose developmental logics have shaped the modern age.


## Creativity and the autonomy of the political Subject

The idea of the autonomy of the Subject captures the subjective dimension of modernity: modernity as a ruptural event marked by the birth of the political Subject, who is the measure of all things. The turn to the Subject was the event that inaugurated modern thinking from the Renaissance through the Reformation to the Enlightenment. In this epochal shift a new *episteme* – an epistemological subject and a cognitive system – came into existence: the self-assertion of the human being whose advent was marked by the rejection of a transcendent being. The turn to autonomy more broadly marked the end of natural history and the beginning of human history, a theme suggested in the historicist conception of history from Vico through Hegel to Marx. Human history thus becomes a narrative of self-realization as opposed to the manifestation of a divine plan.

In his classic work, *The Legitimacy of the Modern Age* ([1966] 1983), Hans Blumenberg showed how the turn to the Subject was characterized by a great faith in the self-legislating power of human reason. The birth of the Subject entailed a view of the modern as legitimate in its own terms and therefore as authentic. Blumenberg was criticizing a commonly held view that the modern world-view was a mere secularized copy of the Christian medieval world-view and was therefore illegitimate because of being inauthentic.[3] His argument was that modernity was, indeed, more than a mere copy of something prior to it, but entailed a radical break from tradition. The modern age was self-creating. To speak of modernity, he argued, is to recognize the authenticity and therefore the legitimacy of the birth of the Subject in its struggle for self-assertion.

In the early social and political theory of modernity, from the sixteenth century to the nineteenth century, the vision of the modern Subject as self-legislating and creative emerged as a challenge to the older ideas of the medieval age which subordinated subjectivity to the natural order and theocratic principles. With the break-up of that cosmology, modernity posited the self-legislating Subject as autonomous. This autonomy was the basis of the cognitive structure of modernity; that is, it constituted its epistemic framework or model of knowledge. Thus the modern world-view, in contrast to the medieval world-view, entails a turn to subjectivity, a shift that was epitomized by certain developments in the Renaissance (which witnessed a turn to subjectivity in art – the portrayal of subjectivity by new artistic techniques which facilitated the representation of subjectivity; in politics – with the rise of the secular prince; and in science – with the New Learning of the Scientific Revolution), the Reformation (which rejected the hierarchical and clerical authority of the church in favour of the consciousness of the individual) and the early modern revolutions (in particular in the seventeenth century when religion finally ceased to be a causal factor in war and the modern state system emerged under the economic policy of mercantilism).

The notion of the consent of the governed became fundamental to the self-understanding of the modern project. This concept served for some three centuries as the framework for the self-assertion of the modern Subject. From the scientific revolution to the Protestant Reformation to the American and French Revolutions to the October Revolution, modernity unfolded as a project that sought to reconstruct the world in its own image. What varied was exactly how the Subject was to be understood. Thus, the liberal project identified the Subject with the self-legislating individual, the bourgeois ego, while the socialist project held to a collectivist understanding of the Subject. Underlying the modern turn to the Subject was the idea of popular sovereignty:[4] the idea that sovereignty rests not in the body of the monarch but in the social body. Modern subjectivity was constituted in a bond, known to the early thinkers as a social contract, between society and the state. The basis of this bond was the idea of the autonomy of the Subject, the self-assertion of the Self and the search for a legitimate social order.[5]

Finally, the autonomy of the Subject is expressed in the declaration of universal values, epitomized in the American and French Revolutions. These are the values of humanity, and are universally applicable to all human beings. The concept of universality associated with the Enlightenment was one that stressed the importance of the values of human, civil and political rights, which were constructed as formal rights on the basis of an abstract human being. Thus, universality implied a certain understanding of the person as a normative reference point. In conclusion, it may be said the idea of autonomy was based on the notion of universalizable personhood and reflected the emerging power of knowledge. This brings us to the cognitive question of the reflexivity of knowledge.

## Reflexivity and the autonomy of culture and knowledge

The second logic of development central to the modern project pertains to the reflexivity that is inherent in the cultural model of modern society. This was defined by reference to an external nature and to tradition, both of which modernity had triumphed over. The foundation of cultural autonomy was encapsulated in modern secularism, which was a product of the emancipation of knowledge, the cognitive framework, from tradition. It was also epitomized in the rationalizing drive of modern science which was based on a model of mastery over nature.

The great architects of modernity – Francis Bacon, the British empiricists, Descartes and the French rationalists and positivists, Kant and Marx – never doubted that nature was a domain external to human subjectivity which had emancipated itself from the state of nature, the original condition of humanity. Indeed, the fable of the state of nature, which was the metaphor of liberal political modernity, was precisely aimed to express the emancipation of humanity from nature, the condition of whose brute reality always presented itself as a condition in which civil society could lapse if it did not develop political institutions of constraint. Nature and the return of violence were two closely related themes in early modern thinking. The autonomy of subjectivity depended for its very existence on its ability to dominate nature. This sense of mastery rested on the epistemological confidence of modern cognitive rationality: the ability of science to uncover the secrets of nature. The struggle for the mastery of nature was the basis of modern science and of romanticism. It inspired the Enlightenment idea of reason and progress, on the one side, and on the other it was the basis of the Enlightenment's other face, the celebration of emotions (Rousseau, Herder) and the expression of heroic individualism (Byron, Goethe) conquering the forces of nature.

It is instructive to see how Kant, who epitomized the spirit of modernity in his evocation of the autonomy of the Subject, believed that the very condition of the autonomy of the Subject was the separation of morality from nature. For Kant, the self-legislating moral world, the basis of which was the freedom of the will, was radically demarcated from the world of nature, the domain of determinism. It may be suggested that the idea of the autonomy of the Subject was defined by reference to the objective world of nature as a relation of freedom versus determinism. In gaining its autonomy over nature, modern subjectivity also wins its autonomy from the ancient authorities of church and throne. The domination of nature and the critique of tradition were thus the two poles of opposition in the construction of the modern project.

The social theory of modernity, in positing the autonomy of the Subject as the foundation of the modern project, laid the basis of another enduring bastion of the modern: the rise of instrumental rationality. According to Theodor Adorno and Max Horkheimer in their critique of modernity, *Dialectic of Enlightenment* ([1947] 1979), instrumental rationality gets its impetus from the struggle to gain mastery over nature. Nature is the domain of external necessity, an objectivity to be dominated by a self-legislating subjectivity, which eventually uses its newly discovered autonomy to dominate human beings. In this way the domination of nature and social domination are mutually implicated.

While this drive towards the mastery of nature was central to the cultural or epistemic model of modern society, it is essential to recognize that the rationality of knowledge was part of a developmental logic of reflexive understanding, as is illustrated by the self-critical nature of modern consciousness. What this means is that reality began to be seen as a human *construction* and no longer as a *representation* of a natural order. The idea of autonomy suggests a certain degree of what might be called 'self-reference', or self-referentiality: modernity seeks to express its own legitimacy from nothing less than itself. This self-referential character to the modern project demarcates it from the medieval world-view and is the basis of the defence of the modern from the conservative critique of modernity. The autonomy of the Subject is a self-legitimating self which sees its own project as authentic and not in need of legitimation by reference to something anterior or transcendent.

## Discursivity: the autonomy of the social

The spirit of modernity as the autonomy of political subjectivity was initially faced with a problem. If the Subject is autonomous, free of the natural order and self-legislating with respect to political authority, how then is a *social* order possible? For the early social theorists – Hobbes, Locke, Rousseau – it was essentially a social contract formed between autonomous individuals for the purpose of their self-preservation.[6] The social contract set up a state in which civil society could function without recourse to violence, or the return to the state of nature. But there was no doubt for these early theorists that modern subjectivity, while being self-legislating, was rooted in a pre-social natural order. The rights to 'Life, Liberty and Property' were seen as the basis of the social order but were derived not from relations of sociability but from natural rights, which preceded the social. However, with Montesquieu and the moral philosophers of the Scottish Enlightenment the reality of the social *sui generis* became increasingly recognized. Society was not something standing opposed to some kind of a pre-social subjectivity, oppressing it, as Rousseau argued, but the generative reality in which subjectivity was constructed. This recognition of the reality of the social did not fully mature until the time of George Herbert Mead, whose work testifies to the intersubjective nature of subjectivity and the social bond.

The third dimension of modernity, then, is the rise and autonomy of the social as a reality in itself and the related developmental process of the discursive regulation of power in civil society. While we today are faced with the postmodern spectre of the decline of the social under conditions established by globalization and fragmentation – as I shall argue in more detail in the next chapter – the spirit of modernity was originally formed with the recognition of the rise of the social as a world-constituting project. Subjectivity is seen as having the power of social construction: the order of society is no longer seen as reflecting the order of nature or as an appendage to the state, as in the case of the 'court society'. Modern society was a 'civil' society, whose autonomy was defined against nature and the state. The social theory of modernity believed the distinctive feature of the social to be the mediating domain of social institutions which lie between, on the one side, the objectivity and primordiality of nature and, on the other side, an autonomous and self-legislating subjectivity. Hegel, who replaced the dualism in Kant's thought – between nature, which is objective, and a moral Subject, who is self-legislating – with a dialectical conception of history as a process of self-realization, recognized the unfolding of the social as the domain in which objectivity and subjectivity are overcome, an insight that was not fully sociologized by him. Thus the idea developed that in the reality of the social the previously separated spheres of nature and subjectivity are mediated. What is specific to the social is the mediating domain of institutions, the regulated spheres of social relations. According to the social theory of modernity, humanity emerged out of the state of nature and gained its autonomy by means of social institutions. It is this characteristic of social institutionalization that the theorists of the modern believed was distinctive about European civilization and demarcated the Occident from the Orient and primitive worlds.

The need for social institutions in which autonomy could be preserved and attain the fullness of its expression was fundamental to the project of modernity. Faith in social institutions replaced unquestioned obedience to authority and fear of nature. For Weber, this was simply part of the 'disenchantment' of the modern world in which meaning was increasingly becoming scarce and was ultimately retreating into the inner world of subjectivity. In his diagnosis of modernity, the institutions of society and the cultural frames of reference are unable to give meaning to the individual. It was his conviction that the fate of times cannot be reversed and the individual must accept the objective loss of meaning with only the compensations of an inner nature and charisma in the public domain for comfort. This loss of meaning, which characterizes modernity, is compensated for by social institutions: institutions mediate between the internal and the external worlds, the world of subjectivity and the world of culture, which for Weber is disenchanted as a result of sundering the idea of totality. The sense of the importance of institutions was much more evident in the writings of Durkheim, for whom modern institutions, in particular occupations and education, could provide an antidote for the anomie he believed pervaded modern society in its transitory stage between mechanical forms of integration and the organic ones of a not too distant future. Durkheim had greater faith in the institutions of modernity to provide a meaningful order than Weber, whose profound pessimism committed him to a much more ambivalent stance on modernity.

The problem of modernity in the classical conceptions, it may be suggested, is how the internal and the external worlds, the world of subjectivity and the world of nature, can be combined without reversing the principle of differentiation so fundamental to the modern age. As I have already argued with respect to the concept of society in the sociology of modernity, institutions were seen as the essence of the social and the means by which the differentiated world of modernity could preserve a unity which had to be shed at the cultural level: the search for a unified principle of integration cannot be found in the cultural model of society but only in its institutional system, which alone has a capacity to provide enduring norms. This, then, points to the other dimension of modernity: the taming of subjectivity. Institutions, which for the sociology of modernity are coeval with the social, mediate between the external spheres of culture in their autonomous discourses of the cognitive, the moral-practical and the aesthetic, and the internal world of subjectivity. Subjectivity for the sociology of modernity is itself outside the social and must therefore be tamed. It is no coincidence that Descartes, one of the intellectual architects of modernity, wrote his last work on subjectivity – *Passions of the Soul* [1649] – and that Weber's reflections on the rationalized world of modernity incorporated the erotic in private life and the role of charisma in public life.

With the recognition of the mediating function of institutions the dichotomy of agency and structure was born as a tension of social action versus the institutional world of social structures. The modern Subject is autonomous and self-legislating, yet is the product of a social order without which it would revert to the state of nature. The question of the autonomy of the Subject immediately raises the problem of the legitimation of power, since the Subject is also a social agent. This tension between the autonomy of the social actor and the objectivity of the social order was reflected in a tension between an emphasis on social order and social change (Wrong, 1994). The social was itself the site of this conflict. The condition of social order was dictated by the need to demarcate the modern Subject from the external world of nature; social change was the expression of the autonomy of the social actor in its negotiation with social structures.

How did modern society overcome this divide between agency and structure, the autonomy of the individual and the demands of society? The solution that was found was the principle of discursivity, the quasi-institutionalization of flexibly structured public communication. One of the innovations of modern western society was the centrality it gave to discursive procedures in the regulation of power. Culture and power were never reducible to each other. The reflexivity in modern culture was expressed in widely practised discursive innovations which mediated the exercise of power in public communication.

To sum up, the three dimensions of modernity entail the developmental logics of the autonomy of the Subject as a project of creativity, the autonomy of culture as a project of reflexivity and the autonomy of the social as the discursive regulation of power. Thus we may see the modern project of institution-building unfolding as a series of developmental logics, or what I would call discourses of radical constructivism. By theorizing the project of modernity in terms of a threefold model of constructivism – the discourses of creativity, reflexivity, discursivity – I believe we can see more clearly how modernity entails an inner tension with itself and how developments today can be seen as a radicalization, rather than an abandonment, of modernity.

In the following section we look at a tension within what might be called 'high modernity' – namely, the limits set by the societal framework of that epoch on its developmental logics. I shall examine this tension in terms of differentiation versus integration.

## Integration and Differentiation

In the previous section I discussed the rise of the social as a process in which agency, which is essentially creative, is structured in a discursively and reflectively mediated process. My aim now is to outline in more detail what is specific to the institutions of modernity and how we can theorize the project of modernity in terms of radical discourses of constructivism. To this end, I will employ the concepts of integration and differentiation to theorize the central tensions of modernity.

The concept of society associated with modernity entails the structuring of society into four domains: polity, economy, culture and social relations. The social theory of modernity recognized the consolidation of these distinct domains, which are also internally differentiated, to be the foundations of modern society. Modern society differs from traditional society in that it is a differentiated unity and therefore the question of integration is central to it. The social theorists of modernity accepted the notion of the essential unity of society but believed that it was a structured, or differentiated, unity. These two concepts – the integration and differentiation of the social – are essential to an understanding of modern society and provide the key to the analysis of its dynamics. Modern society – in contrast to premodern and postmodern society – is differentiated, yet it contains a central organizing principle. First, I shall discuss the idea of the essential unity of society, before proceeding to the question of the structuring, or differentiation, of the social.

The theme of the unity of society – the idea of social order or social integration – is one of the hallmarks of the modern. The modern concept of the essential unity of society differed from premodern notions of the unity, which were defined in terms of the uniformity of the cosmic order and natural law, in that it was primarily a geo-political idea that did not need recourse to a transcendental order. Aristotle, for instance, believed society was a natural unity, and Augustine believed the earthly city was an imperfect reflection of the City of God. Stephen Toulmin (1992) refers to the dream of a perfect fusion of the Order of Nature and the Order of Society, the harmony of the polis with the cosmos – the vision of the 'cosmopolis' – as one of the great driving forces since the formation of human society.[7]

The modern notion of unity, in contrast to the ancient and medieval, was more an expression of the growing visibility of spatial concepts, which undoubtedly were closely related to the emergence of maps and new methods of representing space (Anderson, 1983).

The Age of Discovery had ushered in a new consciousness of the separation of space from place. The globe became increasingly visible, and geographically delineated territories suggested new concepts for imagining unity. It thus became possible for human beings to experience cognitively the collective imaginary of a spatial unity.

With the consolidation of absolute states in the early modern period and the decline in Christendom, the western world witnessed the gradual emergence of the national state. The world became increasingly ordered into distinct national societies. The unity of the social, presupposed in the discourses of modernity, referred to the self-legislating capacity of these units to be able to institute social orders. Modernity located the unity of society in its political regulation. It was the polity – the political, juridical, administrative and military institutions of the state – that ultimately secured the unity of the social. As a geo-political framework, the social was a domain delimited by the central, bureaucratic state. The modern state, which came into existence in the period of absolutism, was also a military organ, which sought to extend and protect the frontiers of the social through military conquest. External war and the internal repression of dissent were the driving force in the constitution of the modern social project.

National societies were characterized by a high degree of uniformity, albeit one that was frequently enforced by repressive means. In Norbert Elias's (1982) terms, the state pacified society by removing violence to the exterior. This unity or uniformity was manifest in the codification of national programmes designed to cultivate a cohesive social body. By means of the institutionalization of national educational systems, national symbols such as flags, anthems, coinage and national literatures, and the cultivation of a myth of national origins reflected in popular notions of heritage, professional historical writing and, above all, in linguistic nationalism, the idea of the social as a national unity gained credence by the late nineteenth century.[8]

This cultural invention of the nation was consolidated further by six developments: the drive towards industrialism, the imperial quest, the emergence of national welfare states, the international commitment to national self-determination, urbanization and mass education. The nation became rooted in a social reality, which was very much structured by the imperatives of capitalism. Industrialism, in uprooting and relocating populations, created new kinds of social relations, which became homogenized through the class system and the formation of new urban life-worlds. Furthermore, in many countries, especially Germany, industrialism was imposed by the state. The drive towards industrialism was related to imperialism, which had an even greater homogenizing effect on society. National societies became increasingly defined in terms of an identification with empire-building. The politics of what has become known as social imperialism transformed class conscious-ness into national consciousness. The nation becomes the ultimate point of identification, overriding class and political loyalties. With the gradual building of nationally specific welfare states in the first half of the twentieth century, coupled with the worldwide commit-ment to national self-determination for the former colonies, the project of modernity as institution-building reaches completion. By the end of the Second World War the world is divided into dist-inct blocks, which, as a result of centuries of state violence, are relatively homogeneous, save for the presence of immigrants who, with the rise of the mature welfare state of the postwar decades, were absorbed into the national society. Elsewhere, the problem of heterogeneity was solved through genocide, partition, population expulsion or enforced assimilation.

We can say, then, that by the end of the Second World War – as a result of state-building, capitalist modernization, industrialization, population movement, imperialism, the growth of the welfare state – the idea of the social is inseparable from the modern nation-state. Mass education, particularly in the second half of the twentieth century, greatly enhanced the integration of a national society, since it has almost exclusively been tied to national programmes. Society is, first, a national society in terms of cultural identification and the distribution of economic and social resources. Its other defining characteristic is its state-centric nature. Modern society is organized by the state, which has a homogenizing role with respect to the social. In short, it is impossible to conceive of the modern project without due regard to the homogenizing logic of the state. This is also true of the former communist world where society was much more shaped in the image of the state. Soviet totalitarianism repre-sented to an extreme degree the homogenizing logic of modernity, but one which eventually destroyed the other face of modernity: the assertion of autonomy and the radical project of constructivism.[9]

There is another dimension to the myth of integration in modern social theory. The idea of the body – the socialized construction of nature and the naturalization of agency – served as a powerful metaphor for imagining and instituting the social. Since the Renais-sance, the image of the body has been an enduring metaphor of the social order and the polity. Whether in the idea of the personifica-tion of the political body in the body of the ruler, as with Elizabeth I, or in the organic conception of society in social Darwinist theory, the homogeneous image of the body as a functionally integrated organism has served as a means of expressing the drive for the regulation of social relations and the exercise of power.

Modern society, however, as I have already argued, is more than a homogenized realm. The unity of the social must also be seen as a differentiated uniformity. While it is true that, under the conditions of modernity, society was institutionally shaped in the image of the state, the unity imposed by the modern polity was a differentiated one. The core institutional structures of modern society consist of the functionally differentiated structures of polity, economy, culture and social relations. I shall examine each of these in turn.

*Polity*    I have discussed above how the modern polity emerged as part of a drive to 'monopolize the means of violence', to use Weber's term. The essential component of the polity is the state itself, but also includes the centralizing administrative-bureaucracy, law and militarism. It was the distinctive achievement of modern political thought to recognize the autonomy of the polity. In the writings of the sixteenth-century political theorists, such as Bodin and Machiavelli, and in the following century with Hobbes, the modern conception of politics emerged with the argument that the rule of the secular prince can be self-legislating once he gains control of the political. Their question was how legitimate political authority could be possible. The answer they found was in the general recognition that the modern polity is based on an instrumentality of purpose and requires no other legitimation than that supplied by legal structures designed for whatever purposes best suit the ambition of the prince. This conception of the political was a break from the medieval idea of the divine right of kings and theocratic notions of authority which entailed the fusion of the theological with the political. Even though the Renaissance notion of the instrumentality of politics was eventually challenged by the liberal conception of the social contract, it did entail the emancipation of the political from the ancient authorities of God and King. Politics, as the quest for power, became a domain that had to be competed for by all contenders. The separation of state and church was the foundation of the modern project of institution-building. However, this emancipatory process was ambivalent, for, with the rise of absolutism, the state became all-powerful and dominated the political field.

With Sir Thomas More, writing in the first half of the sixteenth century, this idea of the social as embodied in the perfect polity expressed itself in the vision of utopia: modernity opened up the possibility of utopia. The early idea of utopia served largely as a critical norm with which to attack the prevailing order, and was frequently seen as residing in some exotic location. Utopia increasingly came to signify the modern impulse itself. Noteworthy is that in More's classic work, *Utopia* [1516], which can be seen as the first conception of modern social policy, it is the state that is the guarantor of the utopian society. Modernity never solved the problem of the state which always dominated the social. Thus all modern revolutions – 1688, 1766, 1789, 1848, 1917 – sought to gain control of the organs of the state.[10] The consequences of the absolute state continued to dominate state–society relations throughout the epoch of modernity, and no modern revolution ever solved the problem of eliminating traces of the *ancien régime* (Anderson, 1974; Mayer, 1981).[11]

Social theory as such was not born until the eighteenth century, when political theory developed into a broader theorization of the social. The early social theories of Montaigne and Montesquieu, arguably the first sociologists, had been overshadowed by the contemporary theories of modern politics by such figures as Machiavelli, Hobbes and Locke, but by the early eighteenth century the moral philosophers of the Scottish Enlightenment – such as Ferguson and Millar – articulated a novel idea of society which went beyond the purely political to a social vision (Berry, 1997; Eriksson, 1993). However, the full implications of this were not apparent until the later emergence of sociology.

The notion of the citizen served as a bridging concept linking the social to the political. The classic account of modern citizenship is T. H. Marshall's ([1950] 1992) *Citizenship and Social Class*. Marshall's argument was that modern society can be viewed as the progressive institutionalization of citizenship. The eighteenth century witnessed, he argued, the institutionalization of civil rights in the creation of civic citizenship around such rights as free speech, assembly, a free press, the right to own property and enter into contract. These purely formal civic rights were supplemented in the nineteenth century with political citizenship in the widening of the franchise so that citizens could act in the political domain, and in the twentieth century with the creation of social citizenship with the rights to education, healthcare, and social security against unemployment. Marshall's theory of citizenship epitomized the social democratic theory of modernity in the twentieth century. As such, it displayed great confidence in modernity's ability to generate the solutions to its own problems and differed from the liberal theory only in its emphasis on social citizenship (Delanty, 1997a). For Marshall, there was no doubt that the citizen was a category formed by the state and was therefore territorially specific.

*Economy*    The discovery of the social as a domain both distinct and broader than the political realm of the state was a gradual process. One of the features of modernity that greatly impressed the early theorists was the dynamism of the economy, which led to the emancipation of social relations from tradition and subservience. The great liberal thinkers, from Hobbes to Locke and Smith, did not question the assumption that modern man is an economic being whose self-interest and identity derives from his ownership of property. Politics serves to stabilize property relations, which are supposed to emanate from natural rights. Economic man, like political man, is a self-contained being who pursues material goals which can be attained by instrumentalized means. By means of the celebrated concept of the 'hidden hand', Adam Smith outlined the process by which modernity unfolded in the articulation of a narrative of the progressive accumulation of wealth leading to universal happiness.

The modern notion of the autonomy of the Subject received its greatest elaboration in the liberal philosophy of the self-contained Subject. It took two centuries of critique to reach the insight that this bourgeois conception was class- and gender-specific, and thereby rested on exclusion. The economic and political philosophy of liberalism ignored the reality of bourgeois property relations and patriarchal gender relations. It was the product of an economic and social order that was based on the separation of domestic work from waged labour and the separation of work from leisure. Both domestic work and leisure presupposed a certain 'privatism'. Moreover, the economic order of modernity rested on the 'work ethic', a belief in the value of work or a career and the allocation of social merit through personal achievement in the world of work. Modernity ultimately rested on a society of producers and the remnants of pre-capitalist social, cultural and economic institutions.

By the time of Marx the economy became a structure that was capable of determining the political and the social more broadly: the modern economy, organized along capitalist lines, entailed the creation of classes and the commodification of social relations. Thus one axis of the differentiation of modern society was stratification, as opposed to segmentation in earlier societies.

*Culture*    In a tradition from Kant to Weber to Habermas modernity has been understood in terms of a strong emphasis on processes of cultural rationalization. According to Habermas (1981), drawing from Kant and Weber, modernity entailed the differentiation of three cultural spheres of rationality from each other: the cognitive (the question of knowledge), the moral-practical (the normative), and the aesthetic-evaluative spheres (the artistic-expressivist). In earlier ages cultural world-views were unified by one, central authority. The world-view of medieval Christianity was a unified one, which saw science, morality and art as an expression of divine will. The world was seen as emanating from a centre from which all authority flows. Modernity entails a break from this centred and unified notion of culture. Modern culture is characterized by being differentiated: that is, its constitutive spheres – the normative, the cognitive and the aesthetic – are independent of each other and from unifying principles such as those of religion. Thus, science is not subordinated to the normative, and art, for example, ceases to be dependent on religious doctrine and, accordingly, loses its 'aura'. Kant was the first philosopher to give systematic expression to the separation of these three spheres, which were the basis of the autonomy of the Subject. His three great works in critical philosophy, *The Critique of Pure Reason* [1781], *The Critique of Practical Reason* [1788], and *The Critique of Judgement* [1790], addressed the spheres of, respectively, the cognitive, the moral-practical and the aesthetic.

Thus, one of the distinctive achievements of modernity in the aesthetic sphere is the emergence of what has become known as the autonomous institution of art (Bürger, 1984). The aesthetic imagination of modernity involved being conscious of its emancipation from subservience to court and church. With the emergence of a reading public and the commercialization of the artistic objects, artists could attain a degree of autonomy from the older relations of patronage. This autonomy that accompanied the decline in patronage was reflected in the content of their work, which could take on a greater concern with the nascent social world. The autonomy of culture was the basis of its developmental logic of reflexivity and led to the increasing professionalization of the world of art, literature and music, which was no longer required to be representational. The culture of modernity was one that regarded the aesthetic as an end in itself: the aesthetic imagination is autonomous in the social world, which enters it only in a mediated way. Thus, one of its distinctive features is its preoccupation with form; the aesthetic form is what determines content. From the eighteenth century onwards modern European art becomes more and more concerned with the autonomy of the aesthetic form, which eventually discards any concern with normative issues.

With respect to cognitive rationality, modernity expressed itself in the idea of the autonomy of knowledge, which goes back to the 'New Learning' associated with the scientific revolution. An early manifestation came in the creation of the modern university system, epitomized in the foundation of the University of Berlin in 1810, which gave full expression to the Enlightenment's conception of knowledge. This debate was initiated by Kant in a plea to the King of Prussia to grant academic freedom to philosophers. His essay, 'The Conflict of the Faculties' (Kant, [1798] 1978) set the terms for a long debate on academic freedom and the ideal of the western university.[12] Alexander von Humboldt was the most influential advocate of the Kantian idea of the university and the notion of academic freedom, and wrote a famous proposal to the Prussian king in 1809, which was subsequently incorporated into the constitution of the new university. The debate around the foundation of the University of Berlin symbolized the spirit of modernity and its ideal that knowledge can be emancipatory but the pursuit of knowledge must be protected from the rest of society. It is to be noted that the Enlightenment model of the university was developed in the context of the nationalization of knowledge: freedom and knowledge constituted one side of the coin; the other was nation and culture. The neo-humanist von Humboldt epitomized the two sides of the Enlightenment's model of the university in Germany. For him, the university was not just the cradle of autonomous knowledge but was also the custodian of the culture of the nation. It not only provided the state with functionally useful knowledge, but was also an important transmitter of national heritage and, furthermore, it had a significant reflexive component.

Finally, the normative, or moral-practical, domain refers to the tendency of modern morality to be self-legislating. Morality, Kant argued, is derived from nothing less than the moral law itself, which is autonomous of the natural order and manifests itself as 'moral imperative'. The discourses of modernity were constructed out of a critical engagement with tradition. The two dominating themes in the great discourses of modernity were the themes of rights and justice. The liberal conceptions of politics and ethics stressed the priority of rights, above all those of civic and political citizenship – that is, the rights of the modern individual to exercise freedom of speech, membership of associations, the right to protest and, later, in the aftermath of the bourgeois emancipation movements, the right to participate in the political community. Like the wider discourse of modernity, these rights were largely formal in their conception and were not always enshrined in reality. This contradiction between the normative claims of modernity and the social reality of capitalism led to the second great discourse of modernity: the question of social justice. With its origins in socialist revolution, deriving from a whole variety of collective actors

(Moore, 1978; Thompson, 1968), the limits of a rights perspective became apparent. A perspective on social justice emerged to fill the gap. However, it is to be stressed that even the most far-reaching critique of modernity in the nineteenth century, the Marxist critique of political economy, did not question the emancipatory impulse of the project of modernity. For Marx, modernity needed to be completed, not abandoned, for in his view the bourgeois utopia was not itself problematical; the problem was to realize the normative claims of modernity under different social conditions.

*Social relations*    Modern society refers not only to the differentiated structures of polity, economy and culture, but also pertains to the realm of social relations per se. The great conceptions of modernity discussed until now have tended to emphasize the political, the economic or the cultural. With the foundation of sociology as a science, the consciousness of modernity began to express itself in a recognition of the increasing reality of the social as a domain in itself. This awareness entailed a rejection of the reduction of social relations to the purely political or economic. The specificity of sociability became an object of analysis in its own right with the writings of Durkheim, Simmel and Mead, to mention just three theorists who were fully conscious of the reality of the social, though this insight, as I have argued, could be traced back to the moral philosophers of the Scottish Enlightenment, to Montesquieu and even as far back as Montaigne.

   In the discourses of modernity social relations are constituted in the demarcation of a distinctive social domain that is separate from the private. Thus the principal expression of this domain is the idea of civil society and the related concept of the public sphere. Modern social relations are constituted in the public domain of civil society. The idea of civility captures the essence of modern sociability. Modernity entails the structuring of distinct domains, the strict demarcation of the private from the public. Thus, Kant ([1784] 1995) spoke of enlightenment as being the 'public use of reason' to stress the idea of civility or publicity. Some of the classic accounts of the rise of the modern sense of the public were Hannah Arendt's *The Human Condition* (1958), Jürgen Habermas's *The Structural Transformation of the Public Sphere* ([1962] 1989a) and Richard Sennett's *The Fall of Public Man* (1977). Arendt described the rise of modernity in terms of the equation of the social with the public. This was in contrast to earlier times, when the social as such did not have a distinct existence outside the private. The social is distinctive to modernity and it is in the social that the power of the state is challenged. The modern individual for Arendt, Habermas and Sennett is a public person whose identity is formed not in the private world but in the public domain of civil society. In his classic work on the rise and transformation of the public sphere, Habermas ([1962] 1989a) analyses this in terms of the formation of a culture of 'publicity' in the eighteenth century around a bourgeois reading public who met in public spaces, such as coffee houses, literary clubs, political societies, libraries, etc. This was a relatively autonomous domain and challenged the earlier concentration of society in the court. The new relations of sociability, though heavily restricted to the male members of the bourgeois class, were more accessible to the growing numbers of people who formed the social basis of the radical ideas of modernity. Of course, Arendt, Habermas and Sennett bemoaned the decline of 'public man' with the rise of the mass society which commercialized the once autonomous public realm, which, accordingly, lost its commitment to pure publicity. Their conceptions of the public sphere were thus conceived in terms of a pessimistic model of decline: civil society becomes overshadowed by mass society. Thus, one of the central questions for Habermas is how mass society can preserve some of the structures of civil society (see Chapter 3).

The interpretation of modern social relations I am proposing is one that emphasizes the centrality of the idea of publicity, or civility, as the defining tenet of the modern conception of the social, in the strict sense of the term. Modern society is a civil society in that it is constructed in the public domain (Cohen and Arato, 1992; Hall, 1995; Keane, 1988a, 1988b). It presupposes a separate private world which is isolated from social relations as such. While the public domain of civil society is based on relations of sociability and individuality, the private world is the domain of domesticity and intimacy.

At this point something should be mentioned concerning the role of collective actors with respect to civil society and modernity. I have emphasized the dualism of the private and the public as the essential feature of modern social relations, suggesting a model of bourgeois individualism. Attention must also be given to the centrality of collective actors who have the ability to form 'discursive' coalitions with segments of the masses (Tarrow, 1995; Wuthnow, 1989). As argued above, the cultural forms of modernity would be inconceivable without such collective actors, who bring about social change.

Modern collective actors are products of civil society in a number of respects. One of the chief expressions of the public culture of modernity is the figure of the intellectual and the rise of ideology (Bloggs, 1993; Eyerman, 1994). These features of the modern project can be seen as the embodiment of the idea of publicity: the intellectual is the legislator, to use Bauman's (1987) phrase, who occupies a central position in the public domain. Intellectuals came into existence with the demise of clerical authority and formed a group distinct from the rising culture of experts (Lepenies, 1988). They played a crucial role in codifying the great ideologies of modernity. What is meant by ideology is those comprehensive political belief-systems that were codified in the nineteenth century and whose function was the mobilization of the masses. Ideologies – such as those of liberalism, conservatism, nationalism, anarchism, socialism, fascism – had the characteristics of being totalizing doctrines about the political nature of society and served to reorganize social relations in a new key. They were programmatic in their ambitions and were frequently utopian. Ideology was a product of the Enlightenment in that it was a creation of knowledge-codifiers whose existence depended on the nascent culture of publicity, which was primarily a public culture that owed its existence to printing and the existence of a reading public. Without this public culture, modern collective actors would not be able to form discursive coalitions with the wider society.

Finally, I would like to suggest that the public culture of modernity entailed a more general principle of what I have been calling 'discursivity', or the discursive regulation of power. The ideas of civil society and the public sphere point to the opening of a discursive space in society in the sense of an institutional space devoted to communication. While this space changed its institutional form – in the transformation of civil society, which was based on exclusion, to mass society – there was always an orientation to discursivity built into the social project of modernity. Communication in all its forms has been one of the central experiences of modernity and has manifested itself in a great variety of forms, of which the most salient is the printed word. Modernity is ultimately based on the printed, not the spoken, word. The emergence of a reading public was one of the most decisive moments in the formation of modern forms of communication, for printed discourse made possible the separation of discourse from the Subject or social actor. Discourse, institutionalized in the public sphere of civil society, became a medium of communication which was irreducible to any particular social actor. However, the idea of discursivity goes beyond publicity in the sense of a domain that is confined to a public domain separated from the private realm. Collective actors articulated a heightened degree of discursivity, going beyond the restricted cultural and political communication of bourgeois discourse. Their discourses made possible the articulation and formation of broader societal discourses, which have shaped the very way we think about society.[13]

My thesis, then, is that modern social relations, in so far as they are characterized by the culture of publicity and civil society, also entail discursivity, and that the transformation of modernity – from printing press to television to the internet – can be seen as the radicalization of this principle of discursivity and its progressive extension to all areas of society. I hope that the full implications of this will become apparent in the course of this book.

To sum up, the structuring of the social can be seen in terms of two processes of institutionalization: the homogenization of the social, a process that is largely manifest in the formation of national societies which establish a degree of integration, and the structuring of the social, spatially delimited in the national state, into the functionally differentiated domains of polity, economy, culture and social relations. These spheres can be analysed in terms of criteria specific to each domain and exist in relations of mutual tension with each other, constituting the broad contours of the central conflict of modernity.

## Conclusion: The Time-Consciousness of Modernity

I shall conclude this chapter with some remarks on the time-consciousness of modernity. The concept of time that underlies the project of modernity in many ways summarizes the entire experience of the modern and provides us with a point of departure for the analysis of the current situation, which I shall be arguing involves a different conception of time.

Modernity has largely been defined by reference to a temporal trajectory beginning in the early modern period with the Renaissance and Reformation, but reaching maturity in the Age of the Enlightenment and extending into the future, frequently with a utopian horizon. Modernity may therefore be said to be a time-consciousness which links the past to the future. The self-understanding of the American and French Revolutions typified this sense of a transition to a new age which entailed a fundamental break from the old order and the unified world-view of Christendom. History, as the narrative of the Subject, replaced the Renaissance idea of providence. Modernity thus signifies an epochal movement and is closely related to the liberal idea of progress and the Marxist notion of permanent revolution. This sense of a temporal dimension to modernity has been closely linked to the idea of modernization in sociological theories, the theory that the evolution of society is to be explained by reference to processes of progressive rationalization, differentiation and individuation. Both the ideas of modernity as a particular kind of time-consciousness and modernization as a sociological thesis share a common concern with the rise of modern society and the decline of traditional society. The movement from traditional to modern society is thus central to the self-understanding of modernity and constitutes a master trend of change. In the discourses of modernity there is only one trajectory, the master trend of change from the premodern – the origin – to the modern, the *telos* or goal of history.

In this book I argue that this definition of modernity is becoming problematical, since the current situation cannot be defined by reference to the passing of traditional society and the coming of the modern as something post-traditional. The current situation, in fact, points to the passing of the modern itself and the dissolution of the social bond. In order to understand this process we need to go beyond the notion of the post-traditional as well as recognizing the inadequacy of the concept of the postmodern. The older conceptions of modernity, in contrast, held to a vision of the epochal movement of traditional society to modern society. The defining characteristics of this process of social change were industrialization, individualization, the building of nation-states and the experience of revolution, all of which led to new configurations of time and space. The time-consciousness of modernity can be summed up in the phrase 'narrative and closure'. Modernity entailed an evolutionary myth of progress which was conceived as the unfolding of a narrative, the narrative of the manifestation of Reason, the realization of subjectivity, the building of institutions, the mastery of nature and the process of civilization. This conception of historical time was, strictly speaking, one of transition as opposed to transformation, which I shall be arguing is a more appropriate term to designate the present situation. The transition implied by the idea of modernity was one based on the epochal movement from one type of society to another. Thus the shift from traditional to modern society suggests a notion of social change in terms of 'transition' as opposed to 'transformation' since the notion of transition signifies a temporal shift from condition A to condition B.[14] The idea of transformation, on the other hand, implies a greater sense of agency than is implied by the notion of transition.

The conception of time associated with the transition to modernity was one of linearity and symmetrical development. Time was a continuum through which society, as a spatially located geopolitical framework, had to pass. Time was dynamic; space was static. Therefore, societies were seen as relatively ordered and fixed, while it was history that changed. The actual experience of time can

be described as 'clock time': the temporal ordering of experience by
reference to the mechanical movement of clock time as opposed to
the rhythmic time of nature.[15] Moreover, the structures of the social
– polity, economy, culture and social relations – were seen as being
relatively symmetrical in their evolution. Regardless of whether one
structure was seen as having greater determining power, the overall
vision of the evolution of society was one that saw fairly uniform
development of all structures as a result of some kind of
functionalizing logic. In the classical tradition, there was the assumption of a basic underlying force: rationalism, commodification
or differentiation. In sum, the sociology of modernity took for
granted the existence of a single rate of change. As I shall argue in
the next chapter, this is something that can no longer be un-
problematically assumed, as what is changing today is the rate of
change itself.

A further characteristic of the conception of time in the project of
modernity that needs to be stressed was the equation of modernity
with civilization, in particular with occidental civilization. As a
historical process, modernity entailed the ideas of rupture – that
the western world experienced a major historical break with the
past in the period from the Renaissance to the Enlightenment – and
of completion – the notion that the unfolding of modernity is the
completion of a project that can be traced back to an origin. It is this
supposition of an origin whose *telos* must achieve completion that
ties the discourse of modernity to a model of civilization. This can
be taken further: the concept of the essential unity of society ultimately rested on an ideology of civilization, which in turn was
defined in terms of the inherent superiority of the white race. As
Derrida (1977, 1978) argues, the postulation of an Origin was part
of an intellectual strategy whose other face was the construction
of an Other. The concept of civilization was a quintessential
nineteenth-century notion which derived from the Enlightenment's penchant for intellectual mastery, instrumental control and
institution-building. The unity established by nation-states was
held to rest on a higher principle of unity: the unity of European
civilization (Delanty, 1995a). While there is not much left of this
notion of unity today, it was highly influential in the nineteenth
century, providing national societies with a transcendent point of
unity that would be capable of embedding national myths of
cultural origin in a higher order.

Finally, the discourse of modernity entailed the idea of closure –
the completion of the historical project. A narrative has a beginning
and an end. The end of modernity implied by the theory of modernization was its culmination in the worldwide victory of western

ideas and the mutual linkage of capitalism and liberal democracy. This myth gained widespread credence in the period following the Second World War, when the defeat of fascism seemed to confirm the inherent superiority of the forces of the Enlightenment. Even though this myth had dissolved by the 1970s, the collapse of the Soviet Union in the early 1990s seemed for many to confirm the myth. An example of this great faith in the promise of modernity is Francis Fukuyama's *The End of History and the Last Man* (1992). In this infamous book, whose thesis is too well known to recount in detail, Fukuyama defended the spirit of modernity as a 'struggle for recognition', in which the heritage of 1789 finally dominates over the heritage of 1917. We have reached the 'end of history' today, his message was, in the sense that there are no longer any fundamental ideological battles: liberal democracy has been accepted the world over as the order of the day and all other ideological frameworks have been exhausted of evolutionary potential. In his conception of modernity, the project of the Enlightenment has been completed; modernity's work has been done and history has thereby come to a close. This work captures the idea of narrative and closure which, I have argued, express the central impetus of the time-consciousness of modernity.

In the next chapter I shall discuss the limits of modernity with respect to its societal framework of integration and differentiation. We shall see that modernity has become an increasingly problematic discourse whose inner tensions – constituted in its developmental logics – now point to the limits of its relevance for understanding the world today. We are therefore forced to rethink some of its central categories.

# 2

# *The Limits of Modernity:*
# *From Autonomy to Fragmentation*

## Introduction

Looking at the revival of the idea of modernity in social and political theory since the 1980s it is immediately apparent that the new conceptions of modernity, to be discussed in subsequent chapters, are ones that recognize the ambivalence of modernity as a critical discourse of crisis. The very idea of modernity cannot be separated from the idea of crisis and critique (Koselleck, [1959] 1988). Whether we are talking of 'late-modernity', 'organized modernity', 'the second modernity', 'postmodernity' or 'reflexive modernization', there is general agreement that modernity is a problematical framework of reference and yet one that cannot be so easily abandoned.

There were three critical moments of crisis for modernity: first the Marxist critique of liberal political modernity from the mid-nineteenth century onwards; second, the *fin de siècle* critique of the Enlightenment tradition and the experience with totalitarianism; and, third, the attempt to go beyond modernity at the end of the twentieth century. The Marxist critique, as I have argued, broadly accepted the framework of modernity, seeking merely to realize its normative ideals in everyday life. However, this must be qualified, since Western Marxism – Lukács, Bloch, Gramsci, Marcuse, Benjamin and the Frankfurt School – in its reassessment of the foundations of Marxism reflected a disenchantment with cultural modernity that was more profound than was apparent from Marx's writings. Above all, it expressed a deep crisis of the political Subject and the philosophy of praxis.[1]

The really major onslaught on modernity had its origins in the *fin de siècle* era, with the works of Nietzsche, Heidegger and Freud providing new directions beyond both Marxism and liberalism. The historical experience of modernity was increasingly becoming one that tended to highlight the irrational, a pre-social ontology of Being, the previously hidden forces of the psyche, the fragmentation of culture and the decline of western civilization. The Enlightenment's celebration of civilization as the embodiment of reason and progress was challenged by the new, and particularly German, emphasis on culture. This was the age that emphasized the 'decline of the West', the title of Oswald Spengler's famous work ([1918] 1971), the 'revolt of the masses' (Ortega y Gasset [1930] 1932) and 'the tragedy of culture' (Simmel [1914] 1968), and retold the narrative of modernity as one of a descent into barbarism. The *fin de siècle* witnessed a turn to culture and away from civilization which was seen as decadent and irreversibly in decline; culture, in contrast, held out a promise of salvation and the redemption of something spiritual, far beyond the social and the political horizons of modernity. The First World War and the experience of universal violence undermined for many the promise of the Enlightenment and with the rise of totalitarianism the self-confidence of modernity comes to a final end.

In classical sociology the idea of modernity receives its first major critique with Georg Simmel. His concept of the 'tragedy of culture' gives expression to a certain disenchantment with modernity. In 'The Concept and Tragedy of Culture' ([1914] 1968) and 'The Conflict in Modern Culture' ([1918] 1971a) he outlined one of his most important concepts: the dualism of objective and subjective culture, which in his view is the central conflict of modernity. According to Simmel, culture is divided between two forms, the subjective act of creating culture – by which culture is tied to the individual creator – and the tendency for culture to take on an independent life of its own. The tragedy of culture was the increasing separation of these two domains: the loss of autonomy and creativity under the conditions of societal rationalization. The objectification of culture was a result of the rationalization and differentiation of life. Like Durkheim, Simmel made the concept of differentiation central to his sociology, as is evidenced in his work *On Social Differentiation* [1890]. In another famous essay, 'The Metropolis and Mental Life' ([1903] 1971b), Simmel outlines how the modern city is the arena in which objective culture develops at the cost of subjective or individual culture. One of the distinctive features of the metropolis is the experience of distance between people. In the metropolis the money economy becomes all dominant and shapes social relations, bringing about a fragmentation of experience. In a work influenced by Max Weber's theory of rationalization and Marx's notion of commodification, Simmel extended his analysis of the tragedy of culture in a study on money as a cultural category which intensifies the reification of life ([1907] 1978). His theory of modernity gives more explicit expression to the concept of alienation than that of either Weber or Durkheim. However, unlike Marx's concept of alienation, which was tied to labour, for Simmel alienation is an essentially cultural category.

Finally, it may be asked whether Simmel's analysis leads to the end of the concept of society. While Simmel agreed with Durkheim that society was a reality in itself worthy of scientific analysis, he did not share the latter's positivistic optimism on the visibility of society as a coherent and material domain of 'social facts'. Nor did he look at culture from the perspective of solidarity and civic morality, but from the perspective of the experience of fragmentation for the autonomy of the individual. Viewing society less as a set of 'social facts' than a web or network of relationships, he gradually moved to a position that suggested that the very notion of the social may be absorbed by the cultural. One of his abiding questions was how, under the conditions of the tragedy of culture, is society possible.[2]

One of the most far-reaching critical interpretations of modernity is undoubtedly that associated with the Frankfurt School, and in particular Theodor Adorno and Max Horkheimer, whose *Dialectic of Enlightenment* ([1947] 1979) is a famous example. Writing in the German tradition of *fin de siècle* cultural pessimism, with its heavy overtones of romanticism and despair, Adorno and Horkheimer sought to reconcile Marxism with the theories of Nietzsche, Weber, Mannheim and Freud. The principal argument of the *Dialectic of Enlightenment* was that human history is the story of the struggle between nature and myth. Enlightenment, which they project back to the beginning of western civilization, is the expression of the mastery of nature, which is also the mastery over fear, and this is achieved through instrumental reason. Accordingly, as society gains more and more mastery over nature, it must exercise new forms of domination over subjectivity: the price of mastery over nature is domination over the Self. This is the 'dialectic of Enlightenment': the internalization of domination. Enlightenment is therefore instrumental, binding knowledge to the condition of power. For the authors of this pessimistic book, the ultimate expression of the history of civilization was totalitarianism in its Nazi, Soviet and, in their bleak view, modern mass society. Popular culture, entertainment or the 'culture industry', was explained as the continuation of totalitarianism by other means.

The theory of modernity associated with the Frankfurt School and the writings of Herbert Marcuse (1964) reduced modernity to its negative aspects: modernity was conceived as a closed and totalizing system of power. Of the three dimensions of modernity – the moral-practical, the cognitive and the aesthetic – only the latter offered any chance of an alternative to domination in what they called the 'totally administered society'. So long as the aesthetic dimension remained autonomous of mass society, it could preserve a measure of redemptive critique denied to the rest of culture. For this reason, despite their totalizing critique, Marcuse and the Frankfurt School ultimately adhered to the model of Enlightenment modernity (Honneth, 1991, 1995b).[3] Yet this turn to the aesthetic in Western Marxism reflected a more general shift to the analysis of culture – which is seen as absorbing the social and the political – in the social and political theory of the latter part of the twentieth century. Undoubtedly, this tendency has been influenced by the institutionalization – if not the defeat – of the last radical movements of modernity, the defeat of radical socialism in the 1920s and 1930s and the victory of neo-liberalism in the 1980s over the new social movements of the 1960s and 1970s.

## Rethinking Modernity

In this section I would like to focus on exactly how the framework of modernity as outlined in the previous chapter is in crisis today. I would like to demonstrate in some detail exactly how the three central dimensions of modernity have been undermined by developments in the twentieth century, all of which have been intensified in the last decade of that century. Taking the defining themes of the autonomy of the political Subject, the autonomy of culture and the autonomy of the social, I shall outline how developments in the direction of fragmentation in each of these domains have transformed the project of modernity, forcing us to rethink our theoretical categories. My thesis is that the discourses of radical constructivism – creativity, reflexivity and discursivity – are being released from the societal framework of modernity and are shaping the world in which we live today to a far greater extent than ever before. However, I do not see this as an abandonment but as a radicalization of modernity, since these discourses have always been deeply embedded in modernity.

### The fragmentation of the political Subject

In the discourses of modernity there was relative confidence about the autonomy of the Subject. The threat of fragmentation did not call into question the category of the Self as autonomous and self-legislating. Today we are forced to think of these terms in new ways. The problem the current situation presents is one of the fragmentation of the political Subject. In the discourses of modernity the Self was constituted as an active agent resisting state violence and instituting a political project of self-realization. This notion of the Self or Subject was formulated in terms of a process of liberation from constraining structures, principally the absolute state and church. In the great conceptions of modernity the Subject was seen as essentially political. But from the beginning of the twentieth century the Subject became 'linguistified' as a result of the semiotic turn – from Mead to Heidegger and Wittgenstein – and with this 'linguistification' of the social came a certain dissolution in the coherence of its political constitution.

Thus one of the central questions for the sociologists of the first half of the twentieth century concerned the survival of the autonomous Self under the conditions of mass society. The modern Subject was formed in a society of producers, but we are now living in a society of consumers in which creativity is no longer tied to the production of commodities. The question of autonomy is much more complex today, for, in general, the threat to human autonomy does not come from either the state or the church but from a variety of other forces, such as the market, urban violence, environmental destruction, changes in the uses of information and cultural production, and identity politics such as those pertaining to gender and race. Indeed, it may be suggested that we are no longer living in a 'mass' society but in a 'de-massified' network of social relations (Castells, 1996; Maffesoli, 1996). We are living in a de-massified society in the sense that the threat to the autonomy of the individual comes not from the 'mass' which annihilates the autonomous individual but from the very self-expressions of individuality itself. It has increasingly been recognized that our society is far from a mass society. For instance, Maffesoli (1996) speaks of the replacement of mass society with 'tribes' – new 'emotional communities' which establish new relations of sociability which are unstable, open and ephemeral. The problem of autonomy must therefore be posed in different terms: it can no longer refer to a self-contained individual or a political Subject.

What has become questionable today is the very coherence of the idea of the autonomy of the Self, in its personal and collective manifestations. The notion of universalizable personhood, which I have argued underlay the modern project, has collapsed by the end of the twentieth century in an intellectual climate that celebrates difference, the Self as context-bound, and multiple identity projects. We are less inclined to believe in the idea of an abstract and universal person today: the discourse of the Self has unleashed multiple selves whose autonomy is not something that can be articulated in the traditional terms associated with modernity. This does not necessarily imply the obsolescence of autonomy but it does point to a need to rethink its fundamental categories. The discourse of modernity commenced with the self-assertion of the human Subject, who was essentially political, and the search for a legitimate social and political order. The idea emerged of a social contract between society and state in order to preserve the autonomy of the Self. The concept of legitimacy associated with this was self-referential: modernity's legitimacy was derived from a belief in the autonomy of its Subject who as legislator did not have to question the authenticity of its project, which was conceived of as a ruptural event of world historical proportions. It is this self-referentiality – that modernity derives its legitimacy from itself and not by reference to a transcendental principle – that is in question today, for the Self has collapsed into a variety of projects – such as those of creed, race and gender – which do not accept any terms of universal reference. In a world of plurality, difference and the heterogeneity of identity, we can no longer speak of a 'popular sovereignty', for what is in contention is precisely the very coherence of sovereignty itself as a unifying principle. The belief that the world can be integrated around a unified principle is now a deeply problematic notion (Peters, 1993). Yet we hold on to a belief in the desirability of rights and justice as important cultural aspirations.

## The fragmentation of culture and knowledge

Not only has the integrity, or self-legislation, of political subjectivity been rendered problematical with the release of creativity from the bounds of the political, but so too has the epistemic model of modern cultural rationality. Subjectivity and nature are no longer two opposites confronting each other. Nature has become 'socialized' in the extreme sense that modern science and technology have succeeded in fashioning nature in the image of science. The struggle for the mastery of nature is complete as a result of the ascendancy of science. Under the aegis of the risk society, nature has become a new theme in political discourses and identity projects. These discourses and projects have in common the rejection of an ethic of mastery: nature is not constructed as an object of mastery but has become an equal participant. The risk society (see Chapter 6) has brought a new relationship between subjectivity and objectivity into existence. Nature is now seen as a domain of vulnerability and malleability, with risk deriving not from the dangers of nature but from modern science and technology. Accordingly, the notion of a primordial state of nature has been replaced by the vision of the universal destructiveness of the risk society. Instead of being a means of emancipation from primordiality, science has become the source of new dangers which are capable of annihilating both nature and society. In short, we have reached the age of the 'death of nature'.

We have also witnessed an end to one of modernity's greatest myths – the neutrality of science. The discourses of modernity saw science as a 'mirror of nature', to use Richard Rorty's (1979) term, and not as a partner in dialogue. Today, matters are very different, for nature can now be manufactured in the image of science. Developments in biotechnology, for instance, have fundamentally changed the relationship between science and nature (Delanty, 1998c). According to the authors of the Gulbenkian Commission's report (Wallerstein et al., 1996), one of the most significant changes is the collapse of the dualism of society and nature: they are no longer opposites, confronting each other in relations of exteriority. One of the implications of this is the obsolescence of positivism as a scientific methodology even in the natural sciences, which no longer holds to the notion of nature as unchangeable and fixed in time. This collapse of positivism opens up new possibilities for mediation between society and nature.

The transformation of nature is one of the most discussed questions of the 1990s as far as social change is concerned. It may be argued that nature is becoming more and more cultural (Eder, 1996a). According to Ulrich Beck (1992a), nature in the risk society is becoming a construction of society and, as a consequence, the dualism of society and nature, the basis of modern rationalism and the Enlightenment, is no longer relevant in an age that is seeking new mediations between Subject and Object, the world of the social and the world of nature. Thus, politics is becoming increasingly concerned about nature and the embeddedness of the social in nature, and, as a consequence, new political-cultural questions, such as that of collective responsibility, are emerging (Apel, 1991, 1992; Strydom, 1998; Delanty, 1998c). What I think these developments point to is the increasing reflexivity of culture and knowledge. Knowledge is more available and is also becoming more contested.

## The fragmentation of the social

One of the central dimensions to modernity has been the project of institution-building as a search for a legitimate social and political order. The discourses of modernity emerged in the context of the rise of the social as a reality *sui generis*. The distinctive feature of the social was the mediating domain of social institutions which separate subjectivity from nature. Humanity was seen as emerging out of the state of nature and entering the world of institutions which protect subjectivity from the violence of the state of nature as well as from political violence. For the architects of modernity the rise of the social was one of the dominating features of the age, in particular the project of social engineering around the centralizing state. The transition to national-statehood was a fundamental dimension to this search for a legitimate social and political order.

At the end of the twentieth century, however, we are witnessing the decline of the social, not its rise. Just as modernity arose out of the collapse of the institutions of the Middle Ages, so too is a new historical experience arising out of the decline of the institutions of modernity. Processes of globalization have undermined the project of modernity as one of institution-building by an autonomous agency. What has collapsed is a belief in both the autonomy of agency and the legitimacy of the social and political order. Globalization entails a view of society which questions the idea of a legitimate order that is self-contained. Instead of a self-legislating subjectivity, we have the spectre of a world out of control, or at least one that is not controlled by any one social agent. Globalization, in short, challenges one of the presuppositions of modernity, namely the project of the nationalization of society (Sassen, 1996). Modernity was erected on the foundations of national societies whereby the nation was seen as the embodiment of social agency and the basis of a legitimate social and political order. The autonomy of the Subject was a reflection of the autonomy of the state and of knowledge. In the global society now emerging, the nation-state is losing its ability to legislate, having been challenged by many forces. The result is not so much the decline of the nation or state, but their increasing uncoupling. The result: nation and state go their own separate ways, releasing in one direction a politics of identity and, in another, an unfettered instrumentalism.

The implications of these developments, tendentially pointing towards the fragmentation of the social, force us to rethink the social rather than abandon it. The important issue here is the radicalization of the discursive dimension. Thus I do not think that we need to jettison the idea of autonomy but to rethink it in light of the growing importance of the discursive regulation of power. According to Bernard Peters (1993), as a result of societal complexity, social theory must abandon the view that the sovereignty of the Subject can be reflected in a normative order based on consensus. I shall be arguing for a reconceptualization of the social around a model of discursively structured public communication which draws upon creativity and reflexivity.

In the following section I would like to consider in more detail the contemporary challenge to the social, which, I shall be arguing, is less one of the end of the social under the conditions of its total fragmentation than one of new possibilities for mediation which opens up the prospect of a self-regulating society based on discursive institutionalization. Instead of normative integration focused on the nation-state, what is becoming more important is a certain kind of cognitive integration based on knowledge and networks.

## Autonomy versus Fragmentation: The Loss of Unity

One of the enduring tenets of modernity was the vision of society as a uniform entity, a cohesive order shaped in the image of the modern national state. Yet, this homogeneous vision of the social was also one that was seen as relatively differentiated in terms of its structures. Modern society was both a unity and a differentiated order; it offered a model of social integration which was post-traditional in its separation of the institutional spheres. As a national society it was a uniform and cohesive entity which made possible a degree of social integration. As already noted, it was also a differentiated order in that it was functionally separated into distinct cultural, social, political and economic institutions and structures. The challenge for much of the classical tradition was to relate both of these principles – integration and differentiation. The challenge for today, however, is that both of these notions – the uniformity and differentiation of the social – have been replaced by new principles of order, and as a result new zones of tension are opened up.

One of the most far-reaching changes is the gradual shift from *differentiation* to *de-differentiation* and the related shift from *integration* to *fragmentation*. By de-differentiation is meant the blurring of the boundaries between institutional structures, such as culture and economy, the private and the public, rights and identity, work and leisure.[4] We are witnessing growing *interpenetration* of institutional structures with the result that the discourses of modernity – creativity, reflexivity and discursivity – are undergoing far-reaching transformation.[5] Modernity was constructed on the separation of the functionally distinct domains of the state and economy, the separation of the society and state, the demarcation of the private from the public and the autonomy of the cultural. Today, it is increasingly difficult to say that these spheres are differentiated from each other in the same way. The class structure is no longer rigid, and capitalism has entered its 'disorganized phase' (Lash and Urry, 1987; Offe, 1985). In short, what is collapsing is the organic image of the body as the metaphor of the social. As will be apparent from the following chapters, while social theorists differ on what is replacing the metaphor of the body there is much agreement that the idea of a functionally integrated society is at best questionable. I am inclined to agree with Manuel Castells's (1996) claim that the current situation of the social is best described as a 'network society', a web of globalized interlinkages cutting across the economic, the political and the cultural (see Chapter 7).[6] In the present context the point is that the concept of the 'net' – which is diffuse and decentred, with overlapping connections and de-differentiated structures – is more appropriate to characterize the changes that are occurring today than the metaphor of the body, which suggests something more organic and functionally differentiated. The body may grow old and mature, but (cyborgs aside) it retains the same organic structure, while the net is open and diffuse, forever acquiring and losing structures and nodal points.

The notion of de-differentiation does not entail a reversal of the logic of differentiation, or a return to premodern harmony. A de-differentiated society is a product of societal complexity. As I have argued, our society is characterized by ever more complexity in its structures and functions (Luhmann, 1990; Peters, 1993; Zolo, 1992). This condition of complexity is implied in the idea of differentiation, but in its current form differentiation has produced a situation of decentring to a degree that the relevance of the framework of modernity is in question. Essential to that framework was the assumption that the differentiated nature of the social was contained by a central organizing principle which made possible a degree of integration or uniformity. The great social theorists of modernity – Marx, Durkheim, Weber, Parsons – all took for granted that the differentiating and rationalizing logic of modern society was counterbalanced by the search for a principle of integration.[7] For Marx, it was the raising of class consciousness; for Durkheim, it was the belief in the co-operative ties of organic solidarity; for Weber, it was the belief in the virtues of a formal electoral democracy; and for Parsons, it was value consensus and world community. I am arguing that this assumption of cohesiveness is no longer tenable. There are two reasons for this: first, as already argued, the boundaries between the institutional structures are no longer as rigid as they were in past; second, the state is no longer capable of imposing an organizing principle on society, which is becoming increasingly centreless.

The result of this situation of interpenetration and de-differentiation is a reconfiguration of social structures. On the one hand, as a result of the decline in the sovereignty of the nation-state, the domains of economy, polity, culture and social relations are becoming detached from each other more than ever before and, on the other hand, this breakdown in integration is accompanied by new possibilities of recombination. I shall discuss (in a sketch that mirrors that of the preceding chapter) this tendency towards the fragmentation of the model of modernity in more detail with respect to the domains of polity, economy, culture and social relations.

*Polity*   The fragmentation of the polity is one of the more visible manifestations of the wider social fragmentation. This is apparent on a number of fronts. The function of the state is increasingly shifting from being a provider of social goods to a regulator. The rise of the regulatory state (Majone, 1996) has occurred in a context of a more general undermining of the sovereignty of the nation-state, whose power is being eroded upwards by transnational processes, downwards by the resurgence of regionalism and transversally by social movements and organized interests (Dunn, 1995). Globalization (Albrow, 1996; Axford, 1995; Robertson, 1992; Sassen, 1996; Waters, 1995) has undoubtedly been a major factor in the erosion of the sovereignty of the nation-state. The state organized on a national basis is increasingly unable to control financial markets, communication and information systems, international crime and threats to the environment. Of course the impact of globalization has been ambivalent, serving to enhance the power of the nation-state in some respects, while undermining it in other areas (Hirst and Thompson, 1996).[8] Rejecting simple globalization theory (i.e. the view that the world is becoming more homogeneous), I would like to argue that we cannot avoid the conclusion that we have witnessed the end of the self-contained territorial state fully in control of its destiny.

The state today is left in a situation of endemic delegitimation, which has penetrated into the heart of the civic culture. With the erosion of the legitimacy of the state as a result of the decline in its actual sovereignty, the other spheres of what may be broadly called the 'polity' are opened up to public scrutiny: the administrative system, the military and the legal system (Burns, 1999). But it is not just a question of public scrutiny, it is also one of the interpenetration of subsystems. For instance, the sexual politics that have surrounded President Clinton demonstrate the degree to which legal activism has overdetermined politics, even against media and public opposition. It appears that the polity is no longer unified by the state as such, which ceases to be a utopia. Consequently, political struggles lose their sense of focus. Thus citizenship, for instance, is no longer seen as something that can be institutionalized by the state. Citizenship can be seen as membership of a political community and is defined by reference to rights, duties or responsibilities, participation and collective identity. Moreover, citizenship has both an inward and an outside face: internally, it seeks to codify the ties that bind the individual to the state; externally, it defines the membership of the political community by reference to other nation-states. Citizenship has therefore been predominantly equated with nationality. What we are witnessing today is the fragmentation of this model and the growing separation of its four components – rights, duties, participation and identity – into new discourses (Delanty, 1997a; Jacobson, 1997; Janoski, 1998). Thus, rights are becoming a new field of cultural contestation (Lury, 1993). Soysal (1994) has argued how universal rights of personhood are beginning to provide an alternative basis for transnational citizenship. This is particularly apparent in the case of immigrants, who can challenge nationality as an exclusive reference point. She argues that this is leading towards a model of citizenship based on deterritorialized rights, a model indicative of a new post-national order which is emerging in the global and post-Cold War era. The idea of duties and responsibilities is also breaking away from the conservative category of dutiful citizenship and is becoming a key category in the politics of reflexivity. Collective responsibility for the future is no longer a conservative idea but an expression of growing reflexivity. Collective identity and participation is being codified in ways beyond national identity by new social movements. The framework that is emerging is complex, with citizenship being recodified in many different ways. Thus, for instance, the new cultural communitarianism of neo-nationalism takes over the components of identity and rights to produce a new kind of cultural imaginary which mobilizes newly invented nations against states.

*Economy*    Some of the most striking changes have occurred in the transformation of the economy. Technology, in particular information technology, has transformed economic production by making information an ingredient in the forces of production, and frequently replacing labour (Castells, 1996).[9] The emerging information-based economy, though still capitalist, is no longer one that can be seen in terms of the exploitation of labour and the commodification of social relations. A new emphasis has emerged on 'postfordism', or capitalism in its postmodern phase. Postfordist production entails a shift away from economies of scale (or large-scale mass production based on single skilled workers and lifetime employment) to more flexible and smaller firms (often based on part-time and multi-skilled labour). This has led to a blurring of the divide between domestic work and waged work as well as the end of lifelong and full employment, with many entry points into and out of the labour market (Aronowitz and Cutler, 1998). The concept of postfordism points to the overall ability of capitalism to sustain economic growth without full employment.[10] Postfordism also represents a shift in the theorization of capitalism from production towards consumption. Postfordist analyses typically emphasize the extension of commodity production into the cultural sphere of consumption. The emphasis on consumption is related to the break-up of the strict separation of work and leisure and the subordination of the latter to the former.

The notion of the class-based actor, defined in terms of economic interests, is becoming outdated today as a result of the emergence of what may be more generally called a 'postmaterialist' society.[11] This has been best described by Daniel Bell (1979) as the divorce of the economy from its traditional moorings in cultural value systems which stress individual achievement through the 'work ethic'. In this diagnosis these values are being undermined by new cultural values – the quest for hedonism, an obsessive concern with the Self, immediate gratification – which do not supply the economic reproduction with its motivational basis; as a result, a culture of consumerism clashes with a culture of production. While Bell assumed that capitalism still needs a work ethic to sustain it, it can be argued that this, in fact, is no longer the case: the cultural values that economic reproduction requires are precisely those that Bell assumed were undermining it. Lash and Urry (1987) describe the interpenetration of economy and culture in the new production of 'signs' rather than just objects: the penetration of economic production into the production of cultural commodities. In short, it is precisely culture itself that is commodified. The emergence of a consumption-oriented society calls into question the Marxist notion of alienation, which presupposes a rational Subject whose interests are distorted by false consciousness deriving from the separation of use values from market values.

Finally, it may be mentioned that the transformation in the concept of nature in recent times and the emergence of the risk society has led to a fundamental questioning of the ideology of unlimited economic growth. Most governments today are committed to some degree of 'sustainable development'. Though there is no evidence to indicate that this has yet resulted in an appreciable change in economic reproduction, the new sensitivity to the ecological limits to growth may be cited as an example of a questioning of both capitalism and modernity. However, the questioning of capitalist modernity must be qualified, for it no longer appears a likely prospect that capitalism will be abandoned in favour of a new mode of production.

*Culture*  It will be recalled from the previous chapter that the cultural framework of modernity can be characterized as the differentiation of culture into the separate domains of the cognitive, the moral practical and the aesthetic. Modernity as a cultural idea begins with the break-up of the unified world-view of medieval Christendom and the emergence of an essentially differentiated cultural framework whose constituent spheres cannot be subsumed under religion, which becomes just one discourse. According to Weber, who provided one of the most detailed analyses of the rationalization of the modern world-view, modernity is, above all, characterized by disenchantment: the gradual loss of enchantment or magic as a result of the rationalization, secularization and intellectualization of cultural discourses. In the classic conceptions, modernity was thus defined as post-traditional. However, cultural reproduction has not entirely borne out Weber's thesis. Religion, which may indeed have become secularized, has at the same time become – perhaps because of its secularization – a powerful force in the world (Barber, 1996; Beyer, 1994). In the global context, religious fundamentalism presents a challenge of enormous proportions to modernity. How else are we to understand the varied expressions of identity, religion, nationalism and community which have erupted in the late twentieth century? More generally, the view that tradition is in decline must be measured against the thesis that tradition is frequently invented by modernity (Hobsbawm and Ranger, 1983).

  My thesis is that the concept of disenchantment which is so central to the project of modernity is today rivalled by the desire for *enchantment*. However, the kind of enchantment we are faced with today is not the revenge of premodern tradition or the return of irrational historical forces, but the product of late modernity. The spectre of a new enchantment is not confined to the non-western world, but is deeply embedded in the culture and psyche of the western world. The cultural discourses of modernity were a western project, while the new cultural discourses that are emerging in the late twentieth century are products of a globalized world which is no longer entirely shaped by the West (Larrain, 1994; Santos, 1995, Turner, 1994). The penchant for enchantment can be seen in a number of contexts: in nationalism, neo-fascism, the fantasy world of cyberspace and new kinds of communication technology, advertising, popular culture, religious revivalism and the identity projects of a whole range of social movements. In the present context of the limits of modernity I merely wish to argue that re-enchantment has become a real force to be reckoned with. It challenges the model of disenchantment on at least two fronts.

First, the new culture of enchantment releases a spirit of community which undermines the modernist project of society. It may be suggested that community is rapidly becoming the new 'imaginary' of our time. All over the world people are appealing to the idea of community as an antidote to the problems generated by modernity. The desire for re-enchantment undermines the older faith in society, but the kind of community that is now being appealed to is not that of premodern tradition, as in Tönnies's famous concept of community as a cohesive world in which culture and society are perfectly fused. The new discourse of community is a postmodernized discourse in the sense that it suggests the release of culture from society. An extreme version of this might be the 'virtual communities' of cyberspace: communities of images, flows of virtual realities (Meyrowitz, 1986). According to the sociology of modernity, 'community' was to be overtaken by the rationalized and disenchanted world of 'society', which could recapture the spirit of community only in limited ways. The contemporary return of community challenges this prognosis and seriously calls into question the ability of society to provide an enduring basis of integration (Delanty, 1998d).

Second, the idea of re-enchantment captures the contemporary salience of identity projects which seem to challenge, or at least reconfigure, the great ideologies of modernity. These ideologies – liberalism, conservatism, socialism – were primarily codified by intellectual elites and defined the relationship between state and society; they specified a subject and were designed for the purpose of the mobilization of the population. At some level or another ideologies sought to gain state power and were based on comprehensive political doctrines. Today, it has become commonplace to remark that these classic ideologies have come to an end, or at least no longer command mass allegiance (Wallerstein, 1996). What has replaced them is a new politics of identity (Delanty, 1998e). But what is distinctive about this new politics of identity is not so much the disappearance of ideology but its refraction or recombination by new social actors as well as the older ones, who are launching what are essentially identity projects. My contention is that identity politics is very much about the desire for enchantment in a disenchanted age. Ideology may be important to this (as in the case of nationalism) but is not essential. Indeed, the example of the new nationalism – which emerges as a result of the decoupling of nation and space – attests to the decline of ideology and its replacement by identity (Delanty, 1997e, 1997f). It is this drive for a world that gives more place to feelings, emotions, and desires that inspires many social movements.

A few more remarks can be made on the limits of the discourses of modernity in so far as they pertain to the cultural domain. The quest for re-enchantment is mirrored in the internal de-differentiation of the three constituent domains of modern culture – the normative or moral practical, the cognitive (knowledge) and the aesthetic-expressive spheres. Not only is the functional separation of culture from economy, polity and social relations being blurred, but the differentiated nature of culture is itself undergoing far-reaching de-differentiation (Anderson, 1998, pp. 62–3). In other words, the three spheres of culture are losing their autonomy. One of the most notable changes here is the extension of the aesthetic over the normative. With the release of the aesthetic beyond its boundaries in the autonomous institution of art, subjectivity enters the cultural field considerably radicalized. Since the early European avant-garde, the aesthetic has slowly become released from the autonomous institution of art to enter the practice of life. The late-modern alliance of the aesthetic with subjectivity brings to completion the project of aesthetic modernity. This is one of the most far-reaching changes today and its consequences can be seen in the release and politicalization of sexuality and new forces of cultural creativity, including consumption.

Another salient change is the end of the autonomy of cognitive rationality: knowledge is no longer autonomous, an end in itself, but has become instrumentalized as a result of the new production of knowledge (Gibbons et al., 1994). Knowledge is no longer the privilege of an elite nor protected in the ivory towers of the institution of the university, but has become more available to a growing number of people and is a major source of contention in late modern society, a situation that leads to a rethinking of the role of the university as a site of knowledge (Delanty, 1998a, 1998b). It is widely recognized that we are living in a 'knowledge society' (Böhme, 1997; Böhme and Stehr, 1986; Castells, 1996; Stehr, 1992), by which is meant that knowledge has become the social and economic basis of society. With the advent of the knowledge society the modernist assumption that knowledge is an end in itself is called into question: in the knowledge society, knowledge itself is the found-ation of a wide variety of social and economic processes, and therefore no longer belongs to the cultural model. Accompanying this levelling of knowledge is a growing loss of faith in the forms of knowledge celebrated by modernity. Instead of certainty, the most striking feature of knowledge today is its contested nature. More and more social actors have access to knowledge, which is no longer the domain of elites. As a result of, principally, AIDS and biotechnological developments and the related threats, such as radioactivity and BSE, the scientists' monopoly on knowledge has broken down and new definitions have emerged.

Finally, it may be mentioned that the modern discourses of rights and justice, which formed the core of many ideologies, are being supplanted by a new discourse of collective responsibility (see Chapter 4). It is difficult to say precisely what form this will eventually take, but there seems to be widespread agreement that the normative or political-ethical discourse of our time is becoming less focused on rights and justice than on the question of collective responsibility. Some indications of this are the almost universal need for a new political ethic for collective responsibility for the environment. In the extreme version of this thesis, proposed by Ulrich Beck (1992a), there is already evidence that the ecological question will replace the social question as the primary political goal.

*Social relations*    In the previous chapter I argued that modernity entailed a view of social relations which strongly emphasized the idea of civil society, or the culture of publicity. Modern social relations were seen as residing primarily in the essentially public domain which constituted civil society. Intellectuals and 'public man' were thus the paradigmatic expressions of the modern individual. The sociology of modernity recognized the gradual absorption of civil society and its culture of publicity into mass society, with the result that one of its central questions was addressed to the survival of critical and autonomous individuality in a world dominated by the uniformity of cultural reproduction. Social relations no longer correspond to this model. As I have already argued, we have moved from mass society to a de-massified society. The assumptions of an older sociology about the relationship of the individual to cultural reproduction are now no longer accepted. It is generally recognized that cultural reproduction in the area of consumption – advertising, popular culture, tourism, mass media, sport etc. – is not

entirely manipulative and that social actors have powers of interpretation and can act strategically – one of the central insights of the
sociology of Pierre Bourdieu. This emphasis on the creative potentialities of the social actor – the autonomy of action – and the essential openness of cultural production is particularly evident in the
cultural opportunities of the web and 'informationalism'. Modernity entailed the transition from an oral culture to a written one. In
the late twentieth century we are moving from a purely written culture to a cyber-culture, the virtual world of informationalism, a new
culture of signs and images (Castells, 1996, 1997, 1998). In sum, we
can reject the notion of an overwhelming mass society which un-
leashes total domination in the making of what Marcuse (1964)
called 'one-dimensional man'. This vision was based on a pessimistic assessment of the decline of bourgeois written culture and a rejection of popular culture. The emerging 'network society' is a
potentially democratic society, but is based on fundamentally
different kinds of social and cultural structures than what has
preceded it. In this context we can also comment on the weakening
of ascription through social roles. Roles are no longer as rigid today
as they were in the past: the roles set by class, gender and work, for
instance, are more fluid than before, thus bringing about greater
indeterminacy in life chances (Furlong and Cartmel, 1997).

Related to the obsolescence of the idea of mass society and the
uniformity of a work-based society we have probably also reached
the limits of the Enlightenment model of civility in the sense of civil
society. Civil society was defined by reference to the absolute state
and stood for the autonomy of the social. It must not be forgotten
that this model of civility was also defined by opposition to the
private world. Thus, civil society was a domain between the auto-
cratic world of the state apparatus and the private world of domestic relations. The idea of civil society survived into recent times
largely as a result of the opposition to Soviet totalitarianism in
Eastern Europe, where the memory of this Enlightenment tradition
was a powerful source of intellectual and political resistance
(Delanty, 1996b). Today, it is difficult to see the relevance of the
model of civil society, for the two poles of opposition upon which it
was based have lost much of their socially determined power.
Changes in the labour market and four decades of feminism have
undermined the idea of the separation of the private from the public
and the separation of domestic work from paid work. On the other
side, changes in the state and the end of totalitarianism as a political
system call into question the Enlightenment idea of civil society as a
domain separate from the polity which has been rendered diffuse.
In whatever way we are to understand social relations today, it is

evident that we need a concept of society that recognizes the end of the dualism of state versus society and public versus private.

A general thesis can be advanced at this stage: social change over the last four decades has led to a situation that challenges the project of modernity in a number of key respects. If the idea of autonomy as a political, cultural and social project was essential to modernity, the contemporary situation points to the reality of fragmentation. Subjectivity has been released from the older institutions, which are suffering a loss in legitimacy and whose boundaries are becoming de-differentiated in a new and diffuse world. Modernity stood for determinacy and certainty; the twenty-first-century world is moving towards a celebration of indeterminacy, contingency and uncertainty. This does not mean that we are abandoning modernity in total for a new epoch, but for one in which the categories of modernity are being reconfigured, while some are being cast aside. In the most general sense, the current situation can be seen in terms of a movement towards an enhanced discursivity, an increased emphasis on knowledge. It is my thesis that the social can no longer be seen in terms of a model of normative integration and functional differentiation. The above considerations point to the emergence of new integrative mechanisms which operate through cultural patterns such as knowledge and new flows of political and cultural communication, which all have implications for the discursive regulation of power. The upshot of this is that democracy is released from the nation-state and in the uncoupling of nation and state, identity is released into a world of open communicative flows. It is in these flows that the social must be conceptualized. Can democracy be won from a politics of pure identity as well as from a politics of bureaucratic instrumentalism? If mass society transformed the individual from a producer to a consumer, can current developments lead to the age of the citizen?

The subsequent chapters in this book will explore various attempts to comprehend these developments, focusing in particular on the relationship between creativity, reflexivity and discursivity. But first, in order to take the present discussion further, I shall consider in the next section some theoretical concepts which can help us understand social change in relation to these logics of development. This will assist us in the task of critically assessing the social theories to be discussed in later chapters. In this, a central question will be: how can we reconceptualize autonomy under the conditions of the apparent fragmentation of the social? Can the new discursive spaces be captured for democratic politics?

## Beyond the Classical Tradition: Contemporary Theories of the Social

Contemporary sociological theory has moved far beyond the classical theorists in their understanding of social change. While Elias (1987) attacked sociology for retreating into the present, most of the major sociological theories of social change are rooted in the contingencies of the present. What has collapsed is the great myth of modernity and the idea of epochal change which sustained its temporal trajectory and spatial categories. Contemporary social theory does not take the historical model of the transition from traditional society to modern society as the model for understanding social change today but the dissolution of the modern itself into a variety of trajectories.

Before embarking on analysis of some of the major social theories of modernity and their conceptions of social change, I shall briefly characterize some general theorizations of the social in contemporary sociology. The following theories point to important theoretical developments which will guide the analysis in this book: Jeffrey Alexander's neo-functionalist approach; Hans Joas's theory of the creativity of action; Klaus Eder's theory of collective learning and, finally, drawing from a variety of sources, the theory of cognitive practice. I shall outline the central ideas of each of these and in the final section of this chapter I shall attempt to draw some general conclusions which will provide a critical reference point for the subsequent chapters. My central aim is to provide a basis for a theorization of the social in terms of an emphasis on cultural (normative, cognitive and aesthetic) linkages between structure and agency. In other words, the central task is to see how, under the conditions of social fragmentation, social action can be conceived of as autonomous. My thesis is that autonomy can be theorized around a notion of discursivity (the increase in communicative action), reflexivity (the socially determining power of knowledge and cultural models) and creativity (expressivity, imagination and experience in relationship to the Self and identity).

### Culture as mediation

In his revision of classical modernization theory and functionalism, Jeffrey Alexander (1998) proposes a new version of functionalism called 'neo-functionalism'. Rejecting the older versions of functionalism for their conservatism and their neglect of the multifaceted

nature of culture, Alexander places culture at the centre of his
approach, which is less a new departure than a reworking of the
Parsonian heritage. In his view, the most important dynamic in modern societies is the process of differentiation, as originally elaborated
by Spencer and Durkheim and later by Parsons. For this reason he is
reluctant to declare the end of functionalism, although he does recognize the one-sidedness of the classical approach, which failed to
incorporate regional and national variations or the fact that the transition between the various phases of social development was caused
by war. More seriously, Parsons did not provide an explanation of
the processes that lead to differentiation.[12] In order to overcome
the static conception of differentiation in Parsonian functionalism,
Alexander gives greater attention to how particular conflicts and
modes of collective action are linked to particular phases of social
development and are specific to social institutions in different contexts. In his theory differentiation generates discontents, opposition
and backlashes against modernization, which is never a uniform
development. Alexander's most far-reaching revision of Parsonian
functionalism is his rejection of the idea of a master trend of change.
In the present context, what is noteworthy is his retention of Parsons's emphasis on the importance of culture (1998, pp. 60–1). Alexander stresses that the symbolic function of culture is a mediatory
category between structure and agency (1998, pp. 216–21). Action is
exercised through, not against, culture; it is inherently related to
culture and is not a process standing outside it. But action is also
autonomous in that it does not simply reproduce or internalize culture; it can also transform it.

It is Alexander's thesis that one of the principal failures of Parsons was to neglect the linguistic or discursive turn in modern
social theory and philosophy. While this took a variety of forms –
in anthropology, in hermeneutic philosophy, in post-structuralism
– it expressed a common belief in the objectivity of culture which
can be read as a text consisting of symbolic structures. Parsons, in
contrast, reduced the importance of cultural symbols to values
and thus failed to see how symbolic systems can be read in different ways by social actors who have the power of cultural interpretation. At this point the distinctive feature of neo-functionalism
becomes apparent: Parsonian functionalism must be married to
a late-Durkheimian approach. Alexander argues that it was
Durkheim's achievement that in his later writings, chiefly *The
Elementary Forms of the Religious Life* ([1912] 1915), he provided the
basis of a theory of the symbolic.[13] The difference between Parsons
and the late Durkheim was that the former tried to generalize
about culture from actual social behaviour, while Durkheim

looked at the interpretative analysis of the actor's meanings or discourse:

> Durkheim was intent on creating a very different kind of sociology, one that would never confuse the analysis of social functions with the patterned understandings of actors themselves. Rather than the weak cultural theory of values that Parsons recommended – which allowed him so neatly to differentiate sociology from anthropology – the late Durkheimian position implies a strong theory that argues against such a disciplinary separation and, in the process, against any radical disjunction between 'traditional' and 'modern' societies as well. (Alexander, 1998, p. 220)

Alexander goes on to defend a 'strong program for cultural sociology' – one inspired by the late Durkheim. The distinctive feature of this is the irreducibility of action and culture. Action is autonomous, for social actors do not merely affirm a conformity with values and, on the other side, culture, which, codified in symbols and narratives, contains what Paul Ricoeur (1977) called a 'surplus of meaning' over and above the meanings that social actors give to their concrete acts. This surplus creates a certain tension in the relation between culture and action.[14]

In order to see how culture can be conceived more dynamically as a basis of creative action, let us consider the theory of Hans Joas.

## The creativity of action

Hans Joas's (1996) theory of the 'creativity of action' provides a further basis for a non-reductionist theory of action and one that sees social change as historically contingent. Drawing on the pragmatic social theory of John Dewey and George Herbert Mead, Joas argues that the dimension of creativity has been a much neglected aspect of the history of social theory and has been overshadowed by the two predominant models of rational action (in utilitarianism and Marxism) and normatively oriented action (in functionalism). In his view there is a creative dimension to all human action, but this has been marginalized in the history of social theory. The idea of creativity challenges the dominant models of social action in that it aims to overcome the dualism of agency and structure, which generate a residual category of non-creative action. The creativity of action is the hidden history of social theory and is suggested by the ideas of expression in the work of Herder and the ideas of production and revolution in Marx:

The idea of expression circumscribes creativity primarily in relation to the subjective world of the actor. The idea of production relates creativity to the objective world, the world of material objects that are the conditions of the means of action. And finally, the idea of revolution assumes that there is a potential of human creativity relative to the social world, namely that we fundamentally reorganize the social institutions that govern human existence. (Joas, 1996, p. 71)

However, it is Joas's thesis that these attempts to reduce creativity to just one dimension failed, and it was the task of the philosophy of life or the expressivist anthropological tradition in continental philosophy – from Schopenhauer and Nietzsche to Simmel – and the American tradition of pragmatism – from Dewey, James and Peirce to Mead – to place the idea of creativity on a new basis in order to link creativity to social action. Creativity must be rescued from irrationalism and aestheticism as well as the Marxist and historicist emphasis on a macrosubject in the same way that social action must be rescued from rationalism and purely normative concepts of society. Joas believes that pragmatism, modified to incorporate a stronger emphasis on creativity, is best equipped to deal with this, and believes that the idea of the creativity of action is also best able to account for present-day psycho-social developments (1996, p. 252). The implications of Joas's theory is that the idea of the creativity of action is capable of mediating agency, structure and culture.

His approach resembles that of Castoriadis ([1975] 1987, 1994, 1997) in that it is addressed to the question of creativity, but differs in that, in contrast to Castoriadis's Aristotelian Marxism, Joas seeks to derive creativity from the pragmatist tradition and to relate this concept to social change in contemporary society. His thesis is that structural changes – shorter working hours, female employment, team-based organizational structures and the spread of flexible links between work and leisure – allow for new possibilities to infuse creativity into one's biography and enhance personal autonomy (Joas, 1996, pp. 253–4). Joas sees the culture of creativity as being a struggle between three kinds of creativity: primary creativity (which is purely imaginative, fanciful and expresses a kind of playfulness), secondary creativity (which is more concerned with technical solutions as opposed to the production of something new) and integrated creativity (which is a synthesis of primary and secondary creativity). This concept of integrated creativity is one of self-articulation, but is wedded to the responsibility of self-control (Joas, 1996, p. 255). The failure of this kind of creativity to emerge happens when the secondary forms of creativity fail and there is a fall-back into a reactive primary creativity, or irrationalism.

In my view, the concept of creativity in the writings of Castoriadis and Joas is of major importance to social theory, in particular in the context of understanding social change today. Given the increased importance of cultural change, the concept of creativity seems to go to the heart of the current situation. However, it is my argument that we need a broader concept of culture than the notion of creativity, in particular if we are to link it to democracy. What is needed is a perspective on how cultural creativity is expressed in a broader articulation of cognitive transformation to embody processes of social learning. In order to broach this I shall discuss the theory of collective learning as proposed by Eder and then outline some developments in cognitive theory.

## Collective learning

Klaus Eder (1985, 1992, 1996a, 1999), following Habermas (see Chapter 3), has argued for an approach that places social learning at the centre of a theory of social change. Social learning does not refer to the evolutionist myth of modernization through functional adaptation but to the neo-evolutionary theory of collective learning.[15] A central question is: how do societies collectively learn and how does learning relate to evolution, or the capacity for social change? Eder's proposal is a notion of a communicatively mediated conflict which is linked to collective action and the reflexivity that is embodied in it. In his view, cultural change in modern society is produced by a collective learning process whose logic is defined by the logic of discursive communication. Communication is a central theoretical category: social action is not just culturally mediated; it is also communicatively reproduced. His Habermasian approach is a contrast to neo-functionalist theory in that it emphasizes less the codification of symbols and narratives in cultural patterns than the discursive component in human communication. The essence of a Habermasian approach is the belief in the irreducibility of communication, which is prior to culture and structure. This suggests a move from a symbolic view of culture to a cognitive position which emphasizes discursivity.

This thesis suggests a new reading of evolutionary theory. The idea of evolution must be detached from the nineteenth-century myth of progress and functional differentiation: evolution refers to the capacity of society to undergo social or collective learning. It must be stressed that this does not imply an ideal path of historical development: social learning is not articulated through history as an objective process, but in human agency (Strydom, 1987, 1992, 1993).

Along with Moscovici (1993), Eder (1996a, p. 48) argues that 'this history must not be seen as a unilinear, universal cognitive learning process, but instead as the totality of cognitive learning processes that must be situated spatially and temporally'. This conception of social learning entails a rejection of a Eurocentric view of the world, for social learning occurs in all societies, simple as well as complex. In short, the idea of a social learning approach suggests a constructivist theory of social change: the self-construction of society by agency.

This approach, which stresses the cognitive and communicative or discursive capacity of social actors, complements Joas's theory of the creativity of action. His idea of an 'integrated creativity' is insufficiently theorized. Missing is a perspective that sees creativity articulated through communication and cognitive practices. Thus, it is not just a question of creativity but it is also a matter of constructivism in the areas of reflexivity and discursivity. A collective learning approach suggests an emphasis on the constructivist dimension and points to what I would call 'epistemic' changes in the cognitive capacity of a society. Thus, a topic of central importance is that of knowledge and the reconstitution of the social in what might be called 'epistemic communities'.[16] What constitutes knowledge and how knowledge is constituted are questions of paramount importance for social theory today.[17]

## Cognitive practice

It has long been recognized by the tradition known as the 'sociology of knowledge' that knowledge is a social category and not simply the possession of professionals or the formalized knowledge of elites. According to this view, the social world is constructed by knowledge – which is inseparable from culture, which provides social actors with interpretative models. Knowledge informs all of social life and is manifest in everyday life as much as in universities. It refers to the classificatory systems of shared meanings, systems of ideas and beliefs and experiences, and constitutes that which is taken to be real. It can be seen as a set of frames which mediate social relations. This tradition, which has its origins in the philosophy of Kant, is associated with the German school of *Wissenssoziologie* as exemplified in the classic works of Karl Mannheim ([1926] 1936) and Max Scheler ([1924] 1980) who argued that knowledge is a socially located category inseparable from culture and must be studied accordingly. It is now widely agreed that Durkheim, in his late work *The Elementary Forms of the Religious Life* ([1912] 1915) also operated with a sociological view of knowledge as constituted in culture.[18] Thus, what he called collective representations can be seen as constituting the cognitive structures by which a society perceives itself and which have a socially integrative function. In modern sociology Berger and Luckmann's *The Social Construction of Reality* ([1966] 1984) has become a classic of this tradition, and in ethnomethodology Garfinkel made the cognitive dimension central (Cohen, 1996, pp. 128–9). However, in general the tendency has been towards a conservative view of the relationship between knowledge and social reality as one of functional integration and cultural cohesion. Knowledge was not looked upon as something that could radically transform its subject matter and was only superficially democratic. Moreover, the sociology of knowledge became divided between those who studied professional knowledge and those who looked at popular knowledge.

In more recent times the cognitive theory of knowledge and culture has re-emerged.[19] In order to appreciate the significance of this development mention must be made of an alternative tradition to the sociological in the concept of the cognitive. In psychology the concept of the cognitive has been particularly important and is associated with the genetic epistemology of Jean Piaget (1970). A wide variety of authors across the social sciences – anthropology, sociology, social studies of science and technology – has affirmed the salience of a cognitive approach to knowledge and culture (De Mey, 1982; Fuller, 1984; Holland and Quinn, 1991; Nowotny, 1973; Strydom, 1999a, 1999b; Varela et al., 1997). Eyerman and Jamison (1991), in a significant work on social movements, argue that the collective identity of social movements can be seen as what they call a 'cognitive praxis'. They argue that social movements are constituted by the forms of knowledge and identity, which are articulated in their historical projects. Cognitive praxis is a kind of 'deep structure' that allows us to analyse its movement over time as well as its future potential. The importance of this approach is that it does not see a perfect fit between knowledge and social integration: knowledge, when rendered reflexive, can be transformative. Eyerman and Jamison (1991, p. 52) argue for the mediating role for social movements both in the transformation of everyday knowledge into professional knowledge and in providing new contexts for the reinterpretation of professional knowledge. In other words, a cognitive approach to knowledge is one that stresses its discursive nature while focusing on the cognitive structures and cultural models that play a structuring role in the course of the process. However, my approach differs in one respect from Eyerman and Jamison (1991), for I am stressing less a particular kind of agency than public-structured communication, which cannot be reduced to social movements. The public is not a social actor but a domain of discourse. In effect, I am proposing the conceptualization of the Subject as the public. This conception of the Subject entails the importation of a heightened contingency into the constitution of the Subject, which is no longer a social actor but a domain of indeterminate discourse.

Other authors have stressed the importance of linking knowledge to culture in order to appreciate how feminism as an 'engendered knowledge' has succeeded in transforming culture and power (McCarthy, 1996). A cognitive approach has been central to the social theory of Habermas and Bourdieu. In *Knowledge and Human Interests*, Habermas ([1968] 1978) argued that knowledge is based on what he called 'cognitive interests', which can be grouped around the different sciences (human, natural and social). However, Habermas did not extend his notion of cognitive interests to non-scientific kinds of knowledge and as a result the full significance of his argument was left undeveloped.

A more promising development is suggested by Bourdieu who operates with an explicitly developed cognitive approach. His concept of the habitus is elucidated in cognitive terms as a category of knowledge (Strydom, 1999a). The habitus supplies the representational categories and schemata with which social actors construct their cultural codes and engage in cultural struggles. For Bourdieu, social actors construct social structures using cognitive categories: 'To speak of habitus is to include in the object the knowledge which the agents, who are part of the object, have of the object, and the contribution that this knowledge makes to the reality of the object' (Bourdieu, 1984, p. 467). As I see it, the weakness with Bourdieu's approach is that cognitive structures do not facilitate a developmental logic. His actors may act strategically, but do not undergo change since they are constrained by the habitus.[20] It is crucial to see that what might now be called cognitive practice entails a degree of conflict or contention: knowledge and social structure are constitutive of each other, but the relationship is one forever open to change depending on how social actors reflexively deploy their cognitive skills and thus discursively activate different cultural models. As a set of competing frames, knowledge is inherently contentious.

What I think this all amounts to is that social theory must take seriously the mediatory role of culture, which is to be conceptualized as discourses of creativity, reflexivity and discursivity and which provides links between structure and agency. The central theses, I believe, that can be tentatively established are the following:

- Social actors can be seen as discursive agents – that is, as cultural producers and agents of change.
- Agency must be seen as embodying a creative dimension which is increasingly salient today as a result of structural social and economic change.
- The importance of epistemic changes in society – that is, changes in the cognitive capacity of a society which lead to a pronounced 'reflexivity' in cultural reproduction.
- Society can be seen as a network; it is based on a principle of neither differentiation nor integration. This opens up new possibilities for mediation, suggesting an end to the dualistic model of modernity and its central conflict.
- One of the most important expressions of the evolution of cognitive structures is the growth in the discursive capacity of society. As cognitive structures expand with the proliferation of cultural models, so too does the general volume of discursivity. Discourse as open-ended communication suggests a model of a self-regulating society based on discursive institutionalization.
- Society cannot be defined by a particular institutional structure. We are living in a society that is not essentially capitalist, industrial or liberal democratic, for society cannot be reduced to a particular structure. The current situation can be characterized as a 'communication society' (Strydom, 1999b) – that is a society of competing counter-publics in which there is a high level of contingency and therefore a certain anarchy of cultural forms prevails.
- Contemporary societies are no longer defined by a dominant social actor or institution (churches, intellectuals, parties, movements) but by public discourse. Neither elites nor collective actors define 'the situation', which instead has become radically open. We are entering a period in which the specificity of 'the social' can no longer be defined in terms of a particular social actor who can impose his or her world-view on the rest of society. Instead, the projects of social actors are refracted through public discourse, which introduced a high degree of contingency into the construction of social knowledge.

In the next chapter, which deals with Habermas's theory of discursive democracy, I shall discuss the implications of a discursive conception of knowledge and culture for democracy. For present purposes it will suffice to remark that the analysis in this chapter allows us to see the conflict between autonomy and fragmentation – which, I have argued, is replacing the tension between differenti-

ation and integration, characteristic of an early phase in modernity –
as one that brings into greater focus the centrality of the citizen, as
opposed to the consumer of post-industrial society or the producer
in industrial society, and the indeterminacy of public discourse.

## Conclusion: Towards a New Time-Consciousness

I shall conclude this chapter with some remarks on the implications
of the preceding analysis for the time-consciousness of a modernity
radicalized by the developmental logics of creativity, reflexivity
and discursivity. Immanuel Wallerstein (1991) stresses how transformations in time and space radically undermine the paradigm of
social thought that came into existence in the nineteenth century
around the idea of development. He thus calls for 'unthinking' the
nineteenth century in order to break from that era's linear conception of time and to enable us to recognize the multiplicities of time–
space realities that now exist. For instance, it can no longer be
seriously upheld that particular societies can be studied in isolation
from each other, or, indeed, that there is one ideal society which is
paradigmatic.

In the present context, Wallerstein's most important argument is
the obsolescence of the tripartite distinction between the political,
the economic and the socio-cultural. The legacy of nineteenth-
century social thought is that social reality occurs in these different
and separate arenas which have created the illusion of a subjective
world (the socio-cultural) and the objective world of economic and
political structures. Wallerstein's approach is a useful starting point
for any reconceptualization of modernity. His famous works (1974,
1979, 1980, 1984) on the rise of the 'modern world system' were
path-breaking contributions to globalization theory. However, on
the whole he has confined his analyses to historical sociology and
has not written extensively on social transformation today. Perhaps
for that reason his analysis fails to appreciate the tendency of globalization to fragment the world into separate 'global models'. It
was Wallerstein's thesis that the world was becoming progressively
integrated by the capitalist world system, with a single centre or
core dominating a variety of peripheries and semi-peripheries. His
model has been criticized on the grounds that in fact the world is
subdividing into a variety of world systems with their own cores.
While capitalism may be dominating the world system, there is no
one world system as such, but various constellations of economic,
political and cultural centres (Arnason, 1997, pp. 366–8).

Without entering into a debate with Wallerstein, the important point is that social change cannot be understood in terms of a unitary model of globalization. Thus globalization must be detached from modernity, in particular from western modernity. What must be rejected is the idea of a master trend of social change, be it a model of globalization or a theory of modernization. There is no unitary logic regulating history, imposing a master trend of change. Globalization – in economic, political, technological and cultural processes – can equally lead to many varied configurations and temporal sequences (Featherstone et al., 1995; Robertson, 1992). Three developments are important in this regard, all of which undermine the unitary model of modernization theory as well as casting doubt on a world-system theory.

First, there is the question of asymmetrical change. Change is not uniform or symmetrical, but uneven, or asymmetrical. With the formation of global blocs – North America, the European Union, China, Southeast Asia, etc. – we can discern the emergence of asymmetrical change.

Second, what is becoming increasingly visible is the related question of the rate of change. Change can be articulated at different rates or paces, depending on a great variety of factors. Classical modernization theory, as well as Marxist theory, presupposes one rate of change which would be relatively consistent in the economic, political, social and cultural structures. But what is becoming apparent today is the application of different rates of change in these domains. The result is a radical disjuncture between economics, politics, social relations and culture.

Third, as a consequence of different logics of change, the experience of time is also changing. The new time-consciousness can be described as non-linearity, a contrast to the narrative and linear model of time presupposed by classical modernity. According to some authors, such as Castells (1996), what developments such as these amount to is a reassertion of the priority of space over time. Modernity privileged an evolutionary concept of time (as historical transition, linearity, uniform movement) over space (which was static and territorially uniform). Today, it is space, or rather new flows of space and communication, that is organizing social change in the network society.

In more general terms we have now reached a point at which social change can no longer be seen in terms of a model of transition. As argued in the previous chapter, modernity was based on the epochal shift from traditional to modern society. As such, modernity expressed the experience of transition from an origin to a future condition. Today, the experience of change is more diffuse: instead of a transition from one condition to another, we are more conscious of the transformation of society. This emphasis on social transformation as opposed to transition captures the sense with which social change is now bound up with the mediation of agency, structure and culture. We cannot describe this as transition, since there has been no movement to a clearly defined future state. Social change today is characterized by a radicalized contingency and indeterminacy which calls into question some of the categories of modernity.

In the following four chapters I shall develop these arguments by exploring contemporary conceptions of modernity in the work of Jürgen Habermas (Chapter 3), postmodernists varying from Foucault and Lyotard to Bauman (Chapter 4), social movement theorists such as Touraine (Chapter 5) and the theory of reflexive modernization in Beck and Giddens (Chapter 6) .

# 3

# *Discourse and Democracy: Habermas's Theory of Modernity*

## Introduction

In this chapter I shall outline and critically assess the social theory of Jürgen Habermas, focusing in particular on his conception of modernity and discourse. Broadly sympathetic to Habermas's approach, I shall outline some criticisms of his social theory, which, I argue, has difficulty in addressing cultural questions, particularly in the global context, as an implicit 'occidentalism' underlies the cosmopolitan or universalistic claims of his theory. In general, the bias of this approach is more in the direction of discursivity than creativity, which is underplayed. This, I argue, is a reflection of his gradual retreat from social theory to political philosophy.

The importance of Habermas's work for social theory has taken on a new dimension in recent years with the development of the idea of discursive democracy (Habermas, 1996a; henceforth, all references in this chapter are to Habermas, unless otherwise stated). This notion now lies at the centre of his work, which previously was concerned with the theory of communicative action. While the *Theory of Communicative Action* ([1981] 1984, 1987a) has already attained the stature of a classic in modern social theory and is Habermas's seminal work, his social theory has now moved on to new concerns. Discourse theory can be seen as a deepening of the theory of communicative action and a means of linking together his earlier ideas of legitimation crisis, the public sphere and social protest. Discourse theory not only brings these dimensions together but also extends them into a new direction, namely a theory of law and democratic institutionalization. The result is an important contribution to a theory of social change and the basis of a re-conceptualization of modernity.

The idea of democracy expresses the essence of Habermas's theory of modernity. Modernity had been the unifying theme in his entire work, from his early studies on the public sphere to his theory of communicative action and his critique of postmodernism. The idea of modernity captures the central theme in his thought: the conflict between instrumental and communicative rationality. While the notion of modernity in these works was tied to the completion of the cultural project of the European Enlightenment (1981), his new conception of modernity indicates an alternative reading: modernity is to be conceptualized around a relationship between democracy and discourse. This suggests a move beyond occidental modernity to a notion of cosmopolitan modernity. It also points to the abandoning of a model of *dualism* – the reduction of everything to the central conflict between instrumental and communicative rationality – for one of *mediation*.

In this chapter I shall outline, first, how the notion of discursive democracy offers advantages over competing theories of radical democracy; second, how the idea of discourse links up the various dimensions in Habermas's social theory; third, the main argument of the discourse theory of democracy and its relationship to law; and, in the final two sections, some problems with Habermas's approach and some implications for the future with respect to social change and radical democracy. I shall argue that the principal challenge to Habermas's conception of radical democracy and discourse theory is the cosmopolitan question of postnational democracy and the related need to address cultural issues, in particular issues relating to cultural conflict and identity which Habermas downplays. His normative approach, I shall argue, because it tends to be de-contextualized from social contexts, neglects the creativity of agency as well as the reflexivity of culture.

## The Problem of Democracy

The notion of discursive democracy can be placed in the context of debates on participatory or direct democracy as an alternative to liberal or representative democracy. Participatory democracy has been the most important conception of radical democracy for the left and has served as a normative alternative to representative forms of democracy. Thus, the liberal conception of democracy as majority rule within a constitutional framework, as formal rights and as elite decision-making has been widely perceived to have failed to deliver genuine democracy. Social democracy, on the other hand, has not offered an alternative to liberal democracy, for it matured as part of the modern welfare state, which institutionalized social justice but did not transform the basic structures of liberal democracy. The idea of participatory democracy has emerged with the recognition that social democracy has not led to the emergence of substantive kinds of democratic citizenship.

Participatory democracy, in contrast, signifies a more direct kind of decision-making which is often associated with the principle of popular sovereignty: the idea of a self-legislating political community. The conception of rights underlying participatory democracy also shifts from largely negative conceptions of liberty to substantive rights of empowerment. Thus, democracy as collective decision-making can enter new areas of social life denied to it in liberal democracy, such as economic life, and the previously depoliticized realm of the household and gender roles. It goes beyond social democracy in seeking greater citizen involvement in politics. Social citizenship as a welfarist provision is not seen as a complete form of citizenship, for it has mostly taken the form of formal rights.

It is now possible to say that the old debate between liberal or representative democracy and social democracy has been superseded by debates between republican, discursive and cosmopolitan conceptions of democracy.[1] Republican conceptions of democracy argue for a return to the Aristotelian-Rousseauian concept of politics as ethical praxis. In this tradition, democracy is the expression of the civic will of the people. This romantic ideal of democracy as embedded not in the institutions of the state but in the civic community has been an important dimension to radical conceptions of politics. The origin of participatory democracy was the Aristotelian notion of politics as praxis and was later reflected in Rousseau's republican notion of democracy as the expression of the 'general will' or popular sovereignty. This conception of democracy is also to be found in the early political philosophy of Marx and has continued to inspire radical politics into modern times. Since the 1970s, new social movements and, in particular, the green movement, have generally operated with a participatory model of democracy.

Discursive democracy, on the other hand, as proposed by Habermas argues for a separation of politics from morality. Democracy is not rooted in the civic community or in popular sovereignty but in the structures of communication, which for Habermas always presuppose the possibility of consensus and argumentative discourse. Popular sovereignty, according to Habermas, is too simplistic and undifferentiated to be relevant to the highly complex and plural societies of late modernity. In his estimation, republican conceptions of democracy fail to recognize the complexity of modern society and the existence of multicultural value pluralism, both of which challenge the notion of the unity of the civic community and the appeal to popular sovereignty. He rejects their demand for consensus rooted in a shared form of life for a discursively determined consensus.[2]

There are not many competing models of radical democracy to Habermas's corrective to participatory democracy. Postmodern-style politics, for instance, has relatively little to say on democracy. Postmodernism generally ignores questions of democratic organization, reducing politics to rhetorical strategies and cultural politics (see Chapter 4). Habermas's conceptualization of radical democracy can be seen as a deepening of the notion of participatory democracy, which has been too romantically conceived around the ideal of the democratic polis. In his view, the republican and socialist model has a number of failings. First, it has great difficulty in addressing the problem of complexity in contemporary society and the underlying differentiation of social spheres. Second, republican democracy is unable to cope with cultural diversity. The implication of a multicultural value system is that there can be no consensus based on cultural traditions in modern society. Third, it neglects the question of law and institutionalization. Habermas argues, 'we have to move away from cherished notions, including the idea that radical democracy has to take the form of a self-governing socialism. Only a form of democracy conceived of in terms of a theory of communication is feasible in highly complex societies' (1996b, p. 2). This leads to the main challenge to a discursive democracy of participation: Luhmann's systems theory.

In Habermas's view, the problem of complexity and differentiation is a challenge to radical democracy, which tends to see society as a social whole or as having a centre from which decision-making can emanate and penetrate society. Arguing from the perspective of systems theory, Niklas Luhmann (1982, 1990, 1992, 1995) has given one of the most comprehensive criticisms of this conception of democracy which in his view cannot overcome the problem of complexity. In his theory, which is a radicalized version of Parsonian functionalism, modernity entails not merely the increasing differentiation of functions but has also generated the differentiation of subsystems, the result being that there is no regulating centre in society. In Luhmann's social theory, contemporary society has reached a level of complexity that challenges some of the fundamental presuppositions of democracy and citizenship, which give a privileged role to social action. Thus, not only is functionalism surmounted by systems theory but so too is action theory. The crux of this theory is that the political system has become only one subsystem among many others, bringing about a crisis in the 'self-description' of society – the way in which a society represents itself to itself. For Luhmann, law, for instance, is only one discourse in society and does not have a socially integrative function; it has instead become an objectified 'autopoetic', or self-referential, system. Politics cannot offer solutions of an affirmative nature because as a subsystem it works merely by reducing complexity. Defined negatively, complexity means an absence of information. The subsystems are 'operationally closed' to each other in that they have their own logic and while they can be influenced by each other they do so in their own terms. One of the implications of this is that 'society' does not exist in the sense of being a single social system. Luhmann, in short, announces the end of the social. Society does not exist for the same reason that universal communication does not exist. Communication for Luhmann does not have the same meaning as for Habermas, for whom it is connected to language. For Luhmann, communication is a matter of choosing solutions to problems and coping with contingency. Communication is a discourse of what Luhmann ([1992] 1998) calls 'self-reference' and 'external reference', and always entails the construction of differences, since a system must always differentiate itself from its environment.

Luhmann, unlike Habermas, does not try to defend radical democracy, believing that modern society has become too complex to be democratically regulated by citizen participation. Habermas has taken Luhmann's social theory seriously and has attempted to incorporate many of its central insights into his own more normative approach which also recognizes the autonomy of social action. His writings witness an extensive dialogue with Luhmann going back to the early 1970s, and as a result the notion of the functionally regulated 'social system' occupies a central place in his social theory ([1973] 1976, 1996a; Habermas and Luhmann, 1971). Against Luhmann's technocratic functionalism, Habermas argues that while radical democracy must take seriously the fact that we are living in a 'decentred' and 'polycentrically fragmented' society, this does not mean that democratization must be fundamentally limited (1996a, p. 47). In his view, the political culture of modernity still provides a basis for public debate and power has not entirely dispensed with the need for legitimation.[3] This is so, he contends, because the lifeworld still maintains a certain autonomy, however much it may be 'colonized' by the system, and therefore we have not reached the point of the closure of the political. In his most recent work (1996a,

1998), Habermas has embraced a theory of law which is capable of demonstrating a link with a form of democracy rooted in communication.

The question of law and institutionalization cannot be ignored, according to Habermas. Legal theory has been one of his growing concerns since the 1980s (1987a, 1988, 1995, 1996a). The legal system is essential for radical democracy because democratic procedure must be embedded in contexts that it cannot itself regulate. Habermas thus argues for an 'internal' relationship between law and democracy. Participatory democracy must be conceived of around the problem of institutionalizing democratic norms, which cannot always be reduced to foundational acts of public deliberation. In this, the idea of the constitution is crucial and could be used to conceive of a new framework for radical democracy. Habermas stresses the importance of law and democracy because he believes a constitutional state cannot be created without radical democracy. This represents a major departure for Habermas, who previously, along with most left-wing thinkers, conceived democracy in counterfactual terms as something opposed to the legally regulated systems. In his later writings law and democracy are mutually bound up with each other. The key to understanding the connection is the idea of institutionalization: the challenge is to see how existing legal structures can be used to institutionalize democratic forms of organization. What this turn in his thought effectively amounts to is a new paradigm shift in conceptions of radical democracy: the shift from an oppositional – or dualistic – model of democracy to a model of democratic institutionalization. In this, the problem of mediation – conceived in terms of a discursive relationship between law and democracy – becomes more central. In an essay written in 1990 in response to the collapse of communism and German unification, Habermas wrote:

> The non-communist Left has no reason to be down-hearted. It might well be the case that many East German intellectuals will have to adapt to a situation that the West European Left has been in for decades – that of transforming socialist ideas into the radically reformist self-criticism of a capitalist society, which, in the form of a constitutional democracy with universal suffrage and a welfare state, has developed not only weaknesses but also strengths. (1991, p. 45)

Habermas's new conception of democracy presents an important contribution to radical democracy and, moreover, offers the left a new kind of socialism. Defending the democratic ideal in its internal relationship to law as core of the socialist project, he writes:

After the collapse of state socialism and the end of the 'global civil war,' the theoretical error of the defeated party is there for all to see: it mistook the socialist project for the design – and violent implementation – of a concrete form of life. If, however, one conceives 'socialism' as the set of necessary conditions for emancipated forms of life about which the participants *themselves* must first reach an understanding, then one will recognize that the democratic self-organization of a legal community constitutes the normative core of this project as well. (1996a, p. xli)

The theory of discursive democracy outlines how radical democracy must be conceptualized around a notion of communication which operates in the social spaces of the civil society and the public sphere, linking social protest to public opinion and these, in turn, to legitimate decision-making and legal institutionalization. This effectively amounts to a new conception of modernity in which social change and democratization are firmly linked in a theory that seeks to see how law and democracy are mediated in discursivity. It may finally be observed that Habermas's social theory can be located in the context of a critical dialogue with Western Marxism – in particular the German tradition – which never succeeded in developing a theory of radical democracy.

## The Formation of Habermas's Social Theory

Before outlining in detail the notion of discursive democracy, I shall, first, locate it in the context of Habermas's earlier writings, since, as I have already argued, the theory synthesizes the many strands in his work since the early 1960s. By approaching the problem in this way, I hope to be able to simplify the complex philosophical arguments with which Habermas lards discourse theory. I shall take the following themes from his earlier writings, which all play crucial roles in his most recent writings: civil society and the theory of the public sphere; the theory of legitimation crisis, social protest and collective learning; modernity and the theory of communicative action; and law and juridification. As suggested, the dominant theme in his earlier writings is one of dualism, the conflict between instrumental and communicative rationality, whereas his later writings express a stronger notion of mediation.

### The origins of discourse: civil society and the theory of the public sphere

Habermas's first major book, *The Structural Transformation of the Public Sphere* ([1962] 1989a), provided the terms of reference for his subsequent writings: the social conditions of rational and critical debate about society. By means of the concept of the public sphere, Habermas attempted to show how modern concepts of legitimate authority, constitutional norms and rationality emerged in civil society in the eighteenth century. Originally, the public sphere was the sphere between the depoliticized private realm and court society; with the maturing of bourgeois civil society, it later became the sphere that mediated between the individual and the state. The press was one of the most important organs in cultivating an informed and critical public opinion, which had an emancipatory impact on struggles against power. In the nineteenth century the public sphere became invaded by commercial interests and in the twentieth century it has been robbed of its critical function by the mass media, which functionalized it for the requirements of capitalism. The result is that the communicative rationality of the public sphere is undermined by the instrumental rationality of capitalism. The theory of the public sphere was linked to the idea of modernity as an 'incomplete project': the public sphere of the Enlightenment era contained an emancipatory potential which was never realized but which, under changed social conditions, could be re-created.

The significance of this work is that it provided a way of conceiving of modernity in terms of the expansion of communicative structures. Modernity entails the opening of what might be called discursive spaces, allowing for greater public participation. This view allows us to see society as a communicative network of interacting individuals. With this work the fundamental theme in Habermas's entire writings emerges: the formation of modernity around the central conflict of the instrumental rationality of capitalism and the communicative rationality of society.

Since the details of the theory of the public sphere (Calhoun, 1993; Hohendahl, 1979) are well known, I shall confine myself to pointing out two central problems with the theory, which Habermas's more recent theory of discursive democracy has rectified. First, the theory was too much rooted in the unitary notion of the bourgeois public sphere and, consequently, the private sphere was seen as too depoliticized. The theory thus neglected other publics, such as women and minorities, and failed to see how issues of identity are problematized in the public sphere (Fraser, 1995; Landes, 1988).

Second, Habermas's early theory was conceived too much in terms of a model of decline: the Enlightenment public sphere gradually became 'refeudalized' as the press became dominated by capitalism and public opinion became instrumentalized in the new mass-public sphere. Writing under the influence of his great philosophical mentor Adorno, and the heritage of the critical theory of the Frankfurt School with its totalizing critique and promise of redemption, Habermas had yet to develop a theory of modernity as a post-historical and emancipatory process. In this early work he tended to see the discursive institutions of civil society being absorbed by mass society. Overall, Habermas idealized the historical public sphere of early bourgeois society, leaving us with an irreconcilable dualism between the discursive ideal of modernity and its instrumentalizing institutional reality.

## Radicalizing discourse: legitimation crisis, social protest and collective learning

The concept of legitimation plays a central role in Habermas's social theory, which is concerned with the social conditions of legitimate authority. The concept of legitimation is linked to the concept of crisis. Taking up Marx's theory of the crisis-ridden nature of capitalism, whereby crises derive from economic contradictions and lead to social contradictions, a crisis can be defined as a stage beyond a contradiction but which has not yet reached the point of conflict. The crises Habermas is interested in are those pertaining to the ways in which power is converted into authority. In this way he merges Marx with Weber, who was also concerned with the nature of legitimate authority. The core of Habermas's theory, however, is that legitimation relates to the way power is made subject to consensus in society. Legitimation therefore presupposes that power can be challenged. The objective, then, for social theory is to examine the social conditions of protest and the critical questioning of power. In his *Legitimation Crisis* ([1973] 1976) Habermas tended to adhere to a neo-Marxist analysis, looking at how capitalism continuously struggles to offset a crisis in legitimation from reaching the point of a withdrawal of mass loyalty when the existing supply of legitimation becomes exhausted.

In the context of the student movement and the rise of radical politics in the late 1960s and early 1970s, the theme of social protest and civil disobedience played a central role in Habermas's social theory, leading it to a more radical interpretation of discourse. These early concerns with social protest were later reflected in his theory of new social movements. In these early writings Habermas did not explicitly take up the idea of the public sphere, though it was one that clearly continued to inform his thought. Under the conditions of late capitalism, social protest for Habermas is about the creation of a self-critical society in which political enlightenment combats ideology. As a left-wing theorist struggling with the spectre of the exhaustion of Western Marxism, Habermas is ultimately concerned with the question of social change. The question of agency is therefore central to a notion of social transformation. Habermas's approach to this involved an uneasy relationship to Western Marxist thinking, which in general operates with a notion of revolution: social change is revolutionary and inspired by a certain utopianism. Thus social protest is ultimately pointing the way towards a fundamentally new kind of society.

A central idea underlying the idea of agency and protest is a notion of collective learning. In his *Reconstruction of Historical Materialism* (1976; published in English as *Communication and the Evolution of Society* 1979), Habermas outlined a theory of social change in terms of normative learning and collective action. His two central theses are that social change is directly related to new kinds of social learning and that the normative innovation involved is to be attributed to social movements which transform the cultural model of society. In this way Habermas breaks from Marxist approaches in that he emphasizes the role of cultural-epistemic shifts in history. However, he does not deny the centrality of economic forces in bringing about social change – which is why he adheres to the basic premises of historical materialism and the philosophy of praxis – but wishes to highlight changes in consciousness as a major concern for a critical theory of society.

Thus by the late 1970s Habermas succeeded in developing a nonreductionist and post-historicist theory of the Subject in terms of a model of communicative action. The question of autonomy is now expressed as the autonomy of moral consciousness and communicative competence. This position allows Habermas to assert the primacy of cognitive issues which cannot be reduced to material forces.[4] Yet a fundamental ambivalence lay behind his work: the discursive component in modern consciousness both depended on the existence of advanced societal structures to bring it into existence – as formulated by historical materialism – and at the same time reflected the autonomy of the Subject – as expressed by the philosophy of praxis. Exactly what was to be the role of social agents was unclear. The theory of communicative action of the early 1980s set out to solve this paradox – and, it is widely recognized, failed. A decade later Habermas attempted a new mediation of agency and structure with greater success.

Modernity and the theory of communicative action

In *The Theory of Communicative Action* ([1981] 1984, 1987a) Habermas took over Weber's notion of occidental rationalism and made it the basis of a theory of modernity. In doing so, Habermas has incorporated the Weberian ambivalence with respect to modernity and universalism. For Habermas, the problem was Weber's failure to clarify the universalist dimension to his notion of rationalism, which in his view was not sufficiently differentiated. Above all, what was missing was a concept of communicative rationality.[5]

While Weber held to an empirical notion of rationality, Habermas's model testifies to the influence of Kant. Weber's notion of the differentiated nature of modern structures of rationality was, of course, also based on Kant's separation of truth, ethics and aesthetics – but reinterpreted via Nietzsche – whereas Habermas's recasting of the differentiation of value spheres seeks to reveal an emancipatory-normative dimension not present in Weber (1985, p. 199, 1981). Like Kant, he wants to see how universality is possible and finds it in the ability of the individual to transcend limits set by empirical contexts. Thus, Habermas's point of departure is the same as Kant's: reason is defined by the critique of tradition and authority. The emancipatory potentials of modernity are defined in opposition to the unity of premodern tradition. The problem that I shall point to later is that, for Kant, reason was defined primarily in opposition to the unified and authoritarian world-view of Christianity, while today there are other cultural challenges which Kant's model of reason may be unable to answer.

The essential difference between Habermas's and Weber's notion of rationality is that Habermas is concerned with elucidating the nature of how, and conditions under which, a normative kind of rationality is formed: somebody is rational if they can justify, when challenged, their action or belief. It refers not merely to the concretely existing state of affairs but to the validity of norms ([1981] 1984, pp. 15–16). Communicative action must in principle allow the possibility of becoming practical discourse, which is ultimately a form of argumentation in which claims to normative validity are consciously reflected upon. The basis of Habermas's communication theory is that even when we do not consciously reflect on our action we are capable of doing so. Modern moral-practical rationality includes the ability to reflect on the consensual norms inherent in social action. Social action for Habermas is primarily communicative, involving reflexivity and cognitive development. Habermas attempts to provide a foundation for a theory of social learning:

'The universalistic position forces one to the assumption that the rationalization of world-views takes place through learning processes' ([1981] 1984, pp. 66–7). Unfortunately, learning processes are conceived in terms of only one cultural model, namely occidental modernity.

Habermas's aim is to identify those aspects of occidental rationalism which are peculiar to 'modern European-American culture' and which are an expression of the 'universal feature of "civilized man"' ([1981] 1984, p. 178). This commits him to a kind of Eurocentrism: universality is closely associated with western modernity. But this must be carefully formulated, since the point of Habermas's theory is precisely a critique of culturally bound and foundationalist notions of truth. It must also be said that Habermas's approach opposes all attempts to universalize one's own identity. His universalism is a minimalistic universalism of procedure, not of substantive content; it means that:

> one relativizes one's own way of life with regard to the legitimate claims of other forms of life, that one grants the strangers and the others, with all their idiosyncrasies and incomprehensibilities, the same rights as oneself, that one does not insist on universalizing one's identity, that one does not simply exclude that which deviates from it, that the areas of tolerance must become infinitely broader than they are today – moral universalism means all these things. (1992a, p. 240)

Habermas proceeds to argue that the evolution of the western world-view of modernity itself makes possible a universal morality. This consists of 'consensual validity' which is implicit in all social action to the extent to which social actors must be able in principle to recognize the binding force of their norms of action and are therefore capable of normative reflection. This consensual validity is embedded in the life-world context of communicative action ([1981] 1984, p. 70). For Habermas, the value of Weber's approach is that it 'opens up possibilities of learning that are grounded in a developmental logic and that cannot be described in a third-person attitude, but can only be reconstructed in the performative attitude of participants in argumentation' ([1981] 1984, p. 220). In a further clarification of precisely this point, Habermas (1985, pp. 206–7) says Weber's thesis can be plausibly defended in regard to modern Europe not only on the level of cultural ideas and on the level of action, but also in terms of the universal validity claims that are attached to the 'decentred understanding of the world', which is embedded in the value spheres of science, art and morality. The 'burden of proof' thus shifts on to the theory of argumentation. Whereas Weber's starting point was the implications of the Reformation, Habermas takes his orientation from the Enlightenment, which seems to have been relatively neglected by Weber as a formative point in occidental rationalism. In Habermas's view the Enlightenment project is in need of completion, since it held out the unfulfilled promise of emancipation by a post-traditional rationality (1981, 1987b). Unlike Adorno and Horkheimer ([1947] 1979) he does not see the Enlightenment and the project of modernity only in terms of domination (except, strangely, in the case of the relationship to nature). So by shifting the emphasis from the Reformation to the Enlightenment and arguing that it was only partially fulfilled, Habermas breaks from the Weberian pessimistic diagnosis of the age: the thesis that modernity has witnessed a 'loss of meaning'. The essence of his critique of Weber is as follows: 'he does not see the selectivity in the pattern of capitalist rationalization' (1992a, p. 112). A 'selective pattern of rationalization' occurs when one of the three value spheres is insufficiently institutionalized or when one sphere predominates over the others' ([1981] 1984, p. 240). In this way Habermas can also resist the functionalist tendency to reduce modernity to modernization: modernity signifies more than institutional processes and relates to normative structures which are only partially embodied in institutions.

In *The Theory of Communicative Action* (1987a) the new social movements, such as feminism, the peace movement and the ecological movement, are given a central place as the carriers of a communicative rationality embedded in the life-world and capable of challenging the 'system'. Yet, in this work, which recognizes the dissolution of the revolutionary macrosubject, social protest occupies an ambivalent position as a post-revolutionary radical consciousness and as the sign of a new kind of politics. Since the principal conflict in this work is seen as that between forms of social integration and system integration – life-world and system – social protest is conceived of as operating between the life-world and the system. Habermas assumes that ideology has come to an end and in its place is a 'fragmented consciousness'. But fragmentation is not seen as something that fundamentally challenges the autonomy of communicative action. It is his thesis that fragmentation results from the colonization of the life-world by outside, objective forces emanating from the system. Fragmentation is purely a matter of cognition, an 'obscurity' in the late modern condition. Habermas concluded on an uncertain note as to the future of radical politics and social protest, seeing new social movements as divided between their reactive and progressive forms. It is, however, clear that he saw the new social movements as the agents of social change and the carriers of radical democracy and a politics of autonomy, a position that is consistent with his theory of societal evolution through collective learning embodied in the radical social movements.

In sum, the conflict between life-world – the domain of autonomy – and system – from where fragmentation emanates – is seen in dualistic terms, with social movements defending the former against the intrusion of the latter but unable to bring about any mediation.

## Law and juridification

Habermas stressed the importance of law in *The Theory of Communicative Action* (1987a) in the context of the notion of the colonization of the life-world. Juridification refers to the increase in the volume of law in modern societies, and ultimately contributes to their fragmentation. Habermas identifies four waves of juridification: first, the rise of the absolutist state which institutionalized law as a medium of political regulation to set limits to absolute government; second, the rise of the bourgeois constitutional state in the nineteenth century which guaranteed the rights of bourgeois civil society against the state; third, the developments of the democratic constitutional state, reflecting the extension of political rights to the masses; and fourth, the creation of the modern welfare state and social citizenship. But juridification is double-edged: the increase in the quantity of law in modern society has occurred under the conditions of what he called the colonization of the life-world by the system. This results in the subordination of law to the imperatives of instrumental rationality imposed by the functionalized logic of the system. Thus, for instance, legal compensation is articulated through monetary compensation, reducing the demands of the life-world to instrumentalized forms of action such as the roles of client and consumer. Juridification, the increase in the volume of law in society, can be more precisely seen as the expansion and specialization of law, which is both a legal institution and a steering mechanism. Law as a legal institution cannot avoid the need for legitimation, while, as a steering mechanism, law has become a self-perpetuating and formal rationality. Habermas's critique is mostly directed against the instrumentalizing consequences of law as a medium or steering mechanism, which results in a separation of the consensual basis of decision-making from law.

In conclusion, the main problem with the much discussed theory of communicative action is its strong dualistic model of the struggle between life-world and system, a radicalized autonomy pitted against the external forces of fragmentation. Conceiving of the relationship between life-world and system in this way ignores the extent of mediation between communicative and instrumental rationality. Thus, work is seen as a purely instrumental activity and issues pertaining to identity and communication are seen as separate from instrumentalism. In the present context, of particular salience is the mediatory role of knowledge, law and democracy, which cannot be confined to either the purely communicative or the strictly instrumental. The end result is that discourse is located exclusively in the life-world and not in the system and therefore lacks any ability to bring about change in the latter. Later in this chapter a second problem will be discussed: the inability of discourse, which is decontextualized from the creativity of action, to bring about change in the life-world itself.

In the next section I shall outline a shift in Habermas's social theory: radical politics is no longer a question of opposition to the institutional order by means of a radical – albeit defensive – agency, but is one of mediation: discourse now becomes part of the self-construction of society.

## Rescuing Discourse: The Mediation of Democracy and Law

Habermas's major work of the 1990s, *Between Facts and Norms: Contributions to a Discourse Theory of Law and Democracy* ([1992] 1996a; all page references in this section are to this work, unless otherwise stated), can be seen as an attempt to bring the dimensions discussed above together in a new synthesis which also reconciles agency and structure in a theory of mediation. Thus the last vestiges of revolutionary socialism are abandoned in the strong argument that radical democracy must preserve an internal relationship to law. Social protest, while occupying a central role in his conception of democracy, is ultimately a matter of how social integration is possible in a complex and plural society. While operating outside the law, social protest is not opposed to the idea of the democratic constitutional state and is essential to the functioning of a form of democracy rooted in discourse. It is Habermas's belief that social integration in a mature political democracy must allow for social protest and rational debate. One of the most far-reaching innovations in this work is its overcoming of the dualism between life-world and system, which existed in Habermas's earlier work.

## Discursive democracy

The idea of discursive democracy can be seen as a reworking of Rousseau and Kant. While Rousseau suggests a republican reading of political autonomy, Kant suggests a liberal one (p. 100). On the one side, Rousseau's notion of popular sovereignty is rooted in the general will, while on the other Kant's human rights are derived from natural law. For Habermas, both conceptions miss the force of a discursive process of democratic constitution in which will and reason are brought together (p. 103). Discursive democracy is based on the principle of universality: that 'just those norms deserve to be valid that could meet with the approval of those potentially affected, insofar as the latter participate in rational discourse' (p. 127). Deliberation requires participation, therefore there must be guaranteed participation in all relevant deliberative and decisional processes. This conception of democracy is procedural and deliberative. Democracy in a complex society with pluralistic value systems cannot be rooted in a concrete form of life. Instead, it must be procedural and formalistic and, more importantly, deliberative or argumentative; it is based on a universalism of procedure, not one of values. Consensus in this deliberative model cannot be reduced to mere compromise. Consequently, a discursive or deliberative model of democracy replaces the contract model of liberalism: 'the legal community constitutes itself not by way of a social contract but on the basis of a discursively achieved understanding' (p. 449). The normative content of discursive democracy in the final analysis derives from the structure of communication itself, which Habermas believes contains fundamental structures which facilitate communication oriented towards reaching an understanding. Discourse theory refers to a higher level of communication oriented towards reaching an understanding, which involves democratic procedures and a communication network of public spheres. In Habermas's conception, democracy mediates between the public sphere (the domain of debate) and the rule of law (the institutional realm).

## The public sphere reconsidered

Discursive democracy is not possible without a level of public involvement that is prior to the deliberative process itself. The democratic procedure must be embedded in contexts which it does not itself regulate. Deliberative politics 'lives off the interplay between democratically institutionalized will-formation and informal opinion-formation. It cannot rely solely on the channels of procedurally regulated deliberation and decision-making' ( p. 308). Democracy is thus a wider process than the purely institutional; it is informed by public opinion generated in the public sphere of civil society. Thus, only 'after a public "struggle for recognition" can the contested interest positions be taken up by the responsible political authorities, put on the parliamentary agenda, discussed, and, if need be, worked into legislative proposals and binding decisions' (p. 314). It is Habermas's aim to place as much of the democratic process as possible on non-institutionalized public communication. The public sphere is a sounding-board for problems that must be processed by the political system because they cannot be solved within the non-institutionalized domains of the life-world: 'To this extent the public sphere is a warning system with sensors that, though unspecialized, are sensitive throughout society' (p. 359). The role of the public sphere is, first, to detect and identify problems, second, to amplify the pressure of problems and, third, to thematize and furnish them with possible solutions. It is important, however, to see that the public sphere, which is not an institution but a social space, does not itself solve the problems, and that its capacity to solve problems is limited. The public sphere produces public opinion not decisions; it is not an organ of consensus-building: 'The public sphere can best be described as a network for communicating information and points of view (i.e., opinions expressing affirmative or negative attitudes); the streams of communication are, in the process, filtered and synthesized in such a way that they coalesce into bundles of topically specified *public* opinion' (p. 360).[6]

In Habermas's new theory of the public sphere the emphasis is on plurality and the emergence of new political streams which do not require an idealization of the Enlightenment public sphere: 'The public sphere is a communication structure rooted in the life-world through the associational network of civil society' (p. 359). It is not cut off from social identity and the private sphere, as in the bourgeois conception. It is simply a social space or the network in which communication takes the form of critical public opinion. The implication of Habermas's new position is a conception of a new modernity as a break from the historical model of the bourgeois-Enlightenment model. This theory of the public sphere is a major revision of the earlier model, which was based on an idealized view of the Enlightenment public sphere and saw in modern society only processes of refeudalization. He has since recognized the inadequacy of this model, which was blind to alternative public spheres and those which emerged along with new social movements in the 1980s and 1990s.

By separating the public sphere from democracy as an institution,

Habermas has provided an important corrective to radical democracy, which requires its self-limitation and its location in public discourse. Participation is self-limiting in two senses. First, the 'communication structures of the public sphere relieve the public of the burden of decision-making; the postponed decisions are reserved for the institutionalized political process' (p. 362). In this way participation does not have to amount to decision-making. Second, participation is confined to those who are potentially affected (p. 365).

Democracy and the public sphere are rooted in social spaces in which groups mobilize. Civil society is the totality or political culture of these social spaces. It is composed of social movements and organizations such as non-governmental organizations, voluntary organizations and associations which are themselves prior to the public sphere but which provide it with its content. Civil society is characterized by plurality, publicity, privacy and legality (p. 368).

Civil society entails a dual concept of politics. Politics can be offensive, attempting to bring about the transformation of society, or it can be defensive, protecting existing structures (p. 370). Habermas seems to be of the view that a robust civil society, and therefore a functioning public sphere, is possible only in the context of a liberal political culture. Civil society, like the public sphere, must have a self-delimiting kind of politics; 'democratic movements emerging from civil society must give up holistic aspirations to a self-organizing society, aspirations that also undergirded Marxist ideas of social revolution' (p. 372). Habermas summarizes his thesis as follows: 'I would like to defend the claim that under certain circumstances civil society can acquire influence in the public sphere, have an effect on the parliamentary complex (and courts) through its own public opinions, and compel the political system to switch over to the official circulation of power' (p. 373).

The problem of complexity is addressed, then, by conceptualizing discursive democracy in terms of a relationship between the public sphere, rooted in the non-institutional structures of civil society, and the institutional processes of the political system. Habermas thus speaks of a 'substantive differentiation of public spheres' mediating between the political system, on the one hand, and, on the other, of private sectors of the life-world and functionalized systems: 'It represents a highly complex network that branches out into a multitude of overlapping international, national, regional, local, and subcultural arenas' (p. 373). Habermas recommends that planning and decision-making in all spheres of institutional life be shaped by deliberative politics – that is, 'shaped by the publicly organized contest of opinions between experts and counterexperts and monitored by public opinion' (p. 351). By conceptualizing radical participatory democracy in discursive terms, Habermas is able to avoid the problems that accompany the simple model of direct or strong democracy. As with other conceptions of radical democracy, he gives greater weight to the civil–social periphery, in contrast to the political centre. He cites examples such as the arms race, poverty in Third World countries, the spectre of ecological destruction and issues relating to immigration, feminism and multiculturalism to underline his argument that political enlightenment and emancipatory politics are almost exclusively initiated not by the political system of the state but by radical politics emanating from civil society (p. 381). This position is in line with his earlier argument in *The Theory of Communicative Action* which argued that social movements were the carriers of modernity and therefore the agents of social change. However, there is little doubt that his work of the 1990s places a stronger emphasis on the indeterminacy of public discourse than on particular social actors.

In Habermas's social theory legitimation does not simply refer to the formal-legal rationality of decision-making but also relates to the sensitivity of the democratic process to the demands of civil society. Legitimation and protest are interwoven. Protest in the form of civil disobedience is justified in cases where decision-making has short-circuited the deliberative process. Resistance to power is no longer seen in terms of a romantic 'great refusal' or a revolutionary act of social transformation. Habermas seems to be of the view that the modern constitutional state, by virtue of its legal constitution, does offer radical democracy enough possibilities to bring about social change. This position seems to suggest a departure from the argument of life-world and system with respect to the thesis of colonization. Law as a medium links life-world and system together. It is through this medium – which is one of public communication – that power can be challenged. With this insight the conflict between instrumental and communicative rationality loses its central position in Habermas's work.

## Law and discourse

The question of the 'internal relation of law and democracy' lies at the heart of Habermas's new social theory. Law is not only a system of rules and procedures, as Weber argued, but also involves a form of social recognition which entails an appeal to a communicative reason. Law is both a social institution, as described by Weber and

Luhmann, and also a normative system of self-transcending validity claims which can never be reduced to the social facticity of law. The law is considered legitimate because it is based ultimately on self-transcending valid claims. Habermas argues that legitimate law is dependent on democratic discourse and is therefore not an objectified discourse. This is the internal relationship of law to democracy: the relationship between the social facticity of law and its normative validity. The internal tension is a conceptual one and is not simply a historically contingent association between law and democracy (p. 449). Habermas believes that this internal tension can be resolved by enhancing the discursive component which binds law and democracy. The external tension in law can be contrasted to its internal tension. The external tension refers to the social situation of law in society: its facticity. On the one side, law is a normative system and on the other side social power distorts law. Law as facticity is always in tension with law as a normative system, making a legal-philosophical analysis of law inadequate without a sociological analysis. This argument can be seen as a reworking of the thesis of juridification: the tension between law as a steering mechanism and law as an institution.

In *Between Facts and Norms* Habermas no longer sees legal juridification in the same terms as he did when he wrote *The Theory of Communicative Action*. In the later work he emphasizes the opportunity structures that law offers radical democracy. In short, he has abandoned the dualistic 'siege' model of radical politics, which pitted the societal carriers of radical democracy against the state and its legal structures, in favour of a less defeatist and less utopian conception of democracy, which grants law a pivotal position in bringing about social change. His alternative model, the more mediatory 'sluice' model, opens the possibility for a more radical transformation of society using law as a medium to institutionalize new forms of democracy. Thus it is law that brings about the reconciliation of agency and structure.

It should be clear how Habermas's model of discursive democracy involves a rethinking of radical democracy. He draws a distinction between decision-making and the public sphere, whereby the actual process of decision-making is institutionally separate from the informal sectors of civil society. But he goes further than this: democracy is not only linked to bottom-up currents in society, it is also internally linked to law. With this thesis, Habernas has undermined the conception of radical democracy as being extra-institutional and purely oppositional. Law cannot be neglected or dismissed as belonging to the system of domination.

The idea of self-legislation is, then, reducible to moral self-legislation, not to a collectively acting citizenry. Discursive democracy requires the institutionalization of deliberative procedures in a legal system: 'The principle of democracy is what then confers legitimating force on the legislative process. The key idea is that the principle of democracy derives from the interpenetration of the discourse principle and the legal form' (p. 121). Law can no longer derive its legitimacy from a higher moral law, or from natural law or, as in Kant, from its own imperative, but only from the discursively redeemable procedures of communication. Habermas argues, 'this tension between facticity and validity is already built into moral discourse, as it is in the practice of argumentation in general; in the medium of law, it is simply intensified and operationalized' (p. 459).

The discursive connection between law and democracy is best illustrated in the example of the constitution. For Habermas, constitutional law is the most important example of the discursive component of law. The constitution is an 'unfinished project'; it is an 'on-going process' of self-organization in which the legal community defines itself (p. 384). The constitution is the institutionalization of a learning process in which a society reflects upon itself and overcomes its normative deficits. Essential to Habermas's theory is the privileged position of constitutional law in the sense that the legal profession, despite the social facticity of law, remains tied to a normative conception of law. 'Discourse theory', Habermas writes, 'explains the legitimacy of law by means of procedures and communicative presuppositions that, once they are legally institutionalized, ground the supposition that the processes of making and applying law lead to rational outcomes' (p. 414). Law-making, however, is faced with the burden of juridification (the increase in the volume of law) as a result of the expansion of government. The result is that the need for legitimation has grown: 'the more the law is enlisted as a means of political steering and social planning, the greater is the burden of legitimation that must be borne by the democratic genesis of law' (p. 428). In short, law-making cannot be detached from the need for legitimation. So long as this tension, which derives from the internal connection between law and democracy, exists, the possibility for a discursive resolution cannot be excluded in principle.

## Discursive Democracy in the Global Public Sphere

Habermas concludes his study on the discourse theory of law and democracy with a defence of discursive democracy in the global order. Today, 'the state has lost its sacred substance' and the 'international order of world society' offers many examples of the progressive 'denationalization of international law' and the opening of a 'global public sphere' ([1992] 1996a, pp. 443–4). And, on the other hand, as he points out in the preface, the rule of law is challenged by such spectres as ecological catastrophe and the ecological limits to economic growth, the increasing disparities between the North and the South. The only comfort is the realization that the rule of law is not possible without radical democracy (p. xlii). In the context of European integration Habermas has defended the idea of a postnational citizenship based on the tradition of the *demos*, as opposed to the *ethnos* (1992b, 1994, 1998).[7] But how is discursive democracy possible on the global level? Is it to be confined to the constitutional state?

I believe a global dimension must be central to democratic theory when we consider such global challenges for democracy as the media and information, human rights and new cultural conceptions of rights, the ecological problems, population growth and world poverty, and issues relating to security, violence and peace. What I think these problems point to is the question of a global constitution, since none of these problems can be solved on the level of the national constitutional state. However, the really big question is how we are to conceive of a global constitution.[8]

The first critical perspective I wish to bring to bear on Habermas's concept of discursive democracy is that, despite his recognition of the limits of national sovereignty and the need to embrace global issues, his model is constructed in such a way that it depends too much on the constitutional democratic state and the kind of citizenship it presupposes. The argument for discursive democracy and its internal relationship to law is based on the presuppositions of the constitutional state, which Habermas assumes can be generalized to the postnational level. However, this is not quite so simple, for there are major difficulties in transferring the idea of the constitution – which emerged in the context of the nation-state – on to the international realm. Habermas seems to be saying that the constitutional democratic ideal continues to hold out the promise of radical democracy for the global order as well as the national. The problem is that this position presupposes that there is on the global level an equivalent legal framework to that of the constitutional state which will enforce it. Despite the growing importance of international law, it is not apparent that this has the same binding nature as national constitutions. This is one of the big problems with the idea of a European constitution. Moreover, the more citizenship is transferred upwards to the transnational level, the more formalized it becomes. A global constitution, as a national constitution writ large, would be merely a highly formalistic affair and would entail very little participation. This is one of the fundamental problems with transnational citizenship. We might also wonder how a global democratic order will be able to solve problems of participation, when it is apparent that national governments are increasingly unable to do this. We do not have much evidence to suggest that a global order of governance would be more responsible and democratic than national ones. It seems to me that a deepening of Habermas's position will require further thought on the relationship between radical democracy and global institutions in so far as global or transnational democracy is concerned.

## The Question of Culture and Identity

The second criticism I wish to make of Habermas is also addressed to the cosmopolitan question. Habermas's theory not only neglects the wider global context of democracy, presupposing, as it does, the western constitutional state, but it also neglects the question of cultural conflict and identity, in particular cross-cultural conflicts about identity.[9] In other words, Habermas takes an occidental understanding of the world for granted: European modernity is the historical framework for understanding universal morality. Much of the problem stems from his dualism of life-world and system, a distinction that suggests that the life-world is relatively intact and most of the problems derive from the system, which colonizes the former. Thus the cultural conflicts endemic to the life-world are ignored. The problem that this presents for the discursive theory is that it is unable to address conflicts in deeply divided societies where the very cultural form of life is itself the point of contention. In deeply divided societies, or in cases where fundamental disputes about values are at stake, a rationally deliberated consensus is not as easy as in cases where there is a certain commitment to a common normative culture. Habermas's strong emphasis on rational deliberation may be more relevant to disputes such as those in scientific or legal discourse or in cases where the conflict is amenable to a negotiable outcome. But in the global context of conflicting cultures – conflicts between Islam and the West, conflicts between the developed world and the developing world – contention runs deep and penetrates the very cultural form of the life-world. In this context we cannot take for granted the historical model of occidental modernity and its conception of rationality. Habermas speaks too much in terms of completing the project of modernity. The result is that the idea of social learning is too much tied to the historical model of evolution associated with European modernity.

If we shift the focus from western societies, however deeply divided they may be, to the global context, and consider the conflict *between* cultures, the issue becomes yet more complex. It cannot be taken for granted that the world of Islam, for example, holds the same basic value-commitments as the occidental world. It makes little sense to construct a defence of the discourse ethic and the incomplete project of modernity against tradition when the most formidable challenges in the world today are not coming from older European traditions which have been surmounted by modernity but from cultural formations beyond European modernity, e.g. Islam. But the question is not absolute cultural relativism, since it can be argued that universalistic moral principles are deeply embedded in both cultures, and therefore we do not need to take too seriously the counter-arguments of strong contextualists. Yet, the problem will not go away. It is not enough to demonstrate normatively that so long as human society is communicatively reproduced universal moral principles can be reconstructed. The question instead, from a sociological perspective, is whether universal morality may be embodied in *different forms* in the different cultural traditions that exist today (as opposed to in the past, such as premodern tradition). This takes up the issue of whether there are alternative paths to modernity based on different critiques of tradition and whether, therefore, there can be a universal morality without a critique of tradition in the occidental sense. The following discussion suggests that the concept of universal morality as conceptualized by Habermas can be defended against strong contextualism but at the cost of conceding the privileged position of occidental rationalism.

It is worth giving some relevant examples of ways in which the Islamic belief system challenges western notions of universal rationality: Islam as a religion is an active political force in Islamic societies in a way that Christianity in the West is not; European modernity was very much articulated as a critique of Christianity, while there was never a Reformation in the Islamic world; Islam is a religion that is capable of adjusting to the complexities of modernization and even of enhancing it (Allen Roberson, 1988; Esposito, 1983; Gellner, 1981; Mehmet, 1990). Mardin (1995) argues that the western tradition of civil society, essential to Habermas's model of modernity, was not historically part of the Islamic conception of society. It is often argued that the world of Islam holds to an entirely different kind of world-view by which Islam, which is not merely a religion but an integrated way of life, offers a comprehensive code of ethics which derives from the Koran, the Umma (the Islamic community) and the Sharia Law. The world of Islam, while being highly differentiated, composed as it is of two main forms, Shi'ism and Sunnism, is in many ways very different from western culture and, according to Shari'ati (1980), it is capable of offering an alternative global force to that of the West. Islam as an economic and political-cultural world is also far from being a stagnant force. Culturally, economically and politically, it is now one of the most dynamic forces in the world. It cannot also be said to be traditional in the Weberian sense and, like Japan, is possibly in many ways even postmodern (Ahmed, 1992; Sayyid, 1994; Sugimoto and Arnason, 1995).

In sum, in the case of Islam, tradition and modernity cannot be neatly separated as in the West and the model of cultural differentiation does not apply in the same way. A very central problem for Habermas, then, is that in the Islamic world tradition has not been subjected to the critique of tradition *in the same way as in the West* and therefore a notion of modernity cannot be so easily applied as if this were self-evident.[10] Social theory will have to address itself to an understanding of the *transformation of culture* rather than merely the logic of communication, and it will therefore have to address the question of cultural conflict not only in contexts of deeply divided societies, but also cross-cultural conflicts. For Habermas, discourse can somehow be disengaged from culture and provide legitimating norms. Moreover, it presupposes fairly integrated life-world contexts from which, in general, the main problems derive from outside. In the case of deeply divided societies or in cases where fundamental values are at stake, it cannot be assumed that the social conditions exist for argumentative debate. Habermas's model of discourse is closer to the example of deliberation in the court room or that of a community of scholars engaged in argumentative debate. My view is that a more fruitful approach, which will be more historically and sociologically plausible, is to see how principles of moral universalism cannot only be reconstructed out of existing cultural identities but, more importantly, are actually being incorporated into *new* cultural identities in different cultural contexts. For this, a defence of occidental rationalism as the historical carrier of universalistic principles of morality must be abandoned, for it undermines the global significance of the import of Habermas's theory. An important question, then, for the social sciences is the study of the universalistic content in cultures other than the West and to see how new cultural identities are already bringing about social change.[11] A strong model of consensus is unnecessary for this purpose.

### Conclusion: Culture and Discourse

These objections do not invalidate the discourse ethic, but suggest that it must be radically reformulated to take account of the challenges of globalization: the need for a global concept of democracy and citizenship, on the one side, and, on the other, the need to address cultural conflicts relating to identity and values. The problem, in essence, with Habermas's theory is that he sidesteps the question of identity in favour of a normative concept of discursivity: social actors, as private citizens, step outside their identity and values to enter debate in the public sphere, where a discourse free of domination unfolds according to the argumentative logic of a communicative rationality. As an alternative to Habermas's somewhat normative concept of the public sphere, I would suggest that this important idea be accommodated to include culture and identity. The public sphere involves the discursive mediation of cultural conflicts. Instead of locating reflexivity in a decontextualized discourse, it would be more fruitful to see how it is articulated in cultural creativity.

Returning to Hans Joas's notion of the creativity of action outlined in the previous chapter, I would like to conclude by arguing that Habermas's theory of discursive action must be rethought to accommodate creative action. Joas (1996, p. 243), following John Dewey (1927), points the way towards a notion of 'creative democracy' as an alternative to existing models of social action.[12] Such a perspective would involve addressing the cultural dimension of society and ways in which identity is constituted in the creative production of culture. It is apparent that this is something absent in Habermas, whose theory lacks a sense of cultural innovation, preoccupied with a strictly political focus. Indeed, the shift from the problematic of life-world and system to the theory of discursive democracy, which can be seen as a shift from social theory to political philosophy, was at the cost of abandoning the possibility of a broader conception of mediation. This would entail a focus on the creativity of action, conflicts over values and identity and, more broadly, cultural innovation, and would also entail a departure from the historical framework of modernity; developments associated with postmodernity and globalization force us to rethink the normative and cognitive categories of occidental modernity. Finally, it may be argued that an emphasis on the discursive component in cultural reproduction will also allow us to see the broader relevance of the cognitive as a kind of practice, as opposed to something highly intellectualized. Cultural reproduction, which entails a discursive component, is itself a form of cognitive practice.[13]

In the next chapter I examine various cultural approaches to modernity and social change which take on board the postmodern and the global dimensions to contemporary social change. These theories could broadly be termed 'postmodern', for they are centrally addressed to the question of cultural creativity and the fragmentation of the social.

# 4

# Creativity and the Rise of Social Postmodernism: Foucault, Lyotard and Bauman

## Introduction

From a concern with discursivity, as discussed in the previous chapter, I shift the focus in this chapter to the postmodern critique of modernity and the question of cultural creativity. The variety of approaches I discuss – ranging from Foucault and Lyotard to Bauman – share a common concern with the rejection of modernity and the search for a new spirit of creativity irreducible to either a politics of autonomy or social fragmentation. Even though these theorists have very different projects and see their own work from different vantage points (in the case of Foucault and Lyotard a deconstructive critique of the Subject, and in the case of Bauman a redemptive critique of morality), underlying their general approaches is the idea that sociology must address the possibilities opened up by the fragmentation of the discourses of modernity. The social is seen as constructed in cultural contexts and social theory must radically rethink the very notion of modernity. The turn to culture opens up possibilities for understanding social change, which Habermas's social theory tends to ignore. Whereas Habermas emphasizes discursivity, the postmodern challenge addresses the question of cultural change more broadly, calling into question received notions of the autonomy of subjectivity and the social bond (Joas, 1998).

It will be recalled from the previous chapter that for Habermas the primary conflict is between a culturally integrated life-world and a societally integrated system: with the colonization of the life-world by the instrumentally functional imperatives of the system, the life-world reacts by mobilizing its communicative resources which are the basis of the autonomy of the Subject. One dimension to this is the role of the public sphere and social movements which seek to re-establish the sovereignty of the life-world. Thus, in Habermas's conception the normative dimension to social change is paramount with the cognitive and aesthetic relatively underplayed, as is illustrated in his theory of discursive democracy and its relation to the law: since the system is embedded in law which in turn is anchored in the democratic structures civil society, the life-world can maintain normative power over the system. I have suggested that this approach tends to neglect the question of cultural change and in particular cultural creativity which cuts across life-world and system. The problem, in essence, is that Habermas on the whole takes for granted a culturally integrated life-world for which all problems are external. As a result, the discursive space is too confined to areas that exclude the creative field. While his later writings attempt to overcome some of these problems, they do not solve the basic questions of an approach that separates discourse from culture.

The theories I consider in this chapter do not start out from a belief in a normative concept of agency reacting against societal structures or from a radical separation of discourse and culture, but from a perspective on cultural creativity which stresses the autonomy of culture as a reality-creating force. The shift I am documenting, then, could be described as the move from the autonomy of agency to the primacy of culture. While postmodernist approaches have often been criticized for rejecting moral universalism for cultural relativism, it is nevertheless important to appreciate that this concern with culture offers social theory a perspective on the creativity of action, so much neglected in the normative and rational traditions in sociology, as Hans Joas (1996, 1998) has pointed out. However, in eschewing the social and the autonomy of the Subject, the postmodern challenge, deriving as it does from a notion of aesthetic modernity, ultimately retreats into a celebration of cultural and social fragmentation.[1]

In this chapter I begin by examining some of the central theorists associated with postmodernism (principally Foucault and Lyotard). Second, I consider the social theory of Zygmunt Bauman and, third, I examine the idea of cultural production in the move towards what may be termed 'social postmodernism' (Nicholson and Seidman, 1995). Bauman's version of postmodernism offers an important corrective to the post-structuralist tradition – which informs both Lyotard and Foucault – because it places ethics and, in particular, the question of responsibility at the centre of the postmodern experience. My central thesis is that with the shift from post-structuralism to postmodernism – the intimations of which are to be felt in the later writings of both Foucault and Derrida – we find a concern with the Subject emerging in a way that somehow dissolves the conflict between autonomy and fragmentation. However, this move – which I will illustrate in detail with respect to Bauman – ultimately retreats into an overly ethical conception of the self-creating Subject neglecting the reflexivity of cultural models and the discursive regulation of power. As a result, the radical discourse of constructivism which is promised by postmodernity is weakened.

## From Deconstructionism to Constructivism

Michel Foucault and Jacques Derrida are generally associated with postmodernism, even though their writings have been more central to post-structuralism. Undoubtedly, the justification for seeing these theorists as postmodernists lies in their advocacy of a particular methodology and epistemology: namely, deconstructionism. Postmodernism can, to an extent, be seen as the generalization of this method to the condition of society itself: society as a self-interpreting text. Central to their epistemology is the idea of the 'death of the Subject', be it the Subject of history, as in historicism, or the Subject as author, as in literary texts. One of the most influential figures in this context was Roland Barthes (1973), who inspired the turn to literary criticism in social science and philosophy in the 1970s. Barthes argued that texts, whether literary works, the texts of popular culture or the mythologies of everyday life, can be analysed without recourse to a notion of agency. Inspired by structuralist linguistics and developments in modern literature, Barthes effectively announced the 'death of the author'. In the context of the declining influence of Marxism in French intellectual life since 1968 and the attack on existentialism, Barthes's celebration of the authorless text became a model for the apparent 'death of the Subject'. History could now be written without a Subject. This position was also very much influenced by the structuralist anthropology of Claude Lévi-Strauss, for whom history does not contain any possibility of progress or regression because it is simply a repetition of the logics of binary codes. Post-structuralism went only one step further in the denial of developmental logics: in the absence of any possibility of constructivism – which would entail a developmental logic – the role of the intellectual could only be to deconstruct the basic structures of experience.

The writings of Jacques Derrida (1977, 1978) provided a further philosophical basis for post-structuralist deconstructionism. His central argument is that western thought is dominated by the foundationalist logic of 'logocentricism', the search for a universalizing principle of order – the 'logos' – which requires an 'origin' and an 'other' with which to define its project. These 'metaphysical' categories are always present and absent in every discourse, functioning as a kind of regulating device which is also a means of exercising power. Accordingly, his approach is designed to reveal the rhetorical categories – which he calls the 'metaphysics of presence' – that are presupposed in modern western discourses. In particular, he attacks attempts to 'essentialize' identities by revealing how they are constructed in rhetorical strategies of power which reduce plurality to an essence or a fixed order. His deconstruction of essentialism is also a rejection of the very possibility of identity – and ultimately of society – which he argues is based on the illusion of a unifying Subject capable of imposing order on heterogeneity and is therefore an instance of violence.[2]

The deconstructivist position was part of a move to a new hermeneutics of language. However, this linguistic move in French thought differed from both the German hermeneutic tradition and that represented by Paul Ricoeur in France in that it was not tied to a hermeneutics of meaning and a social ontology. Unlike social philosophers such as Gadamer, Winch, Schutz, Ricoeur and Apel, for whom hermeneutics is the interpretation of subjective meaning, the post-structuralists denied the existence of meaning as an illusion of subjectivity. In modern French philosophy agency – and the very possibility of intersubjectivity – is replaced by a notion of discourse, which is conceived of in terms of a system of fluctuating signs. This conception of discourse is very different from that of Habermas, which is related to communication and which has not severed all ties with a philosophy of praxis. Discourse in post-structuralist thought becomes constitutive of a reality which has no existence except in the systems of signs of which it is composed. In the present context, what this effectively amounted to was the disappearance of the actor and the absorption of the social into the 'text'. This concept of the text as a discursive system became very influential in the social sciences, eventually providing the foundation for a new concept of culture as plurality, heterogeneity and difference.[3] It was also, as already noted, a major attack on the very possibility of identity, and denied the feasibility of conceiving the social in terms of a model of the actor. Identity – as political, cultural and biographical – was rejected along with the idea of emancipatory knowledge as illusionary. I shall discuss two influential representatives of the new notion of discourse, Foucault and Lyotard, arguing in the final part of this section that we can detect in their works a gradual shifting away from post-structuralist deconstructionism towards the postmodern concern with the creativity of the Subject.

## Foucault: discourse, knowledge and power

In social theory the deconstructionist turn was best represented by Michel Foucault. Foucault is a difficult figure to locate because his work has primarily been addressed to historical questions in the genesis of modernity and he only briefly turned to issues in contemporary social theory, a move which I believe was highly significant in that it highlighted an orientation in his earlier work. I shall comment on this in more detail shortly. He almost certainly did not consider himself a postmodernist in the sense represented by Lyotard, who brought deconstructionism to a more social direction (see below). Yet there is some justification for considering his work in the present context. In my estimation, apart from his well-known studies on modern institutions – the prison, the hospital, the asylum, the regulation of sexuality – which I am not going to consider here, Foucault's most insightful contribution to the postmodernity of contemporary society consists of his theory of the historical shift from government towards 'governance'. Foucault argued that power is not simply located in the state but located in the social itself. Power is constituted in social relations and cannot be simply reduced to the state apparatus of government or the control of bodies and space. If government suggests the management of society by the state, governance implies the regulation of society by its own structures. Governance refers to the structuring of the field of social action by 'discursive' strategies. In this, structuring power is constituted and the modern Subject is merely a product of power relations. It is important to appreciate that for Foucault power is not merely constraint, or for that matter intentionality: the condition of power is freedom. Power is the capacity to act. Power requires the existence of social actors whose field of action – the discourse of power – is shaped by the relations of power emanating from the field of action itself. Governance thus refers to the shaping of the field of action by determining the rules of discourse. While Foucault outlined his concept of governance and discourse in the context of the rise of modern forms of power, his ideas entered social theory to provide a foundation for a concept of postmodern society of great significance. His concept of power as a system of social relations, shaped in a particular discursive context, has served to give substance to the recognition that state power is not the only kind of power and that where there is power there is resistance. The means by which Foucault approaches this question, with which he became more and more preoccupied in the last decade of his life, lay in a gradual shifting of emphasis from discourse to creativity. In this shift, the possibility of a new subjectivity came into sight – thereby undermining the very possibility of a genuinely deconstructionist critique of the Subject. In the earlier works – with their theme of a captive subjectivity and institutions of total power – there was a more pronounced reduction of creativity to discourse, with the reflective moment denied to both as well as the denial of any logic of development.

The most far-reaching implication of Foucault's approach – as outlined in such seminal works as *The Order of Things* ([1966] 1970) and *The Archaeology of Knowledge* ([1969] 1972) – is the creativity of the discursive field. Discourse and power are not inherently negative or constraining, as may be the impression conveyed by Foucault's famous studies on total institutions of power, the asylum, the prison and the hospital. In fact, if anything, the condition of discourse is, precisely, creativity: discourse is productive. The discursive field is neither controlled by a privileged agency nor by its internal functional logic, the semiotic rules of discourse. Discourse, while being constraining, is open to radical intervention by agency. In order to transform discourse it is necessary to understand its structures and therefore the task of critique is to comprehend the conditions of the possibility of discourse. Once subjectivity grasps its conditions of existence, the possibility of change is in hand. From the perspective of methodology, this is what is meant by Foucault's approach, termed the 'archaeology of knowledge' ([1969] 1972) or the 'genealogical method' (1977): the investigation into the genesis of discourses in order to demonstrate the contingency of the discourse. These were the terms which Foucault used to characterize his version of deconstructionism. Yet, as I have argued, there is much to suggest that this epistemology, while informing the early studies of power – which were concentrated on institutions – did not fully appreciate the modern predicament, which cannot be reduced to surveillance and disciplinary power, but also contains the other logic of what Castoriadis ([1975] 1987) has called the radical imaginary, or, in my terms, the radical discourses of creativity, reflexivity and discursivity. Foucault emphasized the 'gaze' – the exercise of a kind of disciplinary power which emanates from universal surveillance penetrating language and is ultimately focused on the body, a form of power epitomized by Bentham's panopticon. Modernity may indeed have been to a large extent about the culture of the 'eye', but it was also – and it is this that is absent in Foucault – about the culture of the 'voice', which, I have argued, has been one of the radical discourses of modernity.

The kind of politics Foucault stood for was one of refusal and subversion. In short, the theme of social change was central to his project, even though he rejected the illusion of a 'Great Refusal', in Marcuse's sense, or one deriving from a project of autonomy. In its place he argued for the plurality of struggles:

> Where there is power there is resistance, and yet, or rather conse-quently, this resistance is never in a position of exteriority in relation to power. . . . These points of resistance are present everywhere in the power network. Hence there is no single focus of Great Refusal, no soul of revolt, source of all rebellions, or pure law of the revolutionary. Instead there is a plurality of resistances. (Foucault, 1980a, pp. 95–6)

He distinguishes three kinds of struggle:

> either against forms of domination (ethnic, social, and religious); against forms of domination which separate individuals from what they produce; or against that which ties the individual to himself and submits him to others in this way (struggles against subjection, against forms of subjection and submission). (1982, p. 212)

It is his view that the latter is becoming more prevalent today and is present in such new social movements as feminism, the gay move-ment, ethnic and nationalist movements, religious revivalism and environmentalism. These struggles are localized and are not con-centrated in the political realm of the state, but pervade the social. Rather than being concerned with the attempt to seek state power as such, the search for a new subjectivity is more central to their politics. In 1979, for a brief period, Foucault supported the Iranian Revolution, which he believed was about to inaugurate a new spiritual politics in that country (Simons, 1995, pp. 10–11). How-ever, as the authoritarian nature of the revolution became apparent, Foucault withdrew his support and turned to more transgressive politics. Fuyuki Kurasawa (1999) has documented a theme running through Foucault's work, in particular his late work, which sug-gests that, while denying the possibility of a politics of the Subject in the West, Foucault assumed the existence of a radical subjectivity and spiritual redemption in the non-western, 'exotic Other'. How-ever, even though this quest for a lost autonomy and a politically creative subjectivity dominated his thinking in the period since the *History of Sexuality*, it never led him to rethink the genealogical or deconstructive method. Consequently, radical constructivism was never a serious option for Foucault and the rupture with modernity was too great to be bridged.

To transgress the limits of discourse is the political challenge for Foucault. It would appear that the political tradition that Foucault appeals to is more that of Nietzsche and the philosophy of life than· that of Marx. The creativity of action that is required for the act of transgression is closely modelled on the aesthetic impulse of Nietzsche's nihilism, a creative or expressivist act of refusal and self-assertion.

It can be said that Foucault's conception of modernity is a contrast to that of Habermas: where the latter sees the task to be one of completion of a historical model in order to release its emancipatory potentialities, the latter sees only the gradual unravelling of the modern episteme in the subversion of its power structures. Modernity in the Foucaultian framework is not something to be escaped from and is doomed to decline once knowledge, which is constitutive of power, reflects upon itself and opens up the discursive configuration to transformation. The role of social knowledge is therefore central to his approach. A comparison can be made with Habermas's concept of discourse. For Habermas, discourse is something that is entered into in order for social actors to reflect on the possibility of bringing about social change: discourse is liberating and is reconstructed out of something more fundamental, which for Habermas is the communicative structures of the life-world. His discourses have a transcendental role to play in enabling actors to reach an argumentatively achieved consensus and, once entered into, they become compelling: the logic of the argumentative process – 'the force of the better argument' – takes over, driving its participants towards the goal of consensus and thus the closure of the discourse in its concrete and liberating realization in the life-world. In Foucault, the discourse is also doomed by closure and one which is at the same time liberating. However, there is a difference in the two moments of closure: for Foucault, the collapse of the discourse is the result of its transgression by an agency which is unable to step outside the discourse in which its very existence is constituted. Accordingly, the closure of the discourse signifies the end of the Subject contained within it. In Habermas, on the other hand, the closure of the discourse opens up the road for agency to realize its normative and cognitive content in the life-world.

In conclusion, I am arguing that, contrary to many interpretations that emphasize the defeatist dimension to his thought, Foucault was centrally concerned with the possibility of social change, a concern that became more and more pronounced in his later thinking.[4] I have stressed the creative dimension to action that is strongly

implied by his notion of discourse as productive. Related to this is
the central category of social knowledge in his writings. Knowledge
for Foucault permeated society itself and was potentially transformative once the rules of its discourse could be made transparent. His
theory suggested that a social order was always based on what may
be called an 'epistemic' foundation and once this episteme was
rendered problematic, then the entire power edifice collapses. With
this insight Foucault establishes the centrality of a certain kind of
cognitive or discursive practice, which differs from Habermas's in
that it is articulated in real contexts of power.[5]

However, in line with many postmodernist positions, the
downside of his approach is his tendency to see change in terms of
a expressivist or aesthetic model of creativity. As Joas (1996) argues,
creativity also involves the wider responsibilities of institutionalizing democracy. Foucault's model of the social is too much influenced by the literary model of the text: textual subversion cannot be
taken to be an appropriate model for social action. Missing, too,
from his works is a concern with the collective dimension of social
action. Foucault, influenced by the expressivist life philosophy of
Nietzsche, was ultimately speaking to the individual and failed to
appreciate the power of collective actors in transforming society.
His writings were mostly concerned with the rise of modernity and
did not address issues which have become central to postmodern
society: the end of the social and the dissolution of the autonomy of
the Subject. There is no doubt that democracy and collective struggles, such as those associated with the new social movements, were
not central to his concern. In short, his version of deconstructionism
was not fully 'postmodernized'. For this reason we can now turn to
a theorist credited with having introduced postmodernism to social
science.

## Lyotard: knowledge and legitimation

A theorist more conventionally postmodern is Jean-François
Lyotard, whose *Postmodern Condition: A Report on Knowledge* ([1979]
1984; unless otherwise stated, all references in this section are to this
work) has become a classic statement of the postmodern thesis in
sociology. While much of the postmodernist literature is addressed
to developments in the arts, Lyotard is essentially concerned with
the idea of postmodern society.[6] In his view postmodern society is
not something new in so far as a temporal order is concerned but is
a part of the modern (p. 79). Yet, he was one of the first to highlight
the coming of the postmodern society as something innovative:

'What is new in all of this is that the old poles of attraction represented by nation-states, parties, professions, institutions, and historical traditions are losing their attraction' (p. 14). The postmodern is not a stage beyond modernity but is its transformation by cultural innovation and what he calls new 'language games'. But Lyotard goes beyond the purely cultural interpretation of postmodernity in giving it a firm basis in the social order. He takes up Habermas's emphasis on the intensified density of communication in modern society to suggest that the latter has falsely understood the increased importance of language. The explosion of communication cannot be understood in terms of a conflict between language as manipulative or as an emancipatory dialogue. Lyotard's conception of language games is more differentiated: language games constitute the 'social bond' and cannot be separated from knowledge: knowledge is not a meta-narrative of legitimation but is constituted in concrete language games. Language games are not unlike Foucault's discourses in that they shape the parameters of thought and action, though in Lyotard's approach the rules of discourse are more flexible than in Foucault. A conception of social integration is intimated that has broken from the classical assumptions of a normative order integrated by a single principle of order.

It is, however, more instructive to compare Lyotard to Luhmann, who is very much in the background, as is Habermas. Lyotard (p. 17) argues that the postmodern condition entails the '"atomization" of the social into flexible networks of language games'. This is not unlike Luhmann's theory of autopoesis, the functionally separated world of autonomous subsystems which are self-creating. This situation imposes restrictions on the creativity of action, but for Lyotard, unlike Luhmann, the limits of institutional innovation are not set once and for all. Yet, unlike Habermas, he is more conscious of the fragmented nature of the social, a condition which captures the essence of the postmodern condition. Precisely because the social is fragmented intellectuals can no longer speak in the name of a universal truth. Intellectuals, as knowledge producers, must accept the fate of knowledge in the postmodern age. As the subtitle of the book indicates, Lyotard's preoccupation is with knowledge in the aftermath of the end of the great narratives of modernity.[7] He equates modernist knowledge with 'grand narratives' or 'meta-narratives' which are held to transcend society by legitimating knowledge from a point outside the social. Postmodern knowledge, in contrast, is based on 'non-narratives', or forms of knowledge which are embedded in the social and do not transcend it.

The book can be read as a critique of Habermas's *Legitimation Crisis* ([1973] 1976) which argued that modern forms of power, however functionalized they may be, cannot dispense with the need for legitimation. The public demand for legitimation is something that serves to make a legitimation crisis an ever-present possibility. In Lyotard's view, this presupposes a notion of knowledge as meta-narrative because legitimation requires the existence of a sovereign or autonomous body of knowledge. The reality today, he argues, is that knowledge has lost its legitimating function as a result of science entering the productive process. In other words, knowledge has lost its autonomy and 'science plays its own game; it is incapable of legitimating the other language games' (p. 40). The most important point is that knowledge has been reduced to the condition of information and has been operationalized in the economic structures of the post-industrial or information society.

Lyotard's (p. 60) target is Habermas's wish to hold onto the validity of the narrative of emancipation. Rejecting this and the notion of consensus that goes with it, Lyotard also rejects Luhmann's closed systems for which only power can be a legitimating factor. If Habermas underplays complexity as a threat to consensus, Luhmann under-estimates the pragmatism of social actors and their ability to redefine the rules of the game. Indeed, precisely because the rules of the games can be redefined the discourse ethic is undermined from the begin-ning, making consensus impossible. Habermas, he argues, is also too much guided by the illusion of emancipation, while Luhmann has rejected the striving for justice, which is what is valuable in Habermas's project. To recover a sense of justice and responsibility under the conditions of the postmodern condition is Lyotard's aim. It is of course obvious that Lyotard has misrepresented Habermas, for whom legitimation is not secured by reference to a meta-narrative but by public discourse, which is never closed but highly indeterminate.

Against Habermas and Luhmann, Lyotard proposes a model of legitimation based on what he calls 'paralogy'. Paralogy is opposed to the pragmatic attempt to change the rules of knowledge in order to define the discursive conditions for a new model. Such an en-deavour, which is rooted in the 'performativity' of knowledge, re-quires a new sense of responsibility (p. 66). Paralogism entails the subversion of the rules of the language games, but, as with Foucault, it is unable to name its normative orientation. Thus, in-stead of the search for consensus, Lyotard advocates the under-mining of the very rules which consensus requires as its conditions of possibility. This transformative action is the creative force of paralogism, a notion that is not too far from the Marxist idea of permanent revolution. Lyotard's position is also not too far re-moved from the later Foucault in that he rejects explicitly political movements aimed at social change, since, with the collapse of the grand narratives of modernity there can be no universal alternative but a micropolitics of struggle. Neither Foucault nor Lyotard allow any room for a process of social learning in the transformation of society. They are ultimately committed to an aesthetic kind of politics which rejects the autonomy of subjectivity.

However, the importance of Lyotard is that he operates with a notion of the social which recognizes the changed nature of social relations. Rejecting the older notions of social integration associated with the classical theorists – which emphasized normative integration – he advocates a concept of the social bond as being shaped by new kinds of relations, such as those established by knowledge. Thus, in one sense the social has come to an end, while in another it has been reconstituted in a new form. It is for this reason that Lyotard rejects the illusion of consensus, which underlies Habermas's social theory, since it is his conviction that a society integrated by knowledge will dispense with consensual forms of integration. But his approach is not without its problems. In particular, in eschewing the idea of the autonomy of the Subject as a 'meta-narrative of legitimation', Lyotard rejects the possibility of discursive transformation and a reflexive relationship between knowledge and communication. Instead of reworking the idea of autonomy, the condition of fragmentation is privileged in his analysis. Moreover, he conflates information and knowledge. Information is one kind of knowledge culture, the operationalized application of knowledge. Knowledge itself is distinct from information and contains an inherent reflexivity not available to information. Finally, it may be observed, he draws a too ruptural demarcation of modernity from postmodernity and as a result misses not only the reflexive moment in postmodernity but also in modernity.

## From the end to the return of the social

The theme of the 'end of the social' is also central to the work of Jean Baudrillard (1980, 1983), who has been a major and controversial figure in postmodernism.[8] His central contention is that the category of the social, if it ever existed, is in decline at the close of the twentieth century as a result of the rise of various kinds of symbolic orders which privilege not communication but significations, or ways of constructing reality by the mass media. The mass media, in his view, not only construct the social in their own image, thereby robbing it of any authenticity, but they also neutralize social relations (1983, p. 66). Baudrillard goes so far as to argue that the social is a 'simulation' of the mass media and information technology and has no autonomy of its own. The mass media, he argues, bring about the 'destructuring of the social' (1980, p. 140). Social transformation is a meaningless concept, since every attempt at change will be short-circuited by the hyperreality of the social – the world of signs and 'simulacra'. In a world in which transformation is impossible since everything is transparent and reproducible there can only be different kinds of simulations, and each is as real as the other.

For Baudrillard, this means the end of the social, a condition he describes as the 'implosion of the social' (1980, p. 141). Increased information and communication does not produce more meaning and 'socialization', but the neutralization of the social. The objective of information is no longer, he says, to circulate meaning from one state of reality to another. Marshall McLuhan's notion of the 'medium is the message' is only partly true: if the medium has absorbed the message, then the concept of the medium loses its coherence, 'since both the medium and the real now form a single inscrutable nebula'. Thus implosion means: 'the defusing of polarities, the short-circuiting of the poles of every differential system of meaning, the obliteration of distinctions and oppositions between terms, including the distinction between the medium and the real' (Baudrillard, 1980, p. 142).[9] Baudrillard can be seen as an extreme advocate of the theme of the 'end of the social'. In his case the social has been absorbed by the new cultural logic of the mass media.

So long as postmodernists stress the 'simulated transparency' of the social there can be no chance of a coherent theory of social change.[10] The mistake, as I have already argued, is to take the model of the text as the model of the social. Thus the deconstructive method short-circuits the constructivist dimension in social action and therefore fails to appreciate how the autonomy of the Subject can be conceptualized without entailing essentialism or a false universalism. There is no doubt that the model of knowledge presupposed in the post-structuralist tradition is a narrow one and one that is not centrally concerned with the question of democracy. Knowledge tends to be reduced to power or a fragmented discursive politics that sees no place for democratic politics and collective actors.

However, postmodernism is not quite the same as post-structuralism. In recent years the difference between the two paradigms has grown: postmodernism has developed into a broader school of thought which has become centrally concerned with the question of identity and difference. Whereas the post-structuralist approach as well as that associated with Foucault and Lyotard was predominantly concerned with the denial of subjectivity and the political role of knowledge, recent developments have sought to recover the social dimension, neglected in the older post-structuralist approaches. I have argued that the first indication of the exhaustion of post-structuralism was in the shift in Foucault's later thought, in which he looked more and more to the possibility of a theory of the Subject who could resist power. Feminism and postcolonial studies have been particularly important in linking postmodernism to a theory of agency. In this shift away from the French tradition of post-structuralism, the social dimension – and the wider cognitive dimension – is recovered without a loss of the critical direction of postmodernism. In short, the postmodern break from post-structuralism allows the return of identity and a politics of social knowledge. With this break, the possibility of autonomy and a developmental logic based on creativity comes into sight. In other words, discourse is no longer confined to the theory of the text but can be brought to bear on communicative processes.

In a pivotal volume Linda Nicholson and Steve Seidman seek to defend the idea of a 'social postmodernism' against a purely 'textualizing' deconstructive critique. They attempt 'to show that it is possible for postmodernism to focus on institutions as well as texts, to think about the interrelations of social patterns without being essentializing or totalizing' (Nicholson and Seidman, 1995, p. 9). Their approach is based on the contention that social theorists should defend socially constructed identities without attributing to them essentialistic features and in a way that allows for their politicization. The central question is: 'how do we generate ways of understanding identity as central to personal and group identity while avoiding essentialism?' (Nicholson and Seidman, 1995, p. 21). Their conclusions are that identity is an important part of the social and cannot be simply deconstructed to the point of an empty anti-humanism, as early post-structuralism demanded. The problem, in short, is no longer relativism versus universalism, but is one of expanding the discursive and democratic space. One of the problems with post-structuralist deconstructionism was its surrendering of a political direction or a positive politics. Nicholson and Seidman defend a kind of postmodernism that has not closed itself off from the social:

> Postmodernism, therefore, does not represent an abandonment of 'the social'. Rather, it represents new ways of conceptualizing it. A postmodern conceptualization deviates from a modern one in understanding the categories by which social life is organized as historically emergent rather than naturally given, as multivalent rather than unified in meaning, and as the frequent result and possible present instrument in struggles of power. Whereas in the context of

modernist understanding a negative 'deconstructionist' emphasis may have been and still is necessary, such an emphasis need not be either all that a postmodern approach includes nor understood as that which is removed from institutional analysis. (1995, p. 26)

In their view the separation of postmodernism from the social was the 'wrong turn' because in 'textualizing' critique – the collapse of the social into the text – many of the issues central to social theorists were neglected: 'Postmodern critique narrowed into a critique of representations or knowledges, leaving relatively unattended their social and historical contexts' (1995, p. 9).

Finally, it may be mentioned that the postmodernist approach advocated by Nicholson and Seidman (see also Seidman, 1998) expresses the social and political experiences of the radical social movements that had arisen in the 1960s and 1970s, most of which disintegrated in the 1980s and 1990s. These movements had provided the context for post-structuralism, the critique of the disciplinary, patriarchal and normalized order of society (see Chapter 5). At the turn of the century we are in a different situation. The older social movements have partly realized their project and have subsequently collapsed as unitary agents. As Nicholson and Seidman (1995, p. 34) put it, the postmodern turn is closely connected to the failure of the new social movements to forge coalitions in the face of a well-organized backlash against progressive democratic change. Yet this does not detract from recognizing that the surfacing of different voices within these movements was pivotal in facilitating the deconstruction of essentialized identities and advocating a radical cultural politics of difference. The kind of postmodernism they defend is one that requires a rethinking of the premises and language of social knowledge, identity and politics. In their view, postmodern deconstruction – which is no longer tied to some of the assumptions of the older post-structuralism – can make possible 'a politics of coalition building, a cultural politics of social tolerance and difference, a critical politics of knowledge' (Nicholson and Seidman, 1995, p. 35). Postmodernist deconstruction, they argue, must be allied with the political hopes of the modern tradition of social theorizing.

Viewing postmodernism more positively, it might be suggested that it has opened up a space for a radical reflexivity in contemporary cultural change. It has shown how identities can be revealed to be problematic, since they are multiple, unstable and interlocking. Consequently, the deconstructive critique of essentialism can be invested with a social project. The decentring of received categories as socially constructed, the demonstration that nothing is natural and that our language and social knowledge contains the hidden traces of power struggles are important dimensions to ·democratic politics and an understanding of the social.

In sum, postmodernism, after post-structuralism, is marked by the shift to 'the social'. While this is never fully thematized, we find an increasing sensitivity to the constructive moment and a recognition of the social in Foucault's later writings, in Derrida's recent work and in Lyotard's postmodernism. In the context of the rise of cultural studies, postcolonial studies, feminist theory and marginality studies – where the reception of postmodernism has been greatest – the specific way in which a concern with the social is manifest is in the consideration of 'the Other' and identity. Postmodernism is thus characterized by the positive struggle for a 'politics of difference'. In more general terms it could be said that the question of culture and ethics have become central to it, thus forcing reflexivity and constructivism on to the agenda. This, however, has been at the cost of making the recognition of difference something positive, when, in fact, I would argue it is neither negative nor positive. The influence of this position can be seen in the extraordinary impact it has made on the reformulation of critical theory, as is evidenced in the work of ·Axel Honneth, whose *Struggle for Recognition* (1995a) has in effect made major concessions to the politics of identity.[11]

In order to take this discussion further I shall now look at the work of Zygmunt Bauman, who offers a theory of postmodernity that overcomes some of the normative deficits in much of the literature.

## Bauman: Ethics and Postmodernity

In his recent writings Zygmunt Bauman (1987, 1989, 1991, 1992, 1993, 1995, 1996, 1997) has sought to reconcile postmodernism with morality, a move that contrasts with his earlier, more modernist approach, which sought to link culture to praxis (Bauman, 1973). In *Postmodern Ethics* (1993) he specifically addressed a problem that is generally ignored in the postmodernist literature: how can postmodernist perspectives offer a new ethical understanding? His starting point is the recognition that human beings are moral beings. Morality is more fundamental to human life·than the category of the social itself, constituting an existential condition. What is morality? Bauman's answer is that the moral and existential· condition which defines human nature is 'responsibility for the Other'. The idea of 'responsibility for', or 'being for', is an essential part of the human condition and cannot be reduced to traditional notions of ethics such as the view that human beings are fundamentally good or evil.

This view of morality is not at first sight specifically post-modernist. It is not until the question of choice is considered that the postmodernist implications become apparent: responsibility entails choice, the ability to distinguish between good and evil. But this choice is an open-ended choice, it is far from straightforward and with the collapse of traditional authorities this choice is more open than ever before. Approaching the question of morality in this way, Bauman is able to address the key feature of the postmodernist predicament – the situation of ambivalence: 'Responsibility for the Other is itself shot through with ambivalence: it has no obvious limits, nor does it easily translate into practical steps to be taken or refrained from – each such step being instead pregnant with conse-quences that are notoriously uneasy to predict and even less easy to evaluate in advance' (Bauman, 1995, p. 2). The ambivalence of morality, in Bauman's view, is the very meaning of being moral, for moral life is a life of continuous uncertainty. Ambivalence is built into the moral condition simply because the dividing line between good and evil is not self-evident but must be negotiated by the individual in the course of social action. It is in action that choices are made. The choices that social action presents to the individual are tied to a certain loneliness in the face of the ambivalence of morality. Loneliness is one of Bauman's great themes and is very much connected with his understanding of morality as responsib-ility for the Other.

In Bauman's schema, earlier societies solved the problem of the burden of responsibility by recourse to religion, which greatly sim-plified the need for choices. By means of repentance and redemp-tion the problem of choice in the face of a life of perpetual sin was partly solved by the power of a transcendent authority who can make false choices reversible. The modern project provided an alternative solution. Legislation, the rule of law, provided an ethical code which was designed to prevent evil from entering the world. This was a contrast to earlier societies which had reconciled them-selves to the problem of evil. The modern project, in fact, sought to eliminate the inherent ambivalence of choice by designing secular authorities which took over the burden of choice from the shoulders of the individual. The result was that the epoch of modernity post-ulated the severance of the existentially moral choice from the normative framework of society. This normative framework is em-bodied in the ethical rulings of the law-governed state under which individuals exist as citizens who have rights and duties. This shift from the open-ended nature of moral choice to the ethical rule of law is fundamentally liberating, since it allows for the autonomy of the individual who is 'unencumbered' or 'disembedded' and can therefore achieve self-assertion. In this space – between the ethical rule of law and the loneliness of the moral individual – self-identity emerges as the hallmark of the modern. In as much as modernity is characterized by a penchant for legislation and intellectual and political mastery, it is also marked by a concern with identity.

However, and it is Bauman's main thesis, this concern of the modern project with the autonomy of the individual and the related quest for identity is not fully unleashed until the coming of the postmodern era. Under the conditions of postmodernity the tyranny of choice returns, but does so in a way very different from that of earlier times. The open-ended nature of choice is to be found in the ever-expanding world of social action. With the emphasis on the market in the late twentieth century there is the suggestion that choice is once again contingent on the resources of the individual. With the waning of central authorities, the burden of responsibility has shifted back on to the individual. The postmodern world is a world of choices:

> Modernity extolled the delay of *gratification*, in the hope that the gratification will be still gratifying when the delay is over; the postmodern world in which authorities spring up, unannounced, from nowhere, only to vanish instantly without notice, preaches *delay of payment*. If the savings book was the epitome of modern life, the credit card is the paradigm of the postmodern one. (Bauman, 1995, p. 5)

Modernity entailed the triumph of the universal, which was legislated by centralizing secular authorities which have usurped the traditional authorities, while retaining their absolutist principles; postmodernity suggests the collapse of universal and absolute principles and, coupled with the expanding world of the social, we can say as a consequence that the responsibilities of the individual are more profound than ever before. Postmodern ethics does not require universality, for it accepts that we live in a world of uncertainty. The choices that the postmodern condition presents are not merely those that can be satisfied by the market, but require a moral sensibility, an 'ethics of proximity'.

It is to be stressed that Bauman's conception of modernity and postmodernity does not totally pit the one against the other: 'Postmodernity does not necessarily mean the end, the discreditation or the rejection of modernity. Postmodernity is no more (but no less either) than the modern mind taking a long, attentive and sober look at itself, at its condition and its past works, not fully liking what it sees and sensing the urge to change' (1991, p. 272). He describes post-modernity as modernity 'coming of age', a 'coming to terms with its own impossibility' and as a 'self-monitoring modernity'. Yet, it is evident that modernity is a discourse of instrumentalism and mastery. In *Legislators and Interpreters* (1987), Bauman outlines the transformation of modernity into postmodernity: modernity was the age of the intellectual whose role is best characterized as the 'legislator', while the postmodern age is characterized by interpretation. The legislator has access to a privileged and a higher order of knowledge and is legitimated to make authoritative statements on the basis of that knowledge. The interpreter does not have such a privileged role and is confined merely to facilitating communication in society. The postmodern interpreter does not have recourse to a privileged body of legitimate knowledge but seeks to make seemingly incommensurable traditions penetrable to each other. Bauman insists that these two roles are not exclusive, in that the latter is merely the continuation of the former: the modern was already postmodern but the latter role is more thematized in postmodernity. However, there is little doubt that he sees the modern largely in terms of rising instrumentalism and intellectual mastery.[12]

Bauman's main contribution to the theory of postmodernity is his insistence on adhering to the regulative idea of responsibility as a key feature of the current situation. In his view, with the collapse of a single ethical code, a grand narrative of legitimation in Lyotard's sense – the idea of moral responsibility – can become a new regulative idea, albeit one that is radically disembedded and is ultimately highly personal. One aspect to this postmodernist situation of contingency is the awareness of choices, and of the fact that one has made a choice. With this choice also comes responsibility and the experience of ambivalence. Postmodernity is characterized by the disintegration of consensus and the kind of legislating reason that was sustained by the modern project. Viewed in this light, postmodernity as the tyranny of choice can only be an ambivalent development: it opens more and more chances but it can also be dangerous in that it prescribes no solutions. It is a site of opportunity and of danger.

While the idea of responsibility is the core feature of morality and is greatly enhanced by postmodernity, Bauman's concern with the normative dimension of culture is also reflected in his claim that postmodernity, far from being the apolitical world that it is often held to be, offers possibilities for substantive values such as tolerance and solidarity. Bauman (1991, p. 257) says these values are still relevant today but they cannot gain their confidence from something as solid and comforting as social structures, laws of history or the destination of nations and races from which the modernist project derived its impetus. With the transformation of modernity into postmodernity such substantive values can only come from something as vague as a genuine concern with misery and suffering and the knowledge that the postmodern mind has less need for cruelty and humiliation of the Other. But there is a danger that the postmodern sensibility will merely express itself in the superficial culture of 'kindness' and its critique of modernist social engineering that is a product of the information age and the dissemination of globalized images of suffering. The result is that problems such as world poverty are just seen as part of the infinite variety of existence (Bauman, 1991, p. 258). According to Bauman, the postmodern condition has split society into the 'happy seduced and unhappy oppressed selves'. This is the essence of his critique: it neglects the other side of the current form of life which is not characterized by choice. His emphasis on the theme of the Other is in line with the more general postmodernist stress on difference and the release of the Self from previously constraining traditions. However, Bauman's approach differs in that he is more concerned with the need for recognition of the Other and the need to create institutional frameworks in which identity and non-identity can flourish.

Bauman's critique of the ambivalence of the postmodern is a development of his critique of modernity in *Modernity and the Holocaust* (1989). In this work he uncovered the underside of modernity as organized brutality, engineered by the modern bureaucratic state and a dehumanized technology. Following in the path of Elias, Arendt and the earlier Frankfurt School, Bauman seeks to link the genesis of violence and the modern state: the essence of his argument is that the violence represented by the holocaust was an expression of the instrumentalizing logic of modernity and not of innate evil or psychological barbarity as such. The institutions that made the holocaust possible and the individuals themselves were in fact characterized by a certain normality. In his view, two related things made the holocaust possible: a self-perpetuating instrumental rationality and the growing distance between the act and its consequences. Together, they made the suspension of moral judgement possible. A major question for the future will be whether postmodernity will be able to reduce that distance and thereby decrease the production of violence.

Just as the tensions and conflicts of premodernity survived into modernity generating its genocides, so too have the tensions of modernity survived into the postmodern era. It is one of Bauman's most profound insights that the 'unfinished business of modern social engineering may well erupt into a new outburst of savage misanthropy, assisted rather than impeded by the newly legalized post-modern self-centredness and indifference' (1991, p. 260). Postmodern society is in danger of becoming immune to systematic critique and radical social dissent, with revolutionary potential. Because of its uncompromising privatization, postmodern society brings about the privatization of problems – the citizen is reduced to a consumer – and, as a result, the responsibility for their solutions is likewise emptied of a social dimension. In other words, postmodernity results in social fragmentation; instead of leading to enhanced solidarity, its market-promoted tolerance leads to fragmentation, the reduction of the social bond to a surface gloss (Bauman, 1991, p. 274). Thus, in this way tolerance leads to acceptance of injustice. Bauman's quest is to find a new ethics of autonomy in the postmodern world of fragmentation. The problem with this approach is that autonomy is seen in too personal terms as purely ethical. The postmodern may be a world of new opportunities and for a creatively inclined subjectivity, but it does not possess any developmental logics on the social and cultural levels where instrumentalism and cynicism prevail.

To sum up: Bauman brings the debate about postmodernity in a new direction from that of the post-structuralist-influenced approaches of Foucault, Lyotard and Baudrillard. He challenges the reduction of postmodernity to the purely aesthetic that is typical of much of the earlier approaches. His social theory is based on a strong sense of the ethical foundations of social action and thereby gives primacy to the normative dimension of culture and the possibility of autonomy under the conditions of postmodernity. However, Bauman's approach does suffer from one major defect. The ethical moment is seen as too opposed to politics and institutions. Reducing the latter to technological determinism, the former can only be something deeply personal. Consequently, there is no real possibility of mediation, or a sense of praxis, to use a term in his earlier work (Bauman, 1973). There is a certain fatalism in his rejection of collective actors and the reduction of modernity to instrumentalism and mastery, a condition with which he associates politics today.

## Conclusion: Beyond Postmodernism

The principal conclusion to be drawn from this chapter is that postmodernist social theory has rediscovered the autonomy of the Subject but has not solved the problem of its political nature.

Having passed through the deconstructionist critique – which led to the eclipse of the political Subject of modernity – the Subject has now returned. The significance of this move is that the central conflict of autonomy versus fragmentation is rendered diffuse and open to new interpretations.

Postmodernism, in so far as it was tied to post-structuralism, looked at cultural change from the standpoint of the aesthetic, with the consequence that the reflexivity that this entails leaves very little room for normative and cognitive dimensions. However, recent developments in postmodernism (Nicholson and Seidman, 1995) have reinstated the primacy of the social and reveal a concern with reflexivity and social knowledge. I have tried to show how Bauman's version of postmodernism overcomes the normative deficit in much of postmodern thinking, providing us with a strong ethical conception of a potentially creative Subject. However, reflexivity still needs to be rethought in a way that links it to the cultural model of society and to the social itself.

In the next chapter I wish to take the argument a step further by introducing the theories of Alain Touraine and Alberto Melucci. The advantages of their positions is that the question of collective actors is addressed and in a way that links reflexivity fully to a stronger notion of agency, bringing social and cultural processes together.

# 5

# *The Return of Agency: Touraine and Melucci*

## Introduction

My observations in the preceding chapters point towards a major problem in the conceptions of modernity associated with the writings of Habermas and postmodernist theory: the relationship of agency to culture and power. Habermas operates with a too decontextualized concept of agency which is untouched by the fragmentation of the life-world: thus the discursive regulation of power and the reflexivity of cultural models never come together. In short, his model of discourse is at the price of a cultural and social sacrifice, for his actor is a political one who can abstract him- or herself from cultural and social contexts. In contrast, we have seen that postmodern social theory as represented in the work of Bauman succeeds, where earlier post-structuralist attempts failed, in embracing an ethical conception of the Subject but in a way that fails to provide a mediation with the cultural model of society and the social itself. Thus the result is either a retreat into politics or into ethics.

I have argued that the social theories considered until now have one common failure – namely the relative weakness of a theorization of social change around what might be called a cultural politics of citizenship bringing together discourses of creativity, reflexivity and discursivity. In a way, as we enter the twenty-first century, we have moved beyond postmodernism and the need for a deconstruction of the Subject. While Habermas's project is still of great significance, we must look beyond its narrow focus on politi-

cal philosophy. The transformation of society as a result of globalization and its fragmentations presents new questions for social
theory which must rethink the project of autonomy. It is the merit of
the two theorists whom I shall be discussing in this chapter that the
concepts of social change and agency occupy a central role in their
theory. The work of Alain Touraine and Alberto Melucci take collective action as their starting point and thereby bring a heightened
sense of radical constructivism to bear in their interpretation of
modernity. We can thus speak of the 'return of agency' to characterize this turn in the theory of modernity. Their social actor is not a
decontextualized one as in Habermas, but a collective actor and,
unlike Luhmann and postmodernism, an agent of social change.
Their writings have additional merit in that they bring the question
of reflexivity and the cognitive dimension in cultural reproduction
to the fore. While postmodernism was a response to the collapse of
the social movements of modernity, the writings of theorists such as
Touraine and Melucci can be seen as an expression of the emergence
of the new social movements (NSM) of the late 1960s and 1970s.[1]
This may in fact also point to the limits of their approach, since the
movements of the late 1960s and 1970s are now in decline having
been overtaken by other ones (Castells, 1996). Touraine has met this
decline, which he has acknowledged, with a theory of the Subject, as
a notion of radical individuation. Problematic as this may be, more
serious is his theorization of the decline of the social under the
emergence of a new dualism – which recalls Habermas's conflict of
life-world and system – between instrumentalism and subjectivism,
which can be bridged only by a politics of the Subject.

At this point in the book we can detect the first intimation of a
theoretical convergence in recent social theory around the recognition of the obsolescence of the older approaches – be they Western
Marxism, post-structuralism, NSMs – and the need for a new
theorization of the central conflict in contemporary society. In different ways the projects of older approaches have been realized in
society, or rendered irrelevant.

## Touraine: From Historicity to the End of the Social

A transformation can be detected in the thought of Alain Touraine
from his writings in the 1960s to his later works in the 1990s. Depending on what one wished to emphasize, this could be termed a
major change or merely a new emphasis in line with a changing
society. Without exaggerating the extent of change in his thought, I
wish to argue that his writings reflect an increasing concern with

the fragmented nature of the social, bringing about a new environment for social actors. From his early concern with social movements as the agents of change, Touraine speaks in the 1990s of the broader concept of the Subject and the possibilities of democracy under the conditions of the end of the social.

In this section I shall outline Touraine's early sociology of action, then discuss his analysis of social movements, and proceed to look at his theory of modernity and democracy. Finally, I compare his approach to that of Foucault and Habermas.

## Historicity and the self-production of society

Touraine's early sociology was what he called a 'sociology of action'. The essential ideas of this theory have remained central to his entire work. Society, in his view, must be seen as a field of social action: structure is constituted by action. His central theme is the idea of the 'self-production of society': the ability of social action to bring about social change. At a time when structuralism was influential in France, where it was associated with Lévi-Strauss and Louis Althusser, Touraine argued for the centrality of the actor.

Society, according to Touraine, does not merely reproduce itself or adapt itself to change, but it transforms itself: change is the permanent condition of society. The agents of change are social movements/collective actors, and not structures. The structure of society is itself the action of the society upon itself. Touraine is a critic of those who reduce society to the status quo or to a system of values or structures (i.e. modernization and functionalist theories). He is also opposed to Marxist approaches which reduce social action to class action. However, Touraine's sociology of action is closer to Marxism in that it is more on the side of change than of order. A preoccupation with order has always been central to sociology, which in his view must be renewed around a dynamic notion of change. One of his main ideas is that society doesn't simply reproduce itself, as in functionalist theories, but acts upon itself.

In *The Self-Production of Society* ([1973] 1977; henceforth all references in this section are to Touraine, unless otherwise stated), Touraine developed his theory of action into a major work in social theory and this has remained the cornerstone of his writings. One of the central ideas of this work is the concept of historicity. Historicity is the term Touraine uses to describe the capacity for self-reflective social action. Unlike Bourdieu, for whom reflexivity transcends social action, Touraine builds the idea of reflexivity into his concept of social action. The concept of historicity suggests the ability of social action to change the course of history by acting on the historical field. There is, then, a close connection between social change and historicity. Historicity signifies the creativity of social action: 'Society is not just reproduction and adaptation; it is also creation, self-production' ([1973] 1977, p. 3).[2]

'Historicity' is made up of three components: the model of knowledge (which constitutes an image of society and nature, i.e. the cognitive dimension); accumulation (the mode of material production); and the cultural model (society's capacity for self-interpretation, i.e. the normative dimension). This tripartite model informs the basis of Touraine's social theory. The cognitive plays a particularly important role in his theory of social change. The cultural model is distinct from ideology, which refers to the identity projects of specific social actors, and to systems of values. Society possesses a capacity to reflect upon itself and to interpret the direction of its movement. The cultural model captures the creativity of social action and gives it a cognitive form, which allows social actors to interpret the social field. This capacity is the cultural model and is the basis of all change; it is the 'image of creativity' and gives society a set of orientations that govern social action ([1973] 1977, pp. 16, 19). It is essential to see that the cultural model is not deterministic but requires an interpretative process before it is realized in social action. Before major social transition happens, change will be primarily centred around the transformation of the cultural model, which is not purely derivative of other structures: 'The concept of historicity . . . refuses to define the actors by their interaction and their participation in shared values. It conceives of society as a set of cultural tensions and social conflicts' ([1973] 1977, p. 62). With respect to 'knowledge', Touraine looks at how it is also an agent of change: knowledge enables a society to act upon itself and to bring about social change. Accumulation, on the other hand, is the process by which economic activity and historicity are linked. However, his principal concern is with the cultural model of society.

The concept of historicity cannot be separated from social struggles, in particular class conflict. Historicity is inseparable from class relations. The proper object of study is not classes but the relations between the classes. In this way Touraine offers an anti-essentialist theory of class. His approach differs from that of mainstream Marxists, for it reflects the changed nature of class conflict which in turn is a product of changes in capitalism. Touraine ([1969] 1971b) was one of the first left-wing thinkers to take on board the idea of the 'post-industrial society', a theory originally proposed by Daniel Bell (1960). In the programmed or post-industrial society the main classes are, on the one side, consumers and, on the other, the managers and technocrats. The state is no longer merely a sub-system but is the focal point of capitalism and the focus for social struggles. In Touraine's version of the theory of the post-industrial society, capitalism is not so much superseded as transformed and – in his main departure from Bell – it is characterized by an increased capacity for historicity. The post-industrial society is a society of many kinds of conflict. These are centrally related to the salience of information: the post-industrial society is an information society and consequently the role of knowledge has a different role to play from that in industrial society. It is evident, however, that Touraine's concept of knowledge includes more than just information, encompassing also the cognitive basis of society.

It is the basis of his social theory that there is one central conflict in every society (e.g., socialism/social democracy in industrial society). However, there is not necessarily one single social agent. In post-industrial society there are many agents and it is not evident which will become the agent of historicity. In *The May Movement* ([1969] 1971a) Touraine explored the possibility that it might be the students who would transform the cultural model of society, which would then open up the way for major social change. In a later book, *Solidarity* (Touraine et al. [1982] 1983), he showed how a social movement could act upon the field of historicity opening up a new field of action. Social movements are at the centre of the post-industrial society:

> whatever the level of project, social movements are not identifiable unless they reveal themselves by means of a durable collective action, one that cannot be reduced to 'reaction' to a crisis or to specific social tensions, and by means of an ideological or utopian production that puts forward, even if only in a fragmentary way, a vision of society. ([1973] 1977, p. 352)

In post-industrial society (which can be defined as the shift from a society based on production to one based on consumption and knowledge) conflict has shifted from the economic to the cultural model as well as to the model of knowledge. The result is that the struggle for historicity may be diverted into a politics of identity and a concern with depoliticized and privatized issues. This is the first suggestion of his mature theory of the fragmentary nature of social change and the view that we are today approaching the end of the social under the conditions of 'de-modernization':[3] 'Our type of society, more than any other, should be thought of as a complex of social relations and movements, cultural products and political struggles' (1981, p. 5).

The central idea of Touraine's theory of change is that social movements initiate social change but do not determine it, for social change is indeterminate. Thus, societies do not merely pass from one state to the next: change is multilevelled. Touraine therefore rejects evolution and progress – post-industrial society is what he calls a 'post-historical society': 'Evolution will continue to exist within this type of society, but the foreseeable transformations of science will occur within the cultural model' and 'Systems of historical action are not situated on a line of progress leading from traditional to modern: they each constitute a particular configuration of the same system' ([1973] 1977, pp. 103, 105). A society's historicity is not a process of change from one type of society to another; it is strictly confined to the synchronic axis. Rather than placing a society in history, Touraine locates a society in its historicity, its self-transformative capacity, and thus rejects the idea of social change as a qualitative leap from one society to another ([1973] 1977, pp. 23–4, 107). In this way Touraine offers a notion of the 'end of history' in the sense of a break from the myth of historical evolution: 'the triumph of historicity is also the end of history' (pp. 103–4). Change and historicity are not coeval. The direction of Touraine's social theory is that change must be brought away from evolution and linked to historicity: 'The greater a society's historicity, the greater its capacity to act upon itself, the more change appears as an internal process' ([1973] 1977, p. 379). He tends to see social change in terms of the tensions and conflicts between the field of historicity, the political system and the social organization. Historicity leads to social change in its relationship with the political system and the social organization of action. Social movements are instrumental in bringing about social change, in translating the cultural model and the field of historicity into a system of social and political organization.

The crisis of sociology is that its nineteenth-century project (which was to find a basis for social integration/order under the conditions of modernization/industrialization) is no longer possible today: society is not a whole, or reducible to a single category, but is diffuse: 'The question that haunted, and which still haunts, what we might call classical sociology is this: On what conditions, through all its transformations and struggles of interests does a society maintain the unity that enables it to define laws, make its institutions work, form new generations, and manage its internal conflicts?' ([1973] 1977, p. 38).

Touraine has always been a critic of the unitarian idea of society, a concept which has been too much associated with conservative sociologies of social order. Society as such does not exist, he argues:

'Society is not merely a system of norms or a system of domination: it is a system of social relations, of debates and conflicts, of political initiatives and claims, of ideologies and alienation' and 'Society is not closed, is not completely integrated either by values or by power. At the level of organizations themselves, the dialectic of historicity and class relations is being pursued in the very praxis of social movements' ([1973] 1977, pp. 30, 58).

## New social movements and social change

In 1978 Touraine published *The Voice and the Eye* ([1978] 1981), which was both a major statement of his interventionist sociology and a theory of social movements. This work has since become a classic work in NSM theory, even though Touraine's concerns go far beyond NSM theory as such. His concern has always been with a wider understanding of social movements, which refers to the movement of society. This is consistent with his view that there is always one major social movement in every historical period and that this is the basis of social change. Yet he is responsive to the NSMs which sprang up in western societies in the 1970s.

In *The Voice and the Eye* Touraine argued that in post-industrial society, which he prefers to call the 'programmed society', there is the appearance of a new societal type which is bound up with the appearance of NSMs. The NSMs are a product of the programmed society because in this kind of society class domination is no longer primarily at the level of organizing industrial work but in organizing consumption. Resistance to this kind of domination cannot be limited to a particular sphere: the struggle between capital and labour has been displaced by a struggle between consumers and a new ruling apparatus:

> That is why the defence against such an apparatus is no longer car-
> ried out in the name of political rights or worker's rights but in sup-
> port of a population's right to choose its kind of life and in support of
> its political potential, which is often called self-management. Political
> action is all pervading: it enters into the health service, into sexuality,
> into education and into energy production. ([1978] 1981, p. 7)[4]

NSMs, he argues, often reject the cultural orientations of industrial society but do not fully develop as historical actors until they cease to be defenders of a threatened form of life and articulate new ident-ities. The change from one cultural model to the next, from indus-trial to the post-industrial, defines the field of sociological research for Touraine. The role of the sociologist is to intervene in historicity by helping to articulate the central conflicts, to indicate what is at stake by going beyond the immediacy of the situation and to help the social actors to understand their action.

Social change is of course complex: it is a question of transition, crisis and transformation, and many kinds of collective action intervene between the two types of society and their kinds of collective action. 'In our type of society', Touraine argues, 'social movements are more than ever the principal agents of history' ([1978] 1981, p. 9). The principal stages in the transition from industrial society to the programmed society are marked by the decline of the old social movements and the emergence of a cultural crisis. The starting point is a decline in the workers' movement and not economic industrial crisis itself. The chief conflict today is not that between worker and owner, but that which mobilizes a population against an apparatus of domination. With this new conflict emerging, a cultural crisis emerges together with a rejection of the older cognitive and normative systems. Thus, in the system of knowledge, for instance, 'evolutionist representation becomes replaced by another form of knowledge, by the idea that society is a system capable of producing, of generating its own normative guidelines instead of having them passed down via an order or a movement that transcends society – no matter whether one call it God, Spirit or History' ([1978] 1981, p. 14). In the cultural model, too, the images that a society forms of itself, of its creative capacity, undergoes change in the emergence of a new model of creativity. In industrial society the image of creativity remains transcendent, whereas in the programmed society the image emerges of society becoming responsible for its action. In rejecting the myth of progress, a rift becomes evident between the existing social institutions and an emergent cultural model, leading to a crisis in socialization. The family, the school, the churches, which have been based on an even older cultural model than that of industrial society, are plunged into a deep crisis:

> The channels of society no longer correspond to the cultural content they are meant to bear. Hence the personality crisis and the critique of power and of institutions which reach beyond politics and infuse the new social movements with a challenging power added to their already existing inclination towards protest and conflict. (1981, p. 15)

This rupture between the cultural model and institutions produces a 'great resistance', as a society turns its back on its former cultural model. This rejection of the older model is not of course total, for it seeks to rescue something from it in order to provide a sense of continuity.

After the experience of events in May 1968, in which he was deeply involved, Touraine is cautious about the possibility of a social movement emerging out of this wider crisis, and suggests that cultural modernization in the context of the decline of the older movements may be the extent of change at the beginning of the twenty-first century. This cultural modernization – as represented by the NSMs of the 1970s – may be merely the sign of a liberal cultural agenda by the rising middle classes and not a genuine social movement. Touraine thus distances himself from the NSMs, which are in danger of remaining on the purely cultural level, preoccupied only with lifestyle politics. Their struggles are more reminiscent of those of the progressive intellectuals of the Enlightenment, such as Voltaire, in that they are more about fighting prejudice and privilege than opposing the system of domination.

Touraine distinguishes three further kinds of movement which have the potential to become a social movement: the struggles of community, populism and anti-technocratic movements. One feature of the current situation is the revival of community and the quest for personal identity. In Touraine's view, 'the retreat into autonomy' runs the risk of becoming impotent, unable to withstand the ravages of history from which it rebels. Ultimately, the quest for community remains on the level of a cultural critique and fails to become a social critique ([1978] 1981, p. 19). To become a genuine social critique, the defence of community must address the global challenge of speaking out for the underdeveloped world without lapsing into romantic anti-modernism. Mindful of the dangers of the utopia of community, Touraine believes utopia to be an indispensable stage in the process of cultural and social change. It can be used against the evolutionist myth of progress to articulate a new cultural model. A second kind of movement is the populist hope, which Touraine associates mostly with the developing world. Populism is anti-traditionalist; it is modernizing but is also anti-colonial. It cannot be reduced to a quest for identity and is often the only kind of progressivist movement possible in the developing world. A third example of a major movement is the anti-technocratic struggles. These mark a decisive stage in the evolution of a social movement and are located between elitist liberation movements and new popular struggles. In Touraine's estimation the anti-nuclear movement is one of the most important of these movements, since it attacks the centre of the apparatus of domination, from which power ultimately emanates. This movement is particularly significant because it brings the producers of knowledge, the scientists and the professional classes closer to the public.

Touraine stresses that these movements do not necessarily amount to a new social movement. Only the latter – anti-technocratic movements – are to be identified with social change. NSMs are not to be equated merely with new causes, demands or disputes, since once these have been resolved the movements frequently disappear or are absorbed into the strategies of other actors. The direction of Touraine's thinking seems to be that as a contradiction appears between, on the one side, institutions and the mode of accumulation and, on the other, the cultural model and the mode of knowledge, new social actors appear on the scene bringing about a reconstruction of the political. Whether or not they will become social movements is a question only the future can tell.

In the present context of understanding social change today, the great significance of Touraine's social theory is his conception of the relationship between social change, social action and the articulation of cultural models of social interpretation. His abstract notion of 'historicity', in effect, means the capacity of a society to produce cultural models and a system of action – which he calls 'class relations' – through which these models become social practices. Social movements are 'the collective action of actors at the highest level – class actors – fighting for the control of historicity, i.e. control of the great cultural orientations by which a society's environmental relationships are normatively organized' ([1978] 1981, p. 26). 'The cultural field,' Touraine argues, 'the historicity of a society, represents the stakes in the most important conflicts' (p. 77). In his analysis of the dynamics of social movements the cultural orientations are given a central role. A social movement is based on a sense of identity, a notion of what it stands for and a focus of opposition (p. 81). A social movement, he also argues, is a knowledge producer, since it acts upon the existing cognitive structures and articulates a new one.

## Critique of modernity: the end of the social?

Touraine's later writings reveal an increasing pessimism about social movements and their ability to bring about social change. He is reluctant to identify with any particular social movement as the primary agent of social change. The central characteristic of contemporary society is the relatively recent development of the collapse of the social. Unlike Baudrillard, Touraine sees this as the result not merely of the absorption of the social into the cultural but as a consequence of the growing separation of the spheres of culture, personality, politics and economy. The idea of society formerly referred to the unity of these domains. In Parsonian social theory society was the functioning totality of all of these spheres. The idea of society represented a principle of unity by which its functional components were held together. Today, however, we are experiencing a separation of these domains, in particular the separation of social life and the state. The concept of society was paramount when modernity brought about a differentiation of its subsystems, but today these have become wrenched apart from each other as a result of what he calls 'de-modernization'. The classic authors – Marx, Weber, Durkheim and Parsons – identified the idea of society with a centralizing principle which could unite these domains – class consciousness, rationality, co-operation, community – but this is less credible today given the extent of fragmentation. For Touraine, this means we must admit that the very category of the social has exhausted itself. The state is no longer at the centre of society – the unity of which is now more likely to be in consumption. This is also the case for social movements, for 'no social movement can bear in itself a model of an ideal society' (1992a, p. 61). Their actions are too limited either because of the cultural and political unity of national societies, or because the spirit of a market individualism has made integration impossible.

However, Touraine is far from Luhmann and postmodernism. His notion of the end of the social is not the expression of political indifference or postmodernist irony but an acknowledgement of a changing world. Even though he is critical of myths of unity, he still holds on to the need for a principle of unity. It is this that marks his social theory off from Luhmann, Foucault and Lyotard and allies him with Habermas and Bauman. Under the rubric of 'post-social movements', Touraine argues that the 'hypermodernity' of our time, in destroying the possibility of society as a unified entity, makes the formation of coherent social movements impossible. The 'main objective is no longer to create an ideal society but to defend the freedom and creativity of the Subject in a universe that appears to be dominated by money and pleasure, technology and war' (1992a, p. 67).

Touraine distinguishes between different kinds of post-social movements, one which can be an expression of individualism addressed to issues relating to war and catastrophes and one which challenges the control of cultural goods. First, it is necessary to distinguish between a social movement and a historical movement. The former deals with the structural problems in society, while the latter seek to control the process of historical development (1992a, p. 68). It appears that the anti-nuclear movement and ecological movement are ultimately more like political than social movements since they seek to define their actions at state level and enter public life. In offering an alternative societal model they resemble historical movements and are to be contrasted to the idea of a social movement, which is more rooted in the transformation of society. The women's movement – as opposed to feminist liberalism – is an example of a social movement in that it goes beyond mere rights to a debate about the very nature of society, addressing issues such as gender and identity. This is an example of a cultural movement which has the potentiality to become a social movement. However, Touraine argues that many social movements can remain purely at the cultural level (1985).

Touraine sees social movements as splintering into various fields, in particular the cultural and the political. Social movements have difficulty in sustaining their project because they are forever divided between the cultural and the political. He remains ambivalent about a new social movement capable of acting on society. He also remains ambiguous as to whether a social movement is a movement as such or the movement of society as a whole. Indeed, there is the suggestion in his writings that the idea of the social movement has passed from particular social actors into the broader field of social action. Underlying this apparent ambivalence is a deeper lack of clarity as to whether the field of historicity and social change are two separate axes on which social movements can act. Touraine speaks of the growing separation of the two axes on which social actors can be situated: the synchronic (which controls the level of historicity) and the diachronic (the process of change) (1992a, p. 68). If social movements, be they cultural or political, are confined to the diachronic, what characterizes the synchronic? Is there a central social conflict in today's society? Touraine apparently has not relinquished his belief in the idea of a central social conflict, which he thinks can survive the apparently irremediable decline of historicist thought and the fate of many collective actors. Touraine has given a precise answer: the notion of a social movement 'designates a general representation of social life rather than a particular type of phenomenon' (1992b, p. 126). As I have argued, Touraine is ambivalent on the status of a social movement: either it is a movement in the sense of an agency or it is the movement of society itself. This ambivalence is, however, an expression of a deeper idea: the possibility that the transformation of the cultural model of society – the self-representation of society – will transform itself into the field of historicity. At the moment, in Touraine's framework, a social movement is forming on the level of a transformation of the cultural model, but it has not consolidated as a social movement. This, then, is the central conflict in today's society: the conflict between a new cultural model and social relations. In order to develop this theme further we need to turn to his *Return of the Actor* ([1984] 1988), to *Critique of Modernity* ([1992] 1995a) and to his writings on democracy ([1994] 1997, 1995b) and other reflections on the end of the social (1998a, 1998b).

*Return of the Actor* was an intermediary book, a concise statement of his earlier social theory and a projection forwards. Some of the main themes are the end of the social, the crisis of modernity, the primacy of social agency and the return of the Subject, and the separation of society and state. Touraine argues that sociology is in crisis because its central category, the idea of the social, is becoming redundant. Society as such does not exist; what exists is social action. Society is breaking up and is being absorbed into the state, a development reflected in the growing prominence of political philosophy at the expense of sociology. Sociology is in danger of being left behind as an ideology of modernity, a theory of social institutions. The words 'society' and the 'social' are beginning to make their way out of our vocabulary, he argues (p. 7). The social is giving way to the political: 'Whereas classical sociology joined culture, social organization, and evolution in order to constitute these large cultural, social, and historical aggregates that it called societies, we will seek to separate them in order to bring forth a space of problems within with sociology can establish itself' (p. 8).

If the social is giving way to the political, it is also sundering its discourse to the cultural. This is evident in the rise of culturalist approaches, such as postmodernism and communitarianism, which all privilege the cultural over the social. If modernity stood for order and uniformity, today, under the rule of the postmodern, diversity is on the rise, with community replacing society. Touraine's question is whether these developments allow for a new but post-historical notion of the Subject: can we speak of a return of the Subject? The Subject is to be defined in an anti-essentialistic manner as creative action ([1984] 1988, p. 42). The task is to see how the cultural model of society can be activated by social actors. Culture must not lose its connection with the social, and the political must be reintegrated into a notion of social action. Unlike postmodernists and communitarians, Touraine emphasizes the importance of social movements and social conflict. Culture cannot be divorced from social action, for it is forever being transformed. Even though Touraine has always argued that there is one central social movement, he has come close to admitting the end of this model:

No social movement today can identify with the whole of the conflicts and the forces for social change in a national society. As a result, the field of struggles becomes more and more autonomous in relation to the action of social movements (although this trend could be reversed in other social situations), and collective behaviour tends more and more toward what I have called social antimovements. ([1984] 1988, p. 67)

In *Critique of Modernity* Touraine seeks to posit a new principle of unity capable of reconciling the dualism of modernity, which threatens to divide society even more. The main objective of this great book is to define the cultural field ([1992] 1995a, p. 361). Given the fragmented nature of contemporary society and the differentiation brought about by modernity, there is no single principle of unity that is capable of uniting the diverse areas of modern life. The illusion of a single myth of unity must be abandoned. The solution Touraine proposes is to reconcile the Subject and Reason, the two strands in the discourses of modernity. The new, or second, modernity will unite these, since neither alone is capable of this task. In order to understand this development in his thought, we need to see how his reconstruction of the critique of modernity relates to the sociology of modernity.

According to Touraine, the distinguishing feature of the critique of modernity has been the revolt of the Subject against Reason. The Enlightenment and the historicist conception of modernity privileged Reason as the god of modernity. This was a western conception of the world and was epitomized in the myth of progress and the myth of revolution as well as in the French myth of the republic. Originally an Enlightenment and rationalistic idea, the myth of Reason as the legislator of modernity entered the social thinking in the nineteenth century via historicism and revolution. Both of these were obsessed with the idea of destroying the old order and the search for a new order. Reason and Subject were absorbed into the totality of history, nation, civilization and world spirit. Touraine points out how these two poles, of Reason and Subject, became divorced in the *fin de siècle* with the realization that modernity had become a fragmented world. The crisis of modernity begins with the liberation of the Subject from Reason. Epitomized in the writings of Nietzsche and Freud, the critique of modernity had two historical moments with a third about to appear on the horizon ([1992] 1995a, p. 95). The first was the exhaustion of the utopian impulse of the early bourgeois emancipation movements and the second was the experience of disenchantment with modernity associated with Weber, the idea of a loss of meaning as a result of the instrumentalization of Reason. Today we are experiencing a third critique: the separation of state and society to a point at which they can no longer be reconciled. Postmodern culture is the condition of fragmentation, according to Touraine ([1992] 1995a, pp. 95–7). However, his approach goes beyond conventional postmodernism, which focuses on the cultural, to address the four key components of modern society, which he terms: sexuality, commodity consumption, the company and the nation. These correspond closely to the domains of personality, culture, economics and politics, which, Touraine argues, are moving in different directions today, bringing about an intensified sense of fragmentation, which cannot be understood as merely differentiation. Underlying the fragmentation of these four orders is a more fundamental separation of the personal order from the collective order: on the one side, we have sexuality and consumption and, on the other, the factory and the nation. The world of modernity, the world of the nineteenth century, was content to call the unity of the private and the collective – personality, culture, economy and politics – 'society', but today these have collapsed into the fragmented spheres of sexuality, consumption, the company and the nation. The latter two involve destruction – in business policy, profit or power tends to outweigh production and nationalism bears within it the seeds of war. While expressing a core area of modernity, these domains are now undermining the culture of modernity to the extent that rationalization is no longer the principle that unites society. In line with postmodernist approaches and the Frankfurt School's critique of culture, Touraine attaches importance to the rise of the consumer society as a challenge to the world of production and the world of nations. But what is happening is that the nation is returning as a new destructive force having become released from modernity:

> The shattering of modernity into four fragments scattered to the four cardinal points of social life is also a fourfold liberation movement. Nietzsche and Freud asserted the rights of Eros in the face of social laws and moralization; national gods rise up and resist the universalism of the market; industrial and banking empires – the lords of industrial society – become concentrated and assert their desire for conquest and power in the face of the frigid advice of textbooks on management; desires escape social controls because they are no longer associated with a social position. Such is the social scene that was born of the decay of the model which identified modernity with the triumph of reason. ([1992] 1995a, p. 145)

In this world ideologies are disappearing and are replaced by neo-communitarian movements seeking to capture the new spaces that have been opened up by a general retreat into subjectivity. We are experiencing a convergence of three great forces: rationalization, an appeal to human rights and a religious communitarianism ([1992] 1995a, p. 59). For Touraine, this can be summed up by saying we are moving from social totalitarianism to cultural totalitarianism (p. 311). This is also apparent in the widespread appeal to community throughout the world today, from Islam to the European Union. Touraine goes so far as to suggest that the national question may dominate the next century in the way that the social question dominated the nineteenth century. In other words, rationalization and subjectivism are becoming divorced from each other and recombined in new ways. Touraine's principle argument is that the domains of Reason and Subject must be brought together. Postmodernity cannot survive by appeal to one, but requires the two. It is essential, he argues, to prevent one element of modernity from absorbing the other. The idea of the Subject, divorced from historicism and the philosophy of the Subject, opens up the possibility of becoming a basis for a new idea of freedom and responsibility. We must look for new ways of reuniting Reason and Subject, the scattered domains of sexuality, consumption, company and nation. By insisting that only a combination of Reason and Subject can achieve a degree of unity, Touraine ([1992] 1995a, p. 250) believes he has answered the challenge of complexity and fragmentation as described by Luhmann and Lyotard. In his view, this reintegration of Reason and Subject is more a continuation of modernity than a break from it, since it is a recovery of the modern project (p. 219). It is also to be defined by the recovery of the creativity of action (p. 242).

It is evident that his notion of the Subject does not refer to the subjectivity of the individual or an essentialist category, but to social movements and is also not constituted in opposition to the Other; it is both autonomy and recognition. Touraine's notion of the Subject seeks to integrate Self and Other into a dynamic social agent. Moreover, by linking the Subject to Reason, he is able to recognize the 're-enchantment' of the world: the disenchantment of the world – the loss of meaning as defined by the older categories of thought – opens the way for the re-enchantment of the world ([1992] 1995a, p. 230). Touraine also believes he can project the Reason–Subject divide back on the social struggles of industrial modernity: the workers' movement was not merely about material and rationalized aims, it was also a struggle for the dignity of workers. A social movement, Touraine has always argued, 'is an attempt on the part of a collective actor to gain control of a society's "values" or cultural orientations by challenging the action of an adversary with which it is linked by power relations' ([1992] 1995a, p. 239). It is both a social and a cultural project. Touraine believes the Subject cannot be dissolved into postmodernity because social struggles still continue. The most important are those between the personal subject and the cultural industries (medical care, education, information). To this extent we do not live in a totally postmodern society ([1992] 1995a, p. 5). Touraine instead prefers to speak of a 'new modernity': the reconciliation of Reason and Subject, which is also a reconciliation of Self and Other.

*Critique of Modernity* closes with a chapter on democracy. Like Habermas, Touraine has made democracy the theme of his later work ([1994] 1997, 1995b), and has also tried to relate the question to European integration (1994). Democracy must be linked to a substantive notion of citizenship, but is caught in the dilemma that if it becomes too substantive it will retreat into identity and if it remains formal it becomes emptied of content. Democracy for Touraine is the politics of the Subject and the challenge is to reconcile the Subject with Reason, or in more concrete terms to provide an institutional framework in which the universalistic conceptions of citizenship can be reconciled with the politics of diversity. The appeal to community will destroy democracy, which is also in danger of becoming an ideology of empty universalism. 'Democracy', Touraine argues, 'allows a society to be both unified and diverse. That is why democracy is a culture and not merely a set of institutional guarantees' ([1994] 1997, p. 127). As in his critique of modernity, Touraine argues that the danger today is the retreat into identity – into ethnicity, gender, nationality – or individualism (the market, consumption) with the result that there is no principle of unity: 'The growing rift between the world of objects and the world of culture is leading to the disappearance of the subject, which is defined by transforming activity into meaning and situations into actions, by producing itself' ([1994] 1997, p. 130). Unlike Habermas, who offers a decontextualized discourse ethic, Touraine speaks of the 'recomposing of the world' around a re-enchanted politics (pp. 138–9). Democracy will be condemned to irrelevance if it does not establish a link between the world of instrumentality and the world of identities. For this reason he emphasizes the need to invent a 'cultural democracy' in order to combine particularity and universality (1995b).

## Between Habermas and postmodernism

Touraine offers a valuable critique of Habermas and postmodernism, while at the same time mediating these two quite different approaches. In his view, there is not a great difference between postmodernist ideas and Luhmann's systems theory, for both assert that there is a dissociation of actor and system ([1992] 1995a, p. 250). Luhmann argues that the system is defined by its self-referentiality, while actors are defined by their cultural differences. Postmodernism, too, asserts the pervasiveness of difference and announces the end of the social. However, the problem with postmodernism according to Touraine is that it 'takes to extremes the destruction of the modernist representation of the world' ([1992] 1995a, p. 190). While emphasizing plurality and heterogeneity, it rejects the functional differentiation of life in so far as it reduces the social and the political to the cultural and the aesthetic. Differentiation does not need to imply either Luhmann's dualism of actor and system or the postmodernist deconstruction of the Subject. Despite the fragmentation of modern society, Touraine still thinks agency is important, and in particular social movements, which of course have no place in postmodernist theory. 'Postmodernism', he says, 'corresponds to decreased creativity and a crisis of collective action' (1992a, p. 77). He rejects the aestheticism of Barthes and Foucault. In demonstrating the origin of the Subject in power and its instrumentalization by Reason, Foucault is left without the normative means of transcending power. Against his vision of modernity in terms of total institutions of power, Touraine defends modernity in terms of a model of conflict.

However, Touraine grants that Foucault's attack on the Subject was important in getting rid of the essentialist idea of the Subject. Now that his critique is over, 'it is time to clear the battlefield and to admit that the Subject, which has survived every insult, is the only idea that allows us to reconstruct the idea of modernity' ([1992] 1995a, p. 172). The Subject, stripped of essentialism and historicism, can be readmitted to a reconstituted modernity. In his view, there are two possible responses to the crisis of modernity: Habermas's answer or the postmodernist answer (p. 178). He is closer to Habermas, but differs in many respects, most notably in his insistence in integrating culture into a theory of democracy (pp. 336–43). His concern with the Subject confirms him to be still in the tradition of the philosophy of praxis. A second difference is that he stresses the centrality of collective action, and, third, while Habermas operates with a normative albeit post-historicist notion of evolution, Touraine remains on the level of historicity. In general, Habermas underestimates the conflictual dimension of society, since he sees the principal conflict between life-world and system, at least in his writings until the 1990s. For Touraine the conflictual dimension of society penetrates into its cultural model, which cannot be transcended by a discourse free of domination. The strengths of his work undoubtedly consist of his recovery of the creative dimension of action, his emphasis on the centrality of the cultural model of society as an interpretative framework for social action and his separation of historicity from evolution.

What then are the problems with Touraine? In my view, the principal weakness of the work is his tendency to overstate the end of the social under the conditions of 'de-modernization'. His critique of classical sociology demolished the unifying myth of society, but has left a void in its place. While he attacks the reduction of the social to the political and to the cultural, he has denied the possibility of an adequate theorization of the social. The idea of the Subject as a unifying principle is unsatisfactory, as it is never spelt out clearly, though there is a strong suggestion that this is to be understood as a cultural politics of citizenship. The problem, in essence, is that the domains of instrumentalism and the world of experience are seen as being too radically opposed, whereas in fact an alternative view would see both as containing discursive spaces.

In order to see how the social can be rescued for social theory, I shall examine the work of Alberto Melucci.

## Melucci: Culture, Identity and Change

The differences between Melucci and Touraine are not substantial. Both theorists take collective action as their starting point and the idea of social change lies at the centre of their sociology. Equally important for both is the question of culture in social change. However, Melucci (1989, pp. 199–204; all references in this section are to Melucci, unless otherwise stated) departs from Touraine in a number of respects, principally emphasizing to a greater extent the non-political dimension of NSMs and collective action. This can be seen in his interest in exploring the role of collective identity in social movements. The function of collective identity was less important for Touraine. The basis of society is not conflict, as appears to be the case with Touraine:

> Even a writer of the stature of Touraine, who has pushed criticism of social philosophies to its furthest and sought to lay a basis for a theory of action, still preserves a sort of metaphysics of conflict as an original dimension of society. The problem, however, is how to explain conflict in terms of social relations without turning it into a primal dimension. (1996a, p. 45)

Melucci's approach stresses conflict over symbolic issues, identity, group membership and the expressivist dimensions to collective action. A further difference is that for Melucci there is not one single social movement, but many. Social movements operate in the microphysics of power and do not always have durability. Finally, constructivism plays a more important role in Melucci's sociology. That is to say, collective identity implies a constructivist view of collective action and affects the practice of research itself. Constructivism operates on two levels as a double hermeneutic; on the first-order level of actors' experiences of their own life and on the second level of social science.

Melucci is a critic of all kinds of reductionism. Marxists emphasize too much that opposition is directed against a centralized locus of power (1996a, p. 176). Unlike Touraine, he goes so far as to abandon the concept of class relationships. The concept of collective action in his approach differs from the holistic assumptions of Marxism: 'Collective action is a multipolar system of action which combines different orientations, involves multiple actors, and encompasses a system of opportunities and constraints which shapes the actors' relationships' (1996a, p. 40). Collective action is constantly being negotiated; it is never fixed in the identity of a class position.

It is also helpful to contrast Melucci to the other approaches considered so far. With respect to Habermas, Melucci agrees with Touraine that the principal conflict is not between life-world and system. Though this conflict is undoubtedly closer to Touraine's concerns, for Melucci the most significant conflicts are those that take place within the life-world itself. Colonization, he argues, is not a one-way process: the life-world can colonize the system (1989, pp. 195–7).

Melucci also opposes postmodernism. The problem with the postmodernist perspective, he argues, is that it 'seems to empty politics of any importance and value, and tries to dissolve interests, social relations and power in a pure game of signs' (1996a, p. 204). His conception of culture is not aesthetic but normative and cognitive: culture offers social actors symbolic resources which can be mobilized in collective action. The connection between collective action, identity and culture is not typical of postmodernism, which emphasizes a different kind of expressivism, one more oriented around consumption and lifestyle issues.

## The location of social movements: everyday life

Social movements emerge from 'everyday life', not in the political public sphere. They are located in the cultural public spheres:

> A necessary condition for the survival of such forms of action is the existence of public spaces independent of the institutions of government and state structures. These spaces assume the form of an articulated system of decision-making, negotiation and representation, in which the signifying practices developed in everyday life can be expressed and heard independently of formal political institutions. . . . The main function of public spaces, then, is to make the questions raised by the movements visible and collective. (1996b, pp. 114–15)

This position is close to Habermas's conception of the public sphere but differs in that Melucci stresses the cultural and symbolic articulation of conflicts. Moreover, the public sphere does not lead to an institutionalization of social movements, for it is essentially a conflictual arena (1996a, p. 221). Social movements 'are situated at the intersection of structure and change' (1996a, p. 53). The kind of social change Melucci is referring to is cultural change. The conflictual dimension of society demonstrates that 'we are living in a society which is increasingly shaped by information and defined by its cultural dimensions; in it, the differences in cultures and the definition of cultures themselves become critical social and political issues which affect economic and social policies' (1996a, p. 161). This is an important contribution to the sociology of social change, for it demonstrates how culture provides a mediatory role between structure and agency. Collective action is articulated through cultural processes, such as the construction of cultural identity. The environmental issue, for instance, 'brings the cultural dimension of human experience to the fore' (1996a, p. 163). Opposition, he argues, 'becomes increasingly "cultural" in character' (1996a, p. 223). Nature is becoming more cultural: 'we are witnessing a denaturalization and culturalization of conflicts' (1996b, p. 149). The ecological question 'highlights the cultural dimension of human action . . . Our salvation lies in the system of ends, that is, in the cultural models which orient our behaviour. Culture – as the capacity to lend meaning to objects and relations – is the unbreachable confine within which questions concerning the destiny of humankind must be posed' (1996b, p. 59). He writes of the importance of 'meaning' in terms of the creation of new cultural codes': 'What lies at the core of contemporary conflicts is the production and reappropriation of meaning' (1996b, p. 145).

The most important dimension to the creation of meaning and the articulation of culture is collective identity. Identity implies the permanence over time of a Subject, a notion of unity (which establishes the identity of the Subject with respect to others or self-identification) and a relation between actors that allows their mutual recognition – i.e. a relational field (1995a, pp. 45–7). Identity entails the paradox of wanting to be different but requiring recognition. The identity of social movements is divided between their self-identity and the way they are perceived by others. Conflict is the expression of this discrepancy. Collective identity ensures the permanence of the movement over time, defining a capacity for autonomous action, for identity is not given but created. It must be seen as a system of relations and representations, and therefore it is not given or fixed. In Melucci's view, a politics of identity is increasingly being displaced from the cultural into the political in the struggles of many groups for recognition in the public domain. This is a consequence of the loosening of the tie between structure and agency.

Social movements have an innovative dimension: they initiate change. 'Contemporary movements are the bearers of the hidden potential for change; they are sensors of forming social needs and they announce new possibilities to the rest of society' (1996a, p. 185). But there is always a difference between the potential for change and that which actually gets realized. This leads us directly to Melucci's theory of modernity. Social change in complex societies is multilevelled. Today, change is 'evolving out of a linear, cumulative, global (if it ever was in the first place) process into a discontinuous, and differentiated one' (1996a, p. 112). Melucci rejects the idea of a central social movement that could lead society forwards. Under the conditions of complexity this is impossible. Power is impersonal; it cannot be equated with an elite: 'in complex societies power has become impersonal; it is dispatched through the great apparatuses of planning and decision making, through the administrative management of all aspects of life' (1996a, p. 106). There is both increased fragmentation and concentration of power, and the distinction between state and civil society has given way to a more complex society (1996a, pp. 217–19). Melucci emphasizes how power is expressed through master codes (1996a, p. 179). A societally complex society is also one that is more interpenetrated by culture: 'Living in a differentiated and rapidly changing society, we belong to numerous systems of relations and perpetually move among them in time and space during our life course' (1996b, p. 35).

For all these reasons Melucci dismisses the socialist society as an 'anachronistic myth' (1996a, p. 210). Contemporary society is a 'centreless society' and therefore change cannot emanate from a centre to the rest of society. In this context he speaks of the obsolescence of revolution (1996a, p. 208). Melucci, like Habermas, has accepted to a degree Luhmann's theory of system complexity, but without his political conclusions. Melucci also emphasizes the increased importance of the world-system in what he prefers to call the 'planetary society', the implications of which undermine the intellectual categories of the nineteenth century, the historicist conception of time and the notion of progress based on the evolution of nations:

> Today we are in the process of leaving behind this linear view of history, and begin to think more in terms of systemic interdependence, in terms of a planetary society which contains in its womb the seeds of no future: when time holds in reserve no future systems to totally and at once transcend the present one, we are left with only different ways of organizing, managing, and politically defining the existing world system from the inside. (1996a, p. 190)

This clearly has implications for the conventional boundaries of the political between right and left, which for Melucci are increasingly becoming redundant, along with the exhaustion of utopian ideas (1996a, p. 213). The political categories of right and left are no longer ideologically distinguishable and have been usurped by a new politics of identity.

## Reflexivity and democracy

In line with Habermas and Touraine, Melucci is very much concerned with a new conception of radical democracy. Touraine, as we have seen, believes the crucial question is the need to extend democracy into both the cultural domain and the instrumental domain, the world of the Subject and the world of Reason. Melucci seeks to extend the idea of democracy to the everyday and argues that social movements are bringing about a democratization of everyday life. In contrast to Habermas, he advocates a notion of reflexivity that is located in everyday life. While for Habermas reflexivity is confined to the discourse ethic, which transcends the everyday, for Melucci social movements, in so far as they mobilize the everyday, are capable of articulating a politics of reflexivity.

Melucci's notion of reflexivity incorporates a constructivist dimension. Identity 'may be defined as the reflexive capacity to produce an awareness of action (that is, a symbolic representation of it above its specific content) . . . From this point of view, one might say that complex societies concern themselves with the production of what Habermas has called "inner nature" ' (1996a, p. 108). Reflexivity implies the capacity for learning. Human societies, he argues, not only have an ability to learn, but they also 'learn to learn' and experience themselves as 'constructed'. There is a connection, then, between the concepts of identity, learning, reflexivity and constructivism. Collective identity is capable of learning, and part of that process is the experience of reflexivity. In so far as social actors experience themselves as agents capable of learning, they see their social world as a constructed one. Constructivism thus has an emancipatory moment, for it reveals the potentiality of change and introduces the creative dimension. The introduction of the ideas of reflexivity and creativity clearly has implications for democracy:

> The problem raised by contemporary social movements . . . concerns a redefinition of what democracy is, can be, and ought to be in a world where information becomes the central resource and where individuals and groups are offered the possibility of themselves constructing their identities instead of remaining simply recipients assigned them from the outside. (1996a, p. 203)

In Melucci's view, political problems can be solved only in a framework that assigns culture a central role. He is primarily concerned with investigating how conflicts are articulated by social movements which construct collective identities. The question of institutionalization is not central to his concerns, in the way, for instance, that it has become for Habermas. While Habermas has turned his attention on the relationship between democracy and law, Melucci looks at the relationship between democracy and culture. This approach, which is often contrasted to so-called resource mobilization theory, confines itself to the relationship between collective action and collective identity. The approaches of Charles Tilly and Sidney Tarrow, for instance, look at collective action in terms of its disruptive tendencies, its ability to mobilize resources and bring about change within an organizational and political system.[5] Melucci prefers to look at the question of how collective action is experienced by social actors and how it is anchored in everyday interactions. For this reason conflict is not the most fundamental condition of collective life, as in Touraine or mainstream NSM theory. This is because there is always a degree of 'symbolic waste' that remains beyond the possibility of institutionalization (Melucci and Lyyra, 1997). This concept refers to the irreducibility of culture to structure and the fact that cultural processes can never be entirely absorbed into the identity projects of social actors.

The critical importance of Melucci's version of NSM theory is that it opens up the question of social change to identity politics. By placing identity in the broad arena of the everyday we can begin to see how social actors initiate social change in the creation of new forms of experience and identities. Collective action is experimental and creative; it is highly diffuse and contingent. Melucci's later writings (1996a, 1996b; Melucci and Lyyra, 1997) suggest a break from a tendency in the literature to equate NSMs with progressive and emancipatory movements of post-industrial society, such as feminism or the ecological movement. Even though these movements were the context for his earlier writings, he has increasingly become more attuned to the plurality of collective actors and the indeterminacy of their outcomes. However, in his earlier writings (1989, p. 200) he claimed that he avoids the normative assumptions of Touraine's supposition of the 'highest possible meaning' of social movements. There is much to suggest that nationalism and various kinds of neo-communitarian and authoritarian populist movements became more prevalent in the 1990s and have captured public space from the social movements of the 1970s and 1980s. Touraine, who appears to have abandoned his search for a single social movement, is more aware of the dangers of a pure politics of identity than Melucci.

In sum, the importance of Melucci to NSM theory resides in emphasis on collective identity and the way in which collective actors appropriate cultural resources in the articulation of collective action. His emphasis on the multifaceted nature of social movements, which can never be reduced to a single historical actor, offers an important corrective to Touraine. More importantly, his work addresses a key concern of the late twentieth century: reflexivity and the transformation of the cultural model of society.

## Conclusion: Reflexivity and Democracy

I began this chapter by arguing how NSM theories, in particular those of Touraine and Melucci, offer an alternative to postmodernism. By focusing on collective action and collective identity, Touraine and Melucci point to a way out of the problems of postmodernism, which is unable to address the question of social change from the perspective of agency. While Touraine establishes a strong connection between agency and structure, Melucci relates agency to culture. Their approaches entail a firm connection between agency, culture and structure: cultural change and political change are becoming increasingly related by a reconstituted democracy which now reaches into the cultural. As with Habermas, the theme of democracy is central to their social theory. But what is distinctive about their understanding of democracy is less its argumentative or deliberative nature than its reflexive constitution and its relation to cultural identity.

Reflexivity is central to both Touraine and Melucci, but the latter takes this much further with a stronger theory of the reflexivity of social action. A reading of their work reveals how social change must be seen from the perspective of a modernity radicalized by reflexivity. The key dimensions of this are: the need to abandon the nineteenth-century paradigm of modernity, the introduction of social learning and the creativity of action. These theoretical developments introduce a strong constructivist dimension into the social theory of modernity. Constructivism entails a view of social action as autonomous and creative, but within a relational and structured context. The notion of knowledge that it presupposes – i.e. different forms, models or codes that are culturally available and activated as competing frames for an observing public by distinct yet related social actors as they draw on them constructively and communicatively – is a far-reaching one that allows us – notwithstanding Touraine's vision of the end of the social – to see how the social can be conceptualized around a model of discursive democratic spaces in which knowledge has a central role. We thus come close to a view of how social integration can be conceived in terms of flows of discursive communication. In order to take this further we need a theory of reflexive modernity.

In the next chapter I shall outline the theory of reflexive modernization in the social theory of Beck and Giddens. The significance of this approach is that it offers a broader concept of reflexivity and also addresses the key question of institutionalization. It will be shown how it is not only social movements that create reflexive forms of communication but also the broader society and its institutions.

# 6

# *Reflexive Modernization: Beck and Giddens*

## Introduction

In recent years the idea of reflexivity has become a major concept in social theory and, it may be suggested, is replacing postmodernity as well as providing a new intellectual framework for the reinterpretation of modernity, which has now become a project of 'reflexive modernization', the theme of a work authored by Beck, Giddens and Lash (1994). As I have argued in the previous three chapters, the idea of reflexivity was central to the approaches of a broad spectrum of theorists, ranging from Habermas and various schools of postmodernism as diverse as Lyotard and Bauman to Touraine and Melucci. I have argued that the idea of reflexivity has become particularly prominent in new social movement theories, in particular the writings of Touraine and Melucci, who discuss reflexivity primarily in terms of social movements, but who also argue that it has major implications for democracy. Melucci's approach brings the analysis of reflexivity into the dynamics of collective identity in social movements. In this chapter I shall be looking at approaches that are centrally concerned with reflexivity but which are not addressed to social movements as such, since they have a wider resonance in the public domain.

The social theory of Beck and Giddens is focused less on social movements than on the wider transformation of society. In short, in their approaches the idea of reflexivity is taken out of social movements and applied to the new kinds of interrelationship between agency and structure that are emerging today. While new social movement theory deals with the reflexivity of collective actors, Beck and Giddens are mostly interested in the reflexivity of the individual social actors, as is apparent in the theme of individualization in their later writings, and, in the case of Giddens, the reflexivity in institutions. My approach, in contrast, aims to shift the focus of reflexivity to public communication, which is where the cultural model of society is rendered reflexive.

I do not wish to suggest that these approaches offer an alternative vision of modernity, for their positions are very much compatible. However, Beck and Giddens point to different issues, which in my view are crucial for an adequate understanding of the social today, though their theories are not without problems. I shall argue that one of the main problems with the positions advocated by Beck and Giddens is the absence of a theory of culture: the thrust of the work is towards a theory of an individualized agency becoming released from previously restraining structures under the conditions of the risk society. Culture, in their approaches, is reduced to a narrowly cognitive dimension, neglecting the wider sense of the cognitive discussed in Chapter 2 (i.e. cognitive praxis, the confluence of knowledge and culture, and the discursive regulation of power).

In this chapter I shall be arguing that reflexivity must be seen as mediated by culture, which has a certain autonomy with respect to agency and culture. Social change must not be seen merely in terms of a duality of structure and agency but is also culturally mediated. I shall first outline Beck's theory of the risk society; I shall then discuss Giddens's social theory; finally, I shall discuss some criticisms of their approaches. The position I shall argue for is that Giddens's social theory represents an advancement on Beck's, but it suffers from a failure to appreciate the implications of discursivity as a mediation of the personal and the institutional – agency and structure, domains that are never adequately mediated in Giddens's theorization.

## Beck and the Risk Society

Few sociological works have become more influential than Ulrich Beck's *Risk Society* (1992a; henceforth all references in this section are to Beck unless otherwise stated). Since its publication in 1986 in Germany, it has become one of the best-known sociological works in recent decades. The public interest in this work is not unconnected to the time of its publication, a year after the Chernobyl catastrophe.[1] For many people, Beck offered an accessible sociological explanation of ecological catastrophe and in the subsequent decade his vision of a 'new modernity' articulated around notions of reflexivity and risk gave expression to the political context of the post-Cold War era. In this section I begin with an outline of Beck's theory of the risk society, which is followed by a discussion of his notion of reflexivity and its implications for politics and social change. I conclude with an analysis of the tension between constructivism and realism in his work.

## Risk and modernity

One of the central contentions underlying Beck's social theory is the shift from industrial society to the risk society. In this shift, a new modernity arises: 'Just as modernization dissolved the structure of feudal society in the nineteenth century and produced the industrial society, modernization today is dissolving industrial society and another modernity is coming into being' (1992a, p. 10). Beck, like Touraine, Melucci, Habermas and Giddens, prefers the idea of a reinterpretation of modernity to the nihilism of postmodernity, the retreat to community in communitarian political philosophy and the instrumentalization of modernity in liberalism. The idea of reflexive modernization is a 'second modernity', a thematization of what Beck also calls 'premodernity' and is not the end but the beginning of modernity.

The contrast to the two phases of modernity can be understood in terms of the end of industrial society and the coming of the post-industrial. For Beck, the defining characteristic of the post-industrial society is its propensity to institutionalized risks arising largely out of science and technology. In the risk society the state is less concerned with maintaining material provision than with safety; the state has become a 'safety state'. In a somewhat exaggerated formulation of this, Beck speaks of the replacement of the welfare state with the risk society, which imposes a new burden on the state's regulatory capacities, leading to a clash between environment and welfare. The welfare state provided security from the ravages of capitalism, while the risk society provides security against the destructive side-effects of modernization, and in particular those induced by science. In the risk society the state is increasingly powerless to act constructively: 'nation-states have become islands of helplessness' (1995b, p. 11). This powerlessness is a consequence of the decreasing salience of political sovereignty based on nation-states whose autonomy has been challenged by new forces. However, the apparent helplessness of the state to cope with risk may also be liberating, for war is being replaced by risk. In the past the nation-state was a political entity organized for war; today it is having to adjust to the primacy of risk, which occurs in peacetime. The idea of the safety state, it must be pointed out against Beck, has little basis in empirical reality, for the increasing importance of science and technology policies is not matched by a fundamental decline in the welfare state. The safety state is best taken as a metaphor or conceptual tool to illustrate a transformation in the system of regulation as a result of the rise of new contingencies which are specific to a risk-ridden society.

The need to regulate side-effects suggests for Beck a transformation in the nature of causation. We can no longer assume a simple relationship between a cause and an effect. In the industrial society the side-effects of modernization were calculable, and science offered a model for the control of the environment. Today the side-effects are incalculable: 'Along with the growing capacity of technical options grows the incalculability of their consequences' (1992a, p. 22). If modernity was an age of goal-aspiration, the age of reflexive modernity is an age of crisis, managing the side-effects of the older goals.

Modernity, in the sense of the Enlightenment project, is exhausting itself in the mood of anxiety that has come to prevail in the risk society. One dimension to this is the formation of global anti-utopias: 'one is no longer concerned with attaining something "good", but rather with preventing the worst. Self limitation is the goal which emerges' (1992a, p. 49). This is all reminiscent of the pessimistic philosophy of modernity associated with Adorno and Horkheimer's ([1947] 1979) thesis that modern rationalism has turned into technocracy and generated barbarism. However, Beck departs from the Frankfurt School in many respects, most notably in his adherence to a strong concept of agency, for the ecological conflicts of the risk society release a political reflexivity which can challenge the new power structures and produce a new discourse of universality:

> The theory of the risk society avoids the difficulties of a critical theory of society in which the theorists apply more or less well justified standards to society and then judge and condemn accordingly (and often counter to the self-conception of those concerned). In a risk society which identifies itself as such, critique is democratized, as it were; that is, there arises a reciprocal critique of sectional rationalities and groups in society. (1996b, p. 33)

Risk, then, is the new site in which the dualism of agency and structure is articulated.

The following are the main characteristics of risk:

1   Risks are to be contrasted to dangers or natural hazards in that they are made by society. That risk derives from society and not from nature is a fundamental characteristic of the risk society in Beck's formulation of the term.

2   The risk society is not only a modern society but one that has entered a specific phase; a phase in which the system of regulation is increasingly having to deal with the side-effects of industrialization. Risks are to be contrasted not merely to natural hazards but also to industrial accidents in that they are global and more endemic. Risk cannot be easily limited and are therefore not insurable or compensatable.

3   Risks are abstract and depersonalized. They are not immediately observable, for they emanate from the new kinds of pollutant such as radioactivity and microbiological entities. These kinds of risk are often detached from agency in that they emanate from forces beyond the control of specific individuals. Therefore, traditional moral categories such as guilt and liability cannot be so easily applied.

4   Risk is global as opposed to being territorially specific. Thus, many risks, such as nuclear ones, transcend national borders. The risk society is a 'world risk society'. The solutions to many of these problems can only be transnational.

5   Risks are not only transnational, but they are also 'democratic' in the sense that they pertain to the entire class structure: pollution is something that effects everyone, rich and poor. This is the 'boomerang effect' (1996a, p. 23) which breaks up the class and national pattern of conflict, for risks sooner or later strike those who profit from them.

6   The testing ground for science and technology is no longer the laboratory or even the workplace, but society itself. For this reason the risks of the risk society are destructive on a massive scale and can bring about the possibility of self-annihilation. This means a change in the temporal horizons of society, for the future has been replaced by risk.[2]

One of the implications of Beck's thesis is that the risk society marks the end of the age-old distinction between nature and society. The foundation of classical modernity and the self-understanding of the Enlightenment was that the social and the natural were separate and that the social guided by science could overcome and dominate nature. Nature was outside the social, and society, armed with the rationalizing and objectivating forces of modern science, could bring it under its control. Today, what in fact has happened is not that the social has gained mastery over nature, but that science has established its rule over both nature and the social. Consequently, the Enlightenment's belief in the ethical neutrality of science must be abolished. Today, as we know from biotechnology, it has become a reality that science can shape nature in its own image (Delanty, 1998c). Science is no longer a tool but a reality-creating force. For Beck, constructivism has penetrated into the very heart of science, bringing an end to the dichotomy of science and nature.

The idea of constructivism captures the central tenet of Beck's social theory: the risk society opens up a new kind of politics which allows for greater constructivism on the part of social actors. The concept of the risk society does not just refer to the instrumentalizing logic of modernization but also pertains to subjectivity and politics. In the risk society, anxiety replaces need. While this may indeed be an exaggerated claim in some respects, Beck wants to argue that modern life is becoming increasingly risky in terms not just of the expanding volume of risks that the individual is faced with and which appear to be impossible to come to terms with, but also with the expansion in the choices that must be made. In his co-authored book on love, Beck (Beck and Beck-Gernsheim [1990] 1995b) argues that love has become a vacuum in which individuals try to shape new meanings and more individualized forms of relations. The social category of love epitomizes the 'chaos' of social relations in the risk society. If risk characterizes the objectivity of society, love is the articulation of a subjectivity that is both disenchanted with modernity and enchanted with its own reflexive powers. Love embodies technocratic elements (the increasing prevalence of contract in relations) as well as deeply emotional dimensions. The risk society is one in which social agency is invested with greater powers of transformation. This can be in personal life or in politics. Love and risk, then, are the two sides of the double-edged coin of modernity, capturing its objectivity and subjectivity. Underlying both is a feeling of anxiety not so much about the future as about the present. Beck endorses Habermas's (Habermas, 1989b) concept of the 'new obscurity' to characterize the politics of the risk society. The nature of risk is precisely that it is obscure: the old poles of opposition are weakening, but it is far from clear where the new politics is going.

## The politics of risk and reflexivity

Beck's writings on risk can be seen as generalizing the ecological question from its association with the politics of new social movements to a broader discourse in society. This new discourse is organized around the central theme of risk and is replacing the older political agendas: 'Like the "social question" in the nineteenth century, the "ecological question" today must be related to social (that is, institutional) opportunities for action that fit the context in which the question arises' (1995b). As he has put it graphically: 'today it is no longer a question of who gets the biggest slice of the cake for the cake has become toxic' (1995a, p. 128). Risk induces reflexivity because there are no absolute or self-evident answers, only discursive outcomes. In the shift from class politics to ecological politics, the political field opens up to an ever widening public. The ecological movement for Beck is not merely an environmental movement but a social movement because its themes extend beyond the strictly environmental to the social, economic and political organization of society.

The politics of risk is characterized by a strong emphasis on the status of knowledge, a discourse of responsibility and sub-politics.

*The status of knowledge*   Knowledge is a central category in Beck's sociology of risk and defines reflexivity. The expansion of science is accompanied by the critique of science and the culture of experts by an ever more critical public. In the risk society 'the sciences' monopoly on rationality is broken' (1996a, p. 29). Reflexive modernization presupposes a scientized society, a society that has been transformed by science and which uses science to undermine the self-legitimating rationality of science. In 'primary scientization' science was applied to the given order of nature, society and people. In reflexive scientization science is applied to itself: 'The second phase is based on a complete scientization, which also extends scientific skepticism to the inherent foundations and external consequences of science itself' (1996a, p. 154). As a result of the penetration of science into all spheres of life, the only responses to the threats of science are ones that have themselves become scientized. The condition of reflexive modernization is the condition of reflexive scientization: the 'opportunity to emancipate social practice from science through science' (1996a, p. 157). The critique of science raises two related issues: the question of the status of knowledge and the delegitimation of the culture of experts. For Beck, the reflexivity that the risk society induces is one that opens the category of knowledge to new definitions. Knowledge is no longer defined by the culture of expertise as a result of its delegitimation. In short, the self-legitimation of knowledge has collapsed. In the risk society everybody becomes an expert, with the result that the objectivity of scientific knowledge is highly contentious: 'science, having lost reality, faces the threat that others will dictate to it what is supposed to be' (1996a, p. 167). The 'chaos of love' in personal relationships is reflected in the chaos of scientific objectivity, the fundamentally contentious nature of reality. In the risk society the relationship between science and society has changed radically: 'Until the sixties, science could count on an uncontroversial public that believed in science, but today its efforts and progress are followed with distrust' (1996a, p. 169).

According to Beck, the kind of politics that is coming to prevail in the risk society is, increasingly, about knowledge. Used in this sense, knowledge refers to the cognitive means by which reality is known. In the risk society reality is mediated by the cognitive, which is ever-widening and is reaching into the political. This is because one of the central conflicts in the risk society is how we define problems. With the collapse of the self-legitimation of science there are more and more views on what counts as a risk and how it should be remedied:

> [the] risk society is tendentially a self-critical society. Insurance experts contradict safety engineers. If the latter declare a zero risk, the former judge: non-insurable. Experts are relativized or dethroned by counter-experts. Politicians encounter the resistance of citizens' initiatives, industrial management that of consumer organizations. Bureaucracies are criticized by self-help groups. (1996b, pp. 32–3)

It is no longer merely a question about the availability of information, for with the multiplicity in definitions of risk the very reliability of information is what is in dispute.

In the risk society political conflict shifts from relations of production to 'relations of definition': it is a question of how a problem is defined. Beck lists the following relations of definition: by what rules do we judge risk? How is the burden of proof distributed? How do we judge compensation? What is the role of scientific expertise in the process? Who can be trusted to enlighten the public? (1995a, p. 129). Under these circumstances politics in the risk society is inherently discursive: reflexive modernization becomes discursive modernization. The risk society is a 'discourse society' (1996a, pp. 128–9). But unlike Habermas's model of discursive democracy, Beck is pointing to more deep-rooted conflict; namely, disputes over the very procedures of debate. In Habermas's model, participants basically accept the normative rules of discourse, whereas Beck's theory of the risk society suggests that scientific rationality itself has collapsed and therefore not even the relatively rational model of scientific disputation is accepted. The result is not just normative uncertainty but also cognitive chaos. Beck's concept of a 'discourse society' is sociologically more useful than Habermas's highly normative concept since it refers to the embeddedness of discourse in cultures of contention and publicity. Industrial and organizational activity, he argues, is becoming discursive and dependent on publicity, and opportunities for external groups to exert influence are growing, but this is also true for parliamentary and governmental policy. Another difference is that in his theory conflicts erupt *inside* institutions, whereas in Habermas they arise *between* the institutional structures of life-world and system (Beck, 1995a, p. 138).

*Discourses of responsibility*   Despite the apparent confusion in the status of knowledge and uncertainty in our normative categories, the risk society offers a new vision of modernity. Beck's social theory points to a discourse of responsibility which is becoming the new master theme in politics today. Against what he calls the 'organized irresponsibility' of the risk society a new kind of responsibility is emerging from society. This is evident on many fronts. There is growing support for the 'polluter pays' principle; a discourse of accountability is rapidly shaping debates on industry, technology and the state's economic planning; there is growing concern about the ethical and social implications of biotechnology. The idea of responsibility is the key to understanding these developments and it may be conflicting with notions of rights. Responsibility for the future and for the environment, previously the key concern of the environmental movement, has now become a public issue and is articulated by a whole range of social actors, which now includes the political parties.

The question of collective responsibility can be said to be one of the central issues facing humanity today. Collective responsibility refers to societal responsibility, as opposed to individual responsibility. It has been widely recognized that the challenges facing society today cannot be dealt with by recourse to individual responsibility. The ecological crisis, developments in science and technology and the increasing specialization of functions in what may be called the 'knowledge society' (Stehr, 1992) have undermined one of the cherished ideas of western culture: the responsibility of the individual. The traditional model of responsibility took for granted that the individual could be responsible for the primary and secondary consequences of his or her action. This conception of responsibility has derived from a philosophical tradition which took epistemological individualism for granted: the individual was a self-contained entity, independent of society which was merely the aggregate sum of individuals. The sociological tradition, on the whole, did not challenge this conception of responsibility since sociology has mostly sought to avoid normative claims. In the late twentieth century the traditional model of responsibility has collapsed as a result of two developments. First, conditions in the social environment no longer make it possible to adhere to a model of individual responsibility. Second, sociology has become increasingly conscious of the need to address normative issues. With the gradual transformation of the old politics of labour into the politics of new social movements, nature has become the central theme in the construction of collective identity.[3]

In sum, then, I believe the idea of responsibility is a positive implication of Beck's theory of reflexive modernization. The political challenges of the risk society undermine the existing system of regulation, which is unable to deal with the multiplication of side-effects. These side-effects have today become the problem and our traditional ethical categories are inadequate since these relate only to individual responsibility.

*Sub-politics*  Sub-politics is a politics of individualization. It refers to the setting free of agency from traditional bonds. 'At the end of the twentieth century', Beck argues, 'people are being cut loose from the ways of life of industrial society, just as at the entry to the industrial epoch they were (and still are being) cut loose from the self-evident feudal and status-based understandings, ways of life societal forms' (1996a, p. 94). Sub-politics is one that overcomes the divide between the private and public; it is the politics of an individualized society. He speaks of the renaissance of a political subjectivity in the 1980s outside the institutionalized forms of politics in the parliamentary system, stretching from the new social movements to citizens' groups. In Beck's view, this refutes systems theory, which supposes that society has no Subject. The reflexivity of sub-politics is far from Luhmann's self-referentiality, which reduced reflexivity to the reproduction of subsystems.

Beck's conception of politics is close to Touraine's notion of the Subject. However, sub-politics is not only the politics of social movements but is also the politics of individuals whose consciousness has been rendered reflexive. 'The individualized everyday culture of the West', Beck argues, 'is simply a culture of built up knowledge and self-confidence: more and higher education, as well as better jobs and opportunities to earn money, in which people no longer must obey' (1994, p. 20). Individualization is linked to social transformation by an emancipated agency which has absorbed structure.

Individualization means the disembedding and re-embedding of industrial society and traditionalism by an emancipated agency which is emerging into a chaotic world of conflicts and institutional transformation. Individualization and reflexive modernization are counterposed to tradition and industrial society. On the one side, industrial society and its political structures are dissolving and, on the other, there is a non-institutional renaissance of the political. The result: 'The individual subject returns to the institutions of society' (1994, p. 17). Beck thus raises the prospect of a new theory of mediation beyond the dualism of agency and structure. Sub-politics is the shaping of society from below; it is a 'self-creation society' (1994, p. 22). Its principal characteristics are the freedom to choose and responsibility for one's actions. I shall argue below that Giddens offers a much more sophisticated theory of social change in terms of mediation. The problem with Beck is that we are left with the irreconcilable dualism of instrumental rationality in the world of institutions versus growing reflexivity in society. Reflexivity can then only be a matter of doubt and, ultimately, anxiety. There is no basis for a discursive mediation which could draw upon creativity and reflexivity.

### Conclusion: constructivism and realism

In this section I have been discussing Beck's theory of risk and his notion of politics and reflexivity. It has been observed that the risk society is not only a society that produces new kinds of danger but is also one that has unleashed possibilities for the emancipation of agency from previously constraining structures. One of the principal dimensions to this is the increased salience of knowledge: risk is mediated through knowledge. But since knowledge is fundamentally contestable, the resulting situation is one of open-ended discourse. This position commits Beck to a thesis of constructivism.

The question of constructivism is a major one, presenting Beck with a dilemma, since he also retains a strong objectivism. This may be summarized as: how real are the risks? Is risk a social construction or does it correspond to something real? On the one side, Beck presupposes that the nature of industrial production, the social organization of technology and the institution of science brings about risk and, on the other, that social actors construct risk in different ways and the politics of reflexivity is increasingly articulated around disputes over knowledge. Risk is thus a key cognitive category in politics but also refers to an objective reality. In Beck's *Risk Society* there is considerable confusion about his epistemological approach. He is certainly no extreme constructivist in the way Baudrillard is, for he wants to argue that risks are real while ecological consciousness varies according to society and age.

The realist-constructivist dualism becomes an acute problem for Beck when we apply his thesis of the chaos of our cognitive and normative structures to his methodology and the epistemology upon which it is based. If the legitimation of scientific knowledge has collapsed as a result of the mobilization of critical publics, the objectivity of risk itself is in question. It would appear that Beck has resisted relativism by retaining a degree of scientism: science, including social science, can reveal the objectivity of risk. In short, if the risk society is a discourse society – in which all claims to the objectivity of knowledge are contestable – realism is highly problematical. So, without wishing to embrace radical semiotic constructivism, how can realism and constructivism be united? This is one of the key issues for social theory and one which I have addressed elsewhere, arguing that constructivism and realism are reconcilable (Delanty, 1997c).[4]

Debating on this, Beck attempts a reconciliation: 'realism conceives the ecological problematic as "closed", whereas constructivism maintains its openness in principle. For the one, it is the dangers (the doomsday scenarios) of the world risk society that are the central focus; for the other, it is the chances, the contexts in which actors operate' (1996c, pp. 6–7). His position is that realism and constructivism do not have to be mutually exclusive. So long as they are both naive and resting on simple counterpositions they are indeed exclusive, but something like a 'realist constructivism' is possible. Naive constructivism tends to be blind to the dangers of risk since they reduce everything to a construction, while, on the other hand, naive realism fails to see that risks are mediated by social actors. Constructions of reality can be distinguished according to whether they have more or less reality (1996c, p. 10). Beck disagrees with Douglas and Wildavsky (1982) for whom risk is a cultural construct: risks are also real and cannot be entirely relativized by culture.

Beck's version of constructivism is tied to reflexivity. A constructivist approach is one that recognizes the capacity of social actors not only to define what constitutes a problem but also how to act. The reflexive moment in his constructivism captures this sense by which social actors can exercise responsibility for society. There is, then, a double constructivism going on: social actors construct risk, which, when rendered reflexive can be the basis of a democratic politics. This reflexivity is also inherent in the very process of science and is a form of social learning in the broader cognitive sense of the term.[5] In the final section of this chapter I shall discuss some criticisms of Beck's theory of reflexive modernization. First, however, I shall discuss the work of Anthony Giddens, who is also one of the principal proponents of reflexive modernization.

## Giddens: Modernity, Reflexivity and Trust

Giddens's concerns are not unlike Beck's but are more systematic and have been articulated in the context of a more general theory of modernity and a sociological theory of structure and agency. Both Beck and Giddens look at reflexivity in terms of the institutional order and the relationship of agency to structures. Reflexivity is a central concept in their works and refers to a broad concept of knowledge. Though they do not write in the tradition of the sociology of knowledge, they employ a broad concept of knowledge to refer to what Giddens calls the 'knowledgeability' of social actors: the process of self-awareness by which the dualism of agency and structure is overcome. There are, however, some differences in the social theory of Giddens and Beck with respect to modernity and reflexivity. For the former, the stress is more on institutional reflexivity and trust, while, for the latter, the emphasis is on risk and the collapse of expert systems. However, the concern of both is the individual in its encounter with structure. Moreover, for both theorists the cognitive question of knowledge is central, albeit, I shall argue, narrowly reductionist.

### The duality of structure: towards a theory of mediation

Giddens's theory of modernity can be seen as an application of this theory of structuration.[6] This theory provides the formal conceptual basis of his later writings on modernity and reflexivity, though he has never demonstrated how the two approaches fit together. Together, the theory of structuration of the 1980s and the theory of modernity of the 1990s represent the abandonment of his early concern with reformulating historical materialism. In order to appreciate his present concerns with the more substantive aspects of social theory, there is much to be gained by briefly looking at the general thesis of structuration. The concepts of structuration and reflexive modernization have in common, it may be suggested, the critical and reflexive use of knowledge or information. Modernity for Giddens unfolds through the progressive mediation of structure and agency through knowledge, which is a mediatory category. Modernity entails the ever expanding production of knowledge – information, scientific expertise, therapy, everyday knowledge – which makes it impossible to separate agency and structure in order that they can be reflexively recombined. Structuration is the process by which agency and structure are mutually constituted in regularized social practices. Giddens takes for granted a certain 'knowledgeability' – or cognitive competence – on the part of social actors, who are more rational than they are in deterministic Marxist and functionalist theories, but not autonomous agents as in rational choice theory. Agents are constituted by structures which they manipulate and constitute. In short, the basic assumption of structuration theory is that social structures are structured by social actors.

Knowledge is the mediating link in the dualism of structure and agency. It takes different forms depending on its degree of reflexivity. The most basic level is what might be called the tacit knowledge of everyday life. For Giddens, the historical unfolding of modernity involves more and more reflexivity. Thus, expert systems have emerged to take on a central role in what has come to be known as the information society or post-industrial society. But knowledge is also essential for everyday life which places increasing demands on individuals for interpretation, both for their own lives in terms of the shaping of their biographies and in the need to make sense of the social world, much of which can be experienced only by information. Knowledge in Giddens is not unlike the idea of cultural capital in Bourdieu: it is a resource that social actors can exploit by means of 'strategies'. Of course, for Bourdieu these strategies by which agency reproduces itself are shaped by the habitus and are predominantly class-based strategies. While Giddens does not give class the same significance, he shares with Bourdieu a concern with reflexivity and the dualism of agency and structure. The habitus was both a contextual situation, in the sense of a structured location, and a field of action, and as such it was an articulation of agency and structure. However, in this double articulation it would appear that it is structure that ultimately has the upper hand. Giddens, in contrast, wants to be able to avoid reductionism and therefore holds to a strong concept of mediation.

The idea of structuration is a very significant contribution to social theory since it effectively lays the basis of a theory of mediation. By this is meant the process by which actors construct an institutional system. Structuration theory is a theory of change: institutions are theorized as perpetually being mediated by social action. In the context of his theory of modernity, structuration can be seen as the process by which social actors increase their knowledge of their structural situation and as they do so they act upon their situation. In this way social change is built into the very nature of modernity. The concept of the 'duality of structure' expresses this double articulation of agency and structure: 'The constitution of agents and structures are not two independently given sets of phenomena, a dualism, but represent a duality. According to the notion of the duality of structure, the structural properties of social systems are both medium and outcome of the practices they recursively organize' (Giddens, 1984, p. 25; all further quotations in this section are from Giddens, unless otherwise stated). According to this view, structure is not external to agency or merely constraining; it is constitutive of agency and is at the same time constituted by it; it is both constraining and enabling: a structure is constituted by 'transformative social relations' (1984, p. 17). In effect, Giddens places the idea of mediation at the centre of his social theory: the duality of structure refers to processes of self-transformation. For instance, structures are, among other things, constituted by rules, but a rule is a discursive practice and the 'discursive formulation of a rule is already an interpretation of it' (1984, p. 23).

Giddens has always emphasized the importance of knowledge in modern society and the degree to which it has brought about social change. Sociological knowledge, for instance, is a particularly reflexive kind of knowledge and, in Giddens's view, has in fact brought about more change than we frequently imagine (1996, p. 6). In this he is not far from Bourdieu, who also believes in the transformative capacity of knowledge. The main difference, however, is that Giddens believes that under the conditions of late or reflexive modernization, individuals are capable of reflexivity to the extent to which they can transcend their concrete situations. Bourdieu, it would appear, reserves the highest form of reflexivity for the theorist. For Giddens, the various kinds of reflexivity feed into each other. By means of what he calls the 'double hermeneutic', there is a complementary relationship between the tacit knowledge of everyday life and social scientific knowledge. Knowledge is always an interpretation of reality. The first order of the hermeneutic process of interpretation is everyday knowledge; the second order is the reflexive interpretation of tacit knowledge by a more heightened form of reflection. Ultimately, for Giddens this role is filled by experts who provide an interpretative system which becomes the basis of a social order of trust.

It might be helpful to compare the notion of a 'discourse society', suggested in different ways by Beck and Habermas (Beck, 1996a, p. 128), to Giddens's notion of a 'sociological society'. The idea of a discourse society refers to the rise of critical publics who are communicatively constituted and do not naively accept traditional or scientistic forms of legitimation. It expresses the way in which established forms of authority are collapsing in what is becoming a more informed and reflexive society. Giddens's conception of contemporary society is similar in that he stresses the self-reliance of individuals and the democratic nature of knowledge. With the declining importance of tradition and nature, knowledge is the defining characteristic of our time. What is different about knowledge is that it is less objectivating and not so easily reduced to ideological manipulation. Indeed, knowledge transcends structure and agency: it is neither a property of individuals nor of structures. The idea of a 'sociological society' thus suggests a kind of society in which individuals become increasingly more self-reliant as a result of having recourse to such resources as knowledge. Basically, then, everybody can become a 'sociologist': reflexive modernization facilitates democratic structuration.

In order to appreciate this it is necessary to see that Giddens has always stressed the hermeneutics of interpretation as constitutive of the social as well as from a methodological and epistemological point of view. It was not until he shifted his focus from the Marxist-influenced critique of historical materialism to modernity that this theme became more explicit. This shift in his work from capitalism to modernity allowed Giddens to reintegrate some of his earlier ideas into his mature social theory. Influenced by such approaches as social interactionism, Simmel and ethnomethodology, which all emphasize the knowledgeable social actor, Giddens developed a more comprehensive theory of modernity, drawing from Durkheim, Weber and Marx. Modernity as a concept offered more advantages than capitalism since it could capture both the hermeneutic process of cultural interpretation as well as socioeconomic and political processes. More importantly, modernity suggests a greater sense of the self-transformative capacity of agency than capitalism, which is too class-specific. Today, more than ever before, social action is operating on levels other than class-specific ones. Thus, between the appearance of the first volume of *A Contemporary Critique of Historical Materialism* (*Power, Property and the State*) in 1981 and the second volume, *The Nation-State and Violence*, in 1985, Giddens had published his influential theory of structuration (1984). His subsequent writing on modernity can be seen as an application of the idea of structuration. Thus, in place of a third volume on historical materialism, Giddens published two works on modernity (1990, 1991), a work on contemporary political culture (1994a) and contributed to the debate on reflexive modernization (1994b), as well as producing a work on intimacy

(1992) and later works on the politics of the 'third way' (1994a, 1998). By the early 1990s, then, the idea of modernity was placed at the centre of social theory, replacing the older framework of historical materialism.

## Modernity and trust

Giddens's theory of modernity can be understood as a framework that links the institutional orders of modernity with processes of reflexivity tied to the experience of risk and trust. The institutional orders of modernity are capitalism, industrialism, surveillance and military power (1990, p. 59). Capitalism is distinct from industrialism in that it is primarily defined as the accumulation of capital in the context of competitive labour and product markets, while industrialism is defined as the transformation of nature. Giddens, who previously was a critic of the idea of industrial society, reintroduced the idea in order to relate nature to an institutional order. Surveillance (the control of information and social supervision) and military power (control of the means of violence in the context of the industrialization of war) are two further dimensions to the institutional orders of modernity and are distinct from capitalism. This sketch of modernity is perhaps closer to what is often called modernization. While modernity is generally related to the cultural dynamics of modern society, modernization tends to refer to the societal dimensions of economy and the polity. Giddens has something like this in mind with his concept of the three dominant sources of the dynamism of modernity: the separation of time and space, the development of disembedding mechanisms, the reflexive appropriation of knowledge.

    The separation of time and space refers to the societal conditions under which time and space are organized. Modern institutions, and society itself, is situated in time and space. This is generally held to be the nation-state, its territory and its shared sense of history and identity. But with the advent of modernity, with its conditions of complexity and anonymity, space and time are separated from each other, and with the emergence of standardized time, the tie between space and time is severed. This also leads to the creation of 'empty space': space and place become distantiated. For instance, in the creation of the space of the nation, local communities with their strong sense of place are thoroughly penetrated by what happens in quite distant places. This is an essential dimension to the dynamism of modernity and opens up possibilities for change. The severing of space and time – the 'disembedding' of time and space – opens up possibilities for their recombination and is an essential dimension to modern organizations. This leads to the second dimension of the dynamism of modernity, disembedding mechanisms.

Disembedding means 'the "lifting out" of social relations from local contexts of interaction and their restructuring across indefinite spans of time-space' (1990, p. 21). Disembedded institutions require media of exchange, such as 'symbolic tokens' which can facilitate communication, e.g. money. Giddens is particularly interested in one kind of disembedding – namely, expert systems. By expert systems is meant the systems of technical or professional expertise that organize large areas of life. According to Giddens, expert systems are becoming increasingly important in the constitution of society. Expert systems, like other symbolic tokens such as money, are disembedded mechanisms because they remove social relations from the immediacies of everyday life to more abstract contexts (1990, p. 28). In other words, they presuppose the separation of time and space. They operate in abstract contexts which do not require strong social bonds or direct involvement in all aspects of the process. Expert systems are paradigmatic of modernity because they involve a separation of agency from process. But there is a social dimension: trust. Premodern society and simple social organizations do not require trust to a significant degree because time and space distantiation is not great. We don't need to invest trust in somebody if they are immediately visible. The problem of trust arises with the formation of abstract and depersonalized systems of organization. Giddens disagrees with Luhmann's theory of trust, which reduces it to the calculation of unanticipated results under the conditions of risk (Giddens, 1990, p. 32). Trust for Giddens is something more continuous and not always conscious; it is a particular kind of confidence in the reliability of institutions. The kind of trust that Giddens is interested in is trust in expert systems. Expert systems are, among other things, interpreters of contingencies and therefore have a reflexive dimension built into their very nature. This leads to the third dimension of the dynamism of modernity, the critical appropriation of knowledge.

Reflexivity – 'the reflexive monitoring of action' – is a defining feature of social action, according to Giddens (1990, p. 36). In premodern societies reflexivity is tied to the reinterpretation and clarification of tradition, while under the conditions of modernity it becomes the basis of societal reproduction: 'The reflexivity of modern social life consists in the fact that social practices are constantly examined and reformed in the light of incoming information about those very practices, thus constitutively altering their character'

(1990, p. 38). What is distinctive about modernity is the application of reflexivity to knowledge itself. Knowledge is becoming more and more reflexively organized, whether in expert systems, in the social sciences or in everyday life. One of Giddens's theses is that knowledge, as a symbolic medium of exchange, when reflexively applied to the conditions of system production, alters the circumstances to which it was originally referred. Knowledge is therefore transformative and can be emancipatory in that it has an enabling role.

We can now clarify the relation between the institutional orders of modernity – capitalism, industrialism, surveillance and military power – and the dynamism of modernity – the distantiation of time and space, disembedding mechanisms and the reflexive appropriation. Institutions in Giddens's framework are not fixed and objectifying entities standing opposed to agency. Institutions, it may be argued, are structured relations of action and have the capacity to be self-transformative; they involve both a disembedding and 're-embedding' mechanism. Under the conditions of modernity, the institutional orders are becoming more and more open to their self-transformative potentialities. In the transition of 'high' modernity to 'late' modernity this tendency is enhanced. A major dimension to this is 're-embedding', which involves the re-anchoring of abstract systems in social relations (1990, p. 87). While modernity involves the expansion of abstract forms of social organization, such as the separation of time and space and the rise of depersonalized expert systems, it also entails the re-embedding of social relations in trust. Trust can refer to abstract and depersonalized or 'faceless' systems, but it can also refer to 'facework' commitments as well as to personal relationships such as professional ethics, friendship or sexual intimacy. Giddens, in effect, seeks to connect these two kinds of trust – trust in abstract expert systems and trust in personal relations – by means of the concept of reflexivity: trust is reflexively mediated in late modernity.

With the transformation of high modernity into late modernity, the experience of life is becoming ever more risk-conscious. Risk emanates from the reflexivity of modernity, the uncertainties and contingencies of a detraditionalized world. This is concretely experienced in two forms, in societal terms and in personal terms. In societal terms, risk has become a permanent feature of modernity largely as a result of the threat of violence which predominantly comes from the industrialization of war. In personal terms, risk is experienced as deriving from the threat of personal meaninglessness. There is a connection between the globalizing tendencies of modernity – which enhance societal risks – and the transformation of personal relations. With regard to the latter, Giddens attaches importance to the building of trust in personal relations as well as in the reflexive use of knowledge by expert systems. The individual in later modernity is forced to be self-reliant and the construction of self-identity becomes a reflexive project, the theme of his later works (1991, 1992).

I have already noted that Giddens is not centrally concerned with collective actors. The individual is his starting point. His individual is a product of a 'post-traditional' world and is a rational and critical being who knows how to use knowledge. Modernity for Giddens 'institutionalizes the principle of doubt and insists that all knowledge takes the form of hypotheses: claims which may very well be true, but which are in principle always open to revision may at some point have to be abandoned' (1991, p. 3). Modernity entails multiple-choice options for the individual who is emancipated from traditional orders of authority but has to come to terms with risk and trust instead. In modernity, tradition does not disappear; it is forced to explain itself. Modernity involves not the disappearance of tradition but its critical reinterpretation (1994b).

The difference between tradition and modernity is that under the conditions of modernity mediated experience is taking over from earlier kinds of direct experience. Mediated experience is occurring in what is both a single and a globalized world and one which is highly fragmented: 'The reflexive project of the self, which consists in the sustaining of coherent, yet continually revised, biographical narratives, takes place in the context of multiple choice as filtered through abstract systems' (1991, p. 5). In a world of multiple authorities and endless choices, risk and trust cannot be simply wished away. But risk can be reflexively appropriated by social actors who use knowledge to shape their biographies and who at the same time transform institutions. In replacing tradition, expertise can be critically actualized in everyday life: 'Expert knowledge is open to re-appropriation by anyone with the necessary time and resources to become trained; and the prevalence of institutional reflexivity means that there is a continuous filter back of expert theories, concepts and findings to the lay population' (1994b, p. 91).

The concept of social reflexivity underlying Giddens's social theory is the basis of this theory of politics. Not unlike Beck's 'sub-politics', he writes of the opening-up of the political to a new 'generative politics', which releases democracy from the twin ideologies of right and left (Giddens, 1994a). Life politics is not located in the domain of the market or state but in the public domain: 'It works through providing material conditions and organizational frameworks, for the life-political decisions taken by individuals and groups in the wider social order. Such a politics depends on the building of active trust, whether in institutions of government or in connected agencies' (1994a, p. 15). Generative politics links the state to the reflexive mobilization of society at large. Giddens thus breaks from the oppositional model of new social movement theories in that generative or life politics has a positive moment because it is concerned with reconstructing the social and political order: it is a politics of mediation. This is not to be confused with civil society, a concept which Giddens thinks is a suspect one since it locates the political between the state and the individual: 'Today we should speak more of reordered conditions of individual and collective life, producing forms of social disintegration to be sure, but also offering new bases for generating solidarities' (1994a, p. 13).

Life politics is a generative politics in the sense that it aims to create new institutional forms of social organization. Some of the central dimensions to this concern the need to create situations where trust can be built, whether in institutions or in personal relations. A further component is securing autonomy for social actors to become active agents. He also seeks to connect the question of collective responsibility with agency. Responsibility is not reducible to duty: it implies the discursive spelling out of reasons, not blind allegiance, and has its own compelling power, 'for commitments freely undertaken often have greater binding force than those which are simply traditionally given' (1994a, p. 21). In *Beyond Left and Right* (1994a, p. 101), Giddens builds his theory of politics into his theory of the institutional order of modernity to produce a framework to characterize alternative socio-political forms of social organization: a post-scarcity economy (capitalism); humanized nature (industrialism); dialogic modernity (surveillance); and negotiated power (means of violence). A post-scarcity economy is one that recognizes the need to impose a regulatory order on growth, limiting it to sustainable levels. The humanization of nature occurs when natural nature has come to an end with the social construction of nature: the age-old relation of nature and human beings is reversed in today's society. Giddens is one of the few thinkers to address the question of violence as a problem for radical politics: a normative political theory cannot concern itself only with peace. Violence must be tamed not by the state but by communication. In this context the concepts of negotiated power and dialogue move to centre stage.

This framework, which links political and social theory, gives central place to democracy. Trust-creating institutions and democracy are inseparable. Defining democracy as dialogical, Giddens connects democracy and trust. There are four domains of democracy: in personal life, in the politics of social movements, in the organizational arena and in the global order (1994a, pp. 117–24). These domains constitute dialogic spaces for the extension of democracy, a theoretical position that is very close to Habermas's discourse theory.

In sum, then, Giddens's social theory is one of systematic proportions: his theory of reflexive modernization can be seen as an application of his more conceptual and formalistic theory of structuration, which offers a theory of agency and structure; modernity is further reflected in a theory of social change and radical politics.[7] Before proceeding to a critical assessment of the theory of reflexive modernization, I shall conclude this section on Giddens by drawing some parallels and differences between his approach and that of Beck and other approaches considered in the previous chapters.

## Conclusion: Giddens in perspective

The social theory of Giddens has much in common with Beck's. Both theorists are concerned with the experience of risk and the kind of reflexivity to which it gives rise. There is little difference in their political theories, Beck's 'sub-politics' being close to Giddens's 'life politics'. As I mentioned at the beginning of the chapter, the principal difference is that Giddens places considerably more emphasis on the reflexivity of institutions than does Beck, whose theme is the crisis of institutions. However, in my view Giddens offers the more coherent theory of how institutions become reflexive and, in the process, how opportunities for social change are opened up. Such a position does not require a dualism of structure and agency but a 'duality' – or mediation – of structure and agency.

Unlike Beck, Giddens links trust to risk, a theme of growing importance in social theory (Sztompka, 1998). The implication of Beck's theory is that all relations of trust have collapsed in the risk society as a result of the delegitimation of expert systems, whereas Giddens is of the view that expert systems survive in the risk society, albeit at the cost of being democratized: everybody can become an expert. It would also appear that Giddens's notion of risk is wider than Beck's; risk permeates all dimensions of life and is a product of the institutional orders of modernity. While undermining expert systems, risk does not lead to their collapse but their democratization. This would appear to be the direction of generative politics, the mediation of institutions and agency.

It may be observed that the question of the transformations of institutions is close to Habermas's theme of the internal relationship between law and democracy. Where Beck and Giddens appear to disagree, with Giddens in agreement with Habermas, is that both theorists hold to a theory of democracy that seeks to mediate life-world and system, agency and structure. The similarities in this respect are also reflected in their view that modernity involves the reflexive appropriation of traditions. Traditions survive the transition to modernity only by becoming reflexive. The notion of post-tradition and the reflexive dialogue are clearly themes central to Habermas's social theory. However, Giddens differs from Habermas in that his notion of politics is far less decontextualized.

Giddens can also be contrasted to postmodern approaches, of which he is critical (1990, p. 150). In the present context, his principal departure is that, for him, reflexivity is also constituted in institutions. He wishes to identify the institutional developments which provide agency with self-transformative capacities. Moreover, the Self is constituted in self-identity whereas postmodernists tend to see the Self dissolved in a system of signs. Finally, Giddens retains modernity as a framework which is radicalized, and therefore prefers the term late or radicalized modernity to post-modernity. Rights and justice are still important, as well as the emancipatory power of knowledge.

## Assessing Reflexive Modernization: The Question of Culture

Having outlined in detail the two main proponents of reflexive modernization, Beck and Giddens, I shall now attempt an appraisal of these approaches. For this purpose I shall take their approaches to be broadly similar, at least in so far as my appraisal here is concerned. I begin by discussing two critiques, both of which are important in developing the concept of reflexive modernization. These are the critiques of Scott Lash and Jeffery Alexander. Coming from quite different perspectives – respectively, postmodern hermeneutics and neo-functionalism – they share a concern with the cultural dimension of reflexivity which tends to be neglected by Giddens and Beck, for whom the cultural is reduced to the interaction of agency and culture.

### Lash's hermeneutic-aesthetic reflexivity

The context of Lash's critique of Beck and Giddens's thesis of reflexive modernization is a modernized hermeneutics. His argument is that Beck and Giddens operate with a cognitive concept of reflexivity and that this is too reductionist. What is neglected, in his view, is the aesthetic dimension to reflexivity, which he explores in the tradition of aesthetic theory associated with the Frankfurt School authors such as Benjamin and Adorno. The absence of an aesthetic dimension is one aspect of the problem which, more generally, is a problem of culture. There are two further dimensions to this. One is that in so far as reflexive modernization is a theory of the ever-increasing powers of agency with respect to structure, it is necessary to introduce a perspective on information and communication structures. Social structures are not just being displaced by an emancipated agency, but are also being displaced by information and communication structures which facilitate the emergence of a more knowledgeable agency. Lash's third criticism is that Beck and Giddens presume a strong programme of individualism to the neglect of collective agency such as community. The upshot of his critique is that Beck and Giddens fail to address themselves to the specifically cultural dimension of reflexivity. In order to introduce this dimension Lash proposes to transform the concept of aesthetic reflexivity into a more hermeneutic direction in order to uncover the cultural foundations of community in late modernity.

Lash's critique is far-reaching and is a crucial contribution to the debate on reflexive modernization.[8] He is critical of the somewhat simple sketch of Beck and Giddens which counterposes two sets of opposites: a high modernity of subjugation being overtaken by an emancipatory reflexive modernization; an emancipated agency setting itself free from constraining structures. In Giddens's case, as we have seen, agency attains reflexivity in two ways; by means of institutional or structural reflexivity and by self-reflexivity. The first refers to the way institutions become more and more reflexive with respect to the rules and resources that constitute their structures. Reflexive structures are also characterized by the high degree of trust that they establish with agency. This is because modern institutions are coming increasingly to depend on experts whose interpretative capacities must be trusted by society, while at the same time being responsive to society. The second kind of reflexivity is self-reflexivity, by which individuals become increasingly reflexive in the organization of their biographies. Cutting across these two levels of reflexivity is the dialectical process of the double hermeneutic, by which the interpretative operations of expert systems enters everyday life, transforming it and in return being transformed by it. For Beck, in contrast, reflexivity is more critical of institutions: his agency is more sceptical of expert systems. For both, knowledge is the key factor that makes reflexivity possible, even though it may lead to different results (for Beck to dualism, for Giddens to mediation).

According to Lash, these approaches fail to see that structure and agency must be mediated by something other than mere knowledge. In his view, this is culture and, in particular, information and communication structures. For instance, why do we find reflexivity in some places and not in others? Can everybody be reflexive? (Lash, 1994, p. 120). Lash argues that reflexivity is not something all-embracing and cognitive but is articulated in a web of global and local networks of information and communication structures.[9] Life chances depend on one's place in the 'mode of information', but this is not reducible to knowledge, for other cultural factors play a role. Taking the examples of economic organization in Japanese and German firms, Lash (1994, pp. 125–6) demonstrates that a high level of trust and economic performance is achieved by symbolic exchanges and a shared sense of identity (which can be contrasted to the Anglo-Saxon world where the cash nexus and non-informational factors predominate in a market-regulated governance). In the corporatist-style governance of these Japanese and German firms, tradition is important for trust and performance and is not inimical to new knowledge flows. In other words, reflexivity is not necessarily linked to post-traditionalism and the disembedding of knowledge but can be articulated through tradition. Lash's conclusion is that tradition and community can be reflexive and therefore purely cognitive factors alone do not define reflexivity.

Thus far, Lash's argument is convincing and suggests an important corrective to the one-sided cognitive approach of Beck and Giddens, for whom knowledge is transparent (i.e. knowledge is a matter of information). His criticism points to a more differentiated understanding of processes of reflexivity and is also able to express more accurately the dark side of reflexivity – namely, patterns of exclusion (which for Lash resides in exclusion from information and communication structures). However, having established the basis of an important alternative to a narrowly cognitive conception of reflexive modernization, Lash then moves in a postmodern direction. Counterposing a cognitive conception of reflexivity to an aesthetic one, he proceeds to argue for the merits of the latter. Lash rejects Habermas's normative approach and, drawing largely from Adorno and Benjamin but also from Bauman, he argues for a postmodern application of aesthetic reflexivity to late modernity. Aware of the obscure results that this has to offer, Lash then seeks to merge this idea of aesthetic reflection with a hermeneutical theory of collective identity and community. Aesthetic reflexivity is important in so far as it breaks away from the objectivism and realism of a purely cognitive theory of Subject, which seems to be presupposed by Beck and Giddens, but which does not solve the problem of the 'we'. In order to develop a wider concept of reflexivity capable of embracing the collective dimension, we must not merely deconstruct but also, he argues, hermeneutically interpret.

Lash's proposal for a more hermeneutically sensitive concept of reflexivity is the idea of a 'cultural community'. His concept of community is far from the traditional communities of Tönnies and includes a reflexive dimension. It is also to be distinguished from Taylor's communitarian interpretation of community in that it is self-critical. A more appropriate model of community is suggested by Bourdieu's reflexive anthropology: the habitus is reflexively constructed and is theorized in terms of cultural categories, or what he calls 'classificatory categories'. Lash argues:

> the notion of reflexivity here is the polar opposite to that of Beck and Giddens. For Beck and Giddens it tends to involve the bracketing of the life-world to arrive at individualized, subject–object forms of social knowledge. For reflexive anthropology it involves bracketing subject–object knowledge and situating knowers in their life world. (1994, p. 156)

Lash approaches a cultural theory of reflexivity when he attempts to move from a narrowly cognitive theory of reflexivity to a hermeneutic one. However, his solution is marred by a too heavy aesthetic import as well as suffering from the inadequacies of a purely hermeneutic approach. Undoubtedly, the introduction of the idea of the Bourdieu-adapted 'reflexive communities' is important and a useful antidote to the individualist bias of Beck and Giddens as well as to postmodernist aestheticism. As Lash says: 'My concentration on the hermeneutic or communitarian dimension has been largely because – in our present age of cognitive-utilitarian and aesthetic-expressive individualism – it is the one I feel is most in need of some sort of operation of retrieval' (1994, p. 165).

While I do not fundamentally disagree with this line of argument, it neglects the most important dimension of cultural transformation in the late 1990s – namely, the discursive transformation of culture. A hermeneutics of community does not exhaust all levels of what Lash calls the *Kulturgesellschaft*, or 'cultural society' (1994, p. 167). Contemporary society is indeed increasingly more and more cultural in that there is a displacement of the social towards the cultural. This is penetrating all aspects of life, including Giddens's expert systems, institutions, economies of 'signs' and social movements, leading us to the conclusion that structure and agency are articulated through cultural forms of interpretation. However, I am not convinced that a hermeneutics of interpretation focused on reflexive communities is adequate to the task of understanding social change and, in particular, cultural change. In the Conclusion I shall be arguing in more detail for a stronger notion of discourse to understand the nature of cultural transformation. My position on this is that the *Kulturgesellschaft* is also a discourse society: culture is a matter of discursivity and is rooted in communication.

## Alexander and symbolic reflexivity

In a review of *Reflexive Modernization*, Jeffrey Alexander (1996) accuses Beck and Giddens of a major theoretical regression: reflexive modernization, he argues, is a dressed-up version of modernization theory with a postmodernist gloss added. Beck and Giddens offer an alternative to Marxism and to Luhmann's system theory, but retain much of the formalism of their approaches. In particular, there is a persistent formalism and atomism in their work which leads, Alexander argues, to a utilitarian and objectivist view of risk. Alexander's objection is based on his conviction that risk is a mediated phenomenon and cannot therefore be understood merely in terms of a reflexive relationship between agency and structure. What is missing is the intermediary variable of culture. Without this variable, reflexive modernization is deeply flawed and is merely a postmodernized version of classical modernization theory, in that it presupposes a simplistic notion of individualistic action as a response to objective situations.

According to Alexander, the mistake Giddens makes is to take too far Beck's argument that the current crisis can lead to a more responsive and democratic way of life. As a result, he effectively turns Foucault on his head, seeing the institutional order of modernity as emancipatory. Thus, 'self-monitoring', which for Foucault was a device by which power could be extended into microforms such as bio-power, becomes for Giddens the basis of an emancipatory reflexivity. This is of course more serious for Giddens than for Beck because the latter attaches less importance to institutional forms of reflexivity, seeing it largely in terms of a critique of institutions. Giddens, Alexander argues, 'turns Foucault on his head, suggesting that contemporary actors have gained enormous control (reflexivity) over their selves and their environments by making wide use of various therapeutic techniques, including science, in the process often becoming experts themselves' (Alexander, 1996, p. 135). In Alexander's view, reflexive modernization is too Parsonian, at least in Giddens's version of the thesis: 'The pathologies and alienations of modernity are converted into positive reaffirmations about the powers of the modern self and the emancipating contributions that apolitical scientific experts make to the reconstruction of society' (Alexander, 1996, p. 135).

A second objection Alexander makes is that the tradition/modernity debate is based on empty categories. Tradition cannot be reduced to dogmatism or ritual and is not irrational or authoritarian: reflexivity is built into tradition. If tradition is seen in a more differentiated light, then the dualism of a detraditionalized modernity superseding tradition is false. However, this latter point, it must be noted, is a misrepresentation of Giddens, who argues that tradition survives in modernity at the cost of becoming reflexive.

Alexander is more favourably disposed to Lash, who has attempted what Alexander regards as crucial – namely, a theory of culture. Both agree that a cognitive approach is too limited and that there is a need for a stronger thesis of constructivism to compensate for what is in effect an epistemology of cognitive realism. However, Alexander is of the view that Lash's aesthetic hermeneutic alternative obfuscates the problem rather than solves it, with the result that none of the three approaches – Beck's, Giddens's or Lash's – 'gets at the kind of universalizing and critical reflexivity that differentiates contemporary democratic, multicultural and civil societies from earlier, more authoritarian, homogeneous and anti-dogmatic regimes' (Alexander, 1996, p. 137). In order to make this transition, it is Alexander's contention that notions of community, such as the idea of reflexive community for which Lash also argues, must be connected to more abstract, universalistic systems of reference. (This of course is not what Lash wishes to argue for and is it is something that is not suggested by Beck and Giddens.) At this point Alexander comes very close to Habermas's most recent social theory, although he criticizes the latter's neglect of a theory of culture. With such a universalistic framework in mind – to be sure, one that is closer to communitarian thinking and neo-functionalism – Alexander concludes: 'What each of the three authors misses, each in his own way, is that this newly gained reflexivity is deeply connected to meaning-making, and that critical action depends on a continued relation to relatively non-contingent, supra-individual cultural forms' (Alexander, 1996, p. 138). But what are these forms? Alexander's answer is at best obscure, but has the merit of being suggestive: in contemporary society cultural forms are more than ever before separated from ascriptive positions, a separation that makes possible greater cultural options for individuals, more possibilities for meaning-creation.

In a separate, co-authored article, Alexander and Smith (1996) turn their critique on Beck and the theory of the risk society. In line with Alexander's critique of Giddens, the claim here is that a certain objectivism underlies the thesis of risk. In their view, Beck fails to develop a cultural perspective on risk and, as a result, reduces risk perception to a thesis of objective visibility with respect to structure and inductive reasoning on the part of agency. This deficiency is because Beck does not grant any autonomy to culture, which is precisely what marks a 'late Durkheimian' approach and one which Alexander and Smith endorse: 'We suggest that a model which acknowledges the autonomy of culture and the role of the mythological, the sacred and the profane in technological discourses enables a more satisfactory understanding of the social dynamics of risk-consciousness' (1996, p. 252).[10] Culture, they argue, has played a mediatory role in defining risk-consciousness. The problem, in essence, for Alexander and Smith is that Beck presents the terrors of the risk society as an objective social fact, one that derives from their visibility. The fact that risk is an objective reality simply leads to inductive reasoning on the part of agency. It is, of course, debatable whether Beck in fact argues that risks are visible, since he makes clear that many risks escape perception because they are invisible to the eye. Yet, it is evident that for Beck risk is real: Chernobyl really happened, even if social actors constructed it in different ways. To put the problem in different terms, the critical question, according to Alexander and Smith, is the time lag between the emergence of risk and its perception by public consciousness: 'Beck wants to portray the risk society as an objective fact, both ontologically, in the sense that it exists as such, in a cold, hard, and material way, and epistemologically, in the sense that these objective facts are perceived directly and accurately in the minds of the citizens themselves' (1996, pp. 255–6).

In order to be able to account for the time lag Beck would have to include the missing variable of culture which mediates between structure and agency. According to Alexander and Smith, the more culturally sensitive theory of risk of Douglas and Wildavsky (1982) offers a promising alternative, but does not really solve the problem because they make culture too dependent on social structure. Thus, where Beck is a prisoner of cognitive objectivism, they are prisoners of structure. Alexander and Smith propose an alternative approach, which in my view is unsatisfactory. In order to explain how risk is culturally constructed they adopt Durkheim's ([1912] 1915) theory of the sacred and the profane which offers an explanation of the symbolic construction of mythological discourses of salvation and destruction. In their view, technologically created risk is symbolically constructed in theological categories such as those of the sacred and the profane, salvation and destruction.[11] The risk discourse is thus nothing more than a secularized salvation discourse of a polluted technology threatening apocalypse.

In my view this is a most inadequate solution to the absence of a cultural perspective. There may be some truth to the view that a Judaeo-Christian discourse of redemption is shot through contemporary risk-consciousness, but this cannot explain all aspects of the cultural construction of risk. Technological discourse cannot be entirely explained by reference to theodicy, however important it may be. Beck's argument is that risk-consciousness results not in apocalyptic prophecies of an expressivist nature but in new forms of political communication which seek to remedy the disorganized responsibility of science and technology policy. Public concern about risk cannot then be explained in terms of mythological discourses and the search for a secular ethic of salvation. I would like to suggest that the most future-oriented dimension of reflexivity – collective responsibility, discussed at length above – which is implied by Beck's theory of risk may be a kind of 'salvation', but one which is bereft of mythological or theological ideas.

In sum, then, a promising critique of reflexive modernization fails to get off the ground as a result of a superficial commitment to a 'late Durkheimian' theory of cultural construction. While Beck and Giddens may have neglected the autonomy of culture by reducing it to its cognitive dimension, Alexander and Smith make the error of collapsing culture into the aesthetic dimension of the symbolic.[12] The result is that they fail to appreciate the different ways in which culture mediates structure and agency.

## Conclusion: Reflexivity and Discourse

In this chapter I introduced the theories of Beck and Giddens, arguing that their conceptions of reflexivity offer social theory with a useful purchase on social change. The importance of reflexive modernization consists of its wide notion of reflexivity and knowledge. I have argued that Giddens's version is particularly rich in that it applies reflexivity to agency and to structure and sees both as mediated by knowledge, albeit a narrow model of knowledge and an individualistic model of action. The main weakness is its reduction of culture – the wider cognitive dimension of cultural reproduction – to agency and structure. If culture were granted autonomy, some of the problems in Giddens's theory could be overcome, such as those identified by Alexander and Lash. I have focused on the critiques of Lash and Alexander since these address the central weakness of the theories of Beck and Giddens. I have argued that this consists of their neglect of culture as a mediating dimension between structure and agency. While the specific alternatives proposed by Lash and Alexander do not really provide the full picture of cultural transformation, they do offer a starting point for a more culturally sensitive theory of social change. Such an approach would have to incorporate the cognitive, normative and aesthetic dimensions of cultural reproduction into a wider theory of structure and agency which would give greater place to the role of public communication. Thus, for example, risk as a cultural discourse has three dimensions: cognitive – in terms of the place of reflexive forms of knowledge; normative – in terms of ethically and politically motivated action; and aesthetic – expressivist and evaluative action, which is symbolically and meaningfully mediated. Beck and Giddens, I have argued, rely too much on a narrow cognitive theory of culture, while their critics (Lash and Alexander) seem to reduce culture to the aesthetic dimension or the purely symbolic. What gets neglected is the overall framework of culture as a cognitive system entailing reflexivity and the growing importance of discursivity in society more broadly. Such a position would require a stronger theorization of the role of the public, which forms the structured and relational context in which reflexivity occurs.

# Conclusion:
# *Knowledge, Democracy and Discursive Institutionalization*

As a new millennium begins, social theory is compelled to rethink the fundamental assumptions of modernity. The idea of modernity was a product of the Age of the Enlightenment, the epoch from the late seventeenth century to the early nineteenth century, when tradition and authority were challenged by an emancipated subjectivity. The self-understanding of the nineteenth and twentieth centuries was very much shaped by the ideas and ideals of that period, in particular the belief in the autonomy of the Subject, the epistemic confidence of modern cultural rationality and the social construction of rationally organized institutions such as the nation-state and the discursive regulation of power. Thus the crisis and critique which characterized the post-Enlightenment period, in effect the last one hundred and fifty years, were always defined by reference to the central conflict of modernity: the tension between the cultural project of modernity and the social reality of modern society, which was increasingly one of fragmentation. Yet, despite that discord, modernity – as it unfolded in the works of Kant through Hegel and Marx to Durkheim, Weber and Simmel – assumed a certain coherence in the social and the cultural; it held out the promise of emancipation and the belief that the dualism of the social and the cultural could be reconciled through politics. To be sure, this was an aspiration that became ever more uncertain, as is illustrated in the thought of Weber and Simmel.

The idea of modernity in the twentieth century, in particular in the aftermath of totalitarianism which haunted the epoch, became increasingly formulated in terms of an ever-deeper sense of crisis, the culmination of which was the rejection of the master theme of the Enlightenment – the autonomy of the Subject. Since the 1970s, when Western Marxism began to lose its intellectual dominance, modernity was gradually discarded in favour of post-structuralism, which entailed the rejection of the entire culture of modernity and its belief in the – ultimately political – coherence of its ideal with reality. In one way or another the social theory of the last three decades of the twentieth century has been an expression of the crisis not just of modernity – the discord between the cultural aspirations of modernity and the social reality of modern society – but of the political Subject and the cultural premises of modernity. The theme of the progressive loss of unity has become one of the main motifs in social theory. The postmodern challenge called into question the very idea of coherence itself: the coherence of the social and cultural project of modernity, the coherence in the identity of the self/ego, the coherence of knowledge and of politics, and the belief that history is the narrative of meaning. Only those who did not accept the rejection of historical actors – such as Habermas and Touraine – could hold on to some of the central categories of modernity. Yet, even in their writings, particularly in recent times, there is a turning away from the completion of the historical project of modernity. Others – such as communitarians and conservatives – who wanted to hold on to the promise of coherence, could do so only at the price of rejecting modernity.

As we enter a new century and millennium we have to reconsider the hitherto existing frameworks. The works of the theorists considered in this book – such as Habermas, Touraine, Bauman, Beck, Giddens – in different ways all point to the need to evolve new terms of debate. In the last four chapters of this book I traced a certain convergence towards a theorization of mediation in their mature writings of the 1990s. For Habermas, this is represented in the shift from the dualism of system and life-world (a debate which still bore the last vestiges of Western Marxism); in Bauman we see the turning away from a version of postmodernism dominated by the post-structural deconstruction of the Subject to an ethical conception of the Self; in Touraine we see the abandoning of a certain philosophy of praxis and collective actors associated with the new social movements which came to dominate in the 1960s and 1970s; in Giddens we also see a turning away from the theory of capitalism and the critique of historical materialism to a theory of structuration and modernity, which stresses less the dualism than the 'duality' of agency and structure. Perhaps convergence is too strong a term, but we can detect in all of these intellectual movements a recognition of the need to theorize new forms of mediation between agency and structure, culture and power, life-world and system, experience and rationalization. All these authors, I have argued, have responded to the changed circumstances of the present with theories of modernity which, in different ways, can be seen as giving varying degrees of weight to the radical discourses of creativity, reflexivity and discursivity. However, in my reading of their approaches the solutions they offer are inadequate in themselves: Habermas's concern, as we have seen, is ultimately in normative political philosophy and, as a result, the sociological implications of discourse theory remain unexplored. Bauman's recasting of postmodernity reveals a retreat into a personal ethics which is politically impotent; Touraine's conception of the progressive loss of unity in contemporary society, and the resulting bifurcation of Subject and Reason, neglects the discursive spaces which exist both in processes of subjectivity and in rationalization; and Giddens's emphasis on reflexivity in institutions and personal life loses sight of discursivity and places too much emphasis on the discord between personal life and the world of institutions. However, it must be said that the foundations now exist for a social theory attuned to current realities and it is my view that the work of these theorists provides an important starting point.[1]

I think one central conclusion here is that not only have the old rivals of Western Marxism and liberal social theory (i.e. modernization theory) become redundant but so too has postmodernism. The postmodern challenge, at least in its post-structuralist form, now no longer sets the terms of debate, for its radical claims have been more or less accepted, having been to an extent realized in social practice today. That is to say, the challenge is no longer to deconstruct the historicist conception of the Subject and the positivistic conception of knowledge. The two key targets of the post-structuralists were the autonomy of the Subject and the related belief in the autonomy of knowledge as a rationalistic and positivistic discourse. In the late 1960s and 1970s these were legitimate targets for intellectual critique, even if in some versions the conclusions were too extravagant. In the late 1990s, however, it is a different story: the historicist Subject and positivistic science have not survived unscathed. In a way, we are now all postmodernists: after three decades of feminism and multiculturalism the idea of an autonomous Subject is no longer credible; and as a result of changes in the social production of knowledge, the collapse of positivism in the natural sciences and the emergence of a new politics focused on commonalities between nature and society, the modernist conception of knowledge as coherent, autonomous and rationalistic is no longer widely adhered to. Postmodernism is exhausted because its work has been done. Politically, it was an expression of a time when the old social movements of modernity were exhausting themselves of their utopian potential but when the impact of the new social movements was not yet apparent. More than three decades later we can say that the challenge is no longer that of the post-structuralist critique – recognizing heterogeneity and difference in homogeneity and unitarian concepts; fragmenting oppressive subjectivities; dissolving the power of identity and ideology, and self-legitimating doctrines of knowledge – but is one precisely of the dissolution of autonomy in a world of sheer fragmentation. In sum, the problem no longer consists of the dangers of a false universalism – the target of the postmodernist critique – but of an uncontrolled relativism which is destroying the possibility of democratic politics and one which frequently appeals to the very notion of autonomy – or self-determination – itself to bring about the determination of the Other (de Vries and Weber, 1997). As Alain Touraine ([1992] 1995a) argues, the challenge now is the overcoming of the division of politics into the dual worlds of pure subjectivity and identity on the one side and, on the other, the release of an unfettered instrumentalism driven by market and technological imperatives. My thesis is that this challenge to overcome an apparently irreconcilable dualism must be seen as one of articulating new possibilities for mediation.

What, then, are the options for a new modernity based on mediation? How can the central conflict in modernity – the cultural idea of autonomy and the social reality of fragmentation – be reconciled without recourse to the illusions of an all-embracing vision of politics? I think we have to reject the solutions offered in the discourses of modernity. The vision of a historical Subject – a social movement, a class, a nation, a church, intellectuals – capable of integrating the fragmented strands in modern society is now discredited, in the wake of the historical experience of the great revolutions and ideologies of the twentieth century – the October Revolution, fascism, nationalism, the Islamic revolution. The class structure has been rendered too diffuse to wield a coherent actor and the social movements which transformed western societies in the 1970s have now ceased to exist as social actors, their projects having been either realized or incorporated into the programmes of other social actors. In short, the changed situation as we enter the twenty-first century is one of uncertainty, contingency, indeterminacy and the collapse of a central social movement, in particular one deriving from western modernity. There is even evidence to suggest that the ecological movement is no longer a coherent agency and its discourse has passed into the public sphere (Eder, 1996b). In this context, a further point of great importance is that the nature of social, political and economic organization has undermined the possibility of revolutionary social change as a transition to a future time.

Many theorists, such as Luhmann, have emphasized the condition of societal complexity and the emergence of what is best termed, following Castells, a network society to characterize the current situation. The implication of this is that the nature of social change makes a notion of *transformation* more pertinent to the current situation than *transition*. Social transformation occurs on an evolutionary plane without a historical trajectory pointing to the transition to a temporal future. The social is no longer based on a centre, an organic structure with fixed and differentiated functions. The most important change that is occurring in our kind of society is one in which 'the social' is shifting from the organic condition of the 'body' – a territorially and functionally integrated society – to the cultural, in which the spatial and temporal categories of modernity are dissolved: the world of the ephemeral and virtual, flows of knowledge and experience, the diffusion of information. The social is increasingly being projected on to the levels of cognitive representations, a tendency recognized by Durkheim in his late work. This phenomenon of what might be called the enculturation of the social is one of the central conclusions of Manuel Castells's theory of the network society (1996, 1997, 1998).

Castells's challenging thesis is that in the network society which is emerging today social relations are being increasingly shaped by flows of information. The emerging network society is a seamless web of relationships that are becoming more and more globalized as a result of the impact of information technology which has transformed social relations in three dimensions: the relations of production, the relations of power and in the relationship of experience. A network is an open and limitless structure that expands through communication and information. According to Castells, the most significant development is the diffusion of information technology, which has transformed economic production, into the political domain of power and the sphere of experience and identity.[2] Power is increasingly residing in access to information exchange and symbolic manipulation of cultural codes. In essence, for Castells the distinctive feature of the current situation is the confluence of information and culture: as economic production is becoming more and more dependent on information, it shifts into the cultural domain, bringing about a transformation in experience and a clash between the 'net' and the Self. With the crisis in the nation-state, collective identities are released from the old structures of power and enter the globalized flows of informationalized culture. Thus politics too is increasingly being played out in the media. In general, power has been taken out of institutions, such as those of the state and organizations such as businesses, the churches and the corporate media; it is diffused in global networks which are not controlled by any particular agency: 'The new power lies in codes of information and in the images of representation around which societies organize their institutions, and people build their lives, and decide their behaviour' (Castells, 1997, p. 359).

This leaves us with a fundamental question: can information become a basis for democratic politics or will it become diffused in a highly fragmented society in which information will be the new tool of domination. What is the relationship between information and democracy? According to Castells, the crucial factor will be whether social movements will emerge and give expression to a new 'identity project' which is not purely defensive and which is able to exploit the culture of information for democracy. There is no doubt that Castells's argument is immensely important: social integration in the kind of society that is taking shape today is neither determined by cultural cohesion, or normative consensus, as the functional school believed, nor by the ideological instruments of class power, as Marxists argued, but by information. The cultural logic of information is the 'glue' that holds 'society' together, to use the vocabulary of an older sociology. Society exists not as a thing or as a particular system but as a network of relations that are nothing other than their communicative content.

In my estimation, Castells's argument can be improved in one respect – namely, we need analytically to separate information from knowledge (Delanty, 1998b). If this distinction were made, then, we could see more clearly how the question of democratic politics can be connected to cultural transformation. Knowledge is more than information, which is knowledge in the context of its economic application. Knowledge is a wider category and pertains to experience, communication and identity; it is primarily social and has many levels, ranging from everyday knowledge to scientific knowledge. The important point is that, as a cognitive practice, knowledge is also a form of experience and is therefore a medium of cultural reproduction.[3] Knowledge is manifested in the three levels of information, communication and reflexivity. It is not reducible to information (Midgley, 1989).

Taking up Habermas's notion of communication as discursive but going beyond his decontextualized approach, we can make the further observation that identity constitutes a form of *contested knowledge*, in such matters as group boundaries and in the fundamental codes of group membership. Thus, what is distinctive about current forms of collective identities is their ability to contest existing social frameworks and cultural codes. The culture of contestation in identity politics is rivalled only by that in knowledge production more generally. Both share the ability to exercise the power to define reality. As I have stressed throughout this book, the old framework of knowledge associated with the Enlightenment is no longer pertinent today, for knowledge has ceased to be autonomous and self-legislating. In the risk society, knowledge is a matter of contestation and of the delegitimation of expertise. This can be seen in such instances as AIDS, BSE, radioactivity, biotechnological developments such as cloning, medical ethics and neurology, which have all opened scientized knowledge to public scrutiny, bringing together discourses of nature, science, law and politics. These cases are also interesting in that the degree of contestation permeates to the cultural model of society itself, and the discourses related to these issues are not dominated by any one particular social actor. The players are organized interests, professional bodies, experts, policy-makers, regulatory agencies, media and social movements. In the absence of a key social actor, it is the public which is becoming more important as a social mediator in disputes which question the very foundations of a society's cognitive and cultural structures. Under these circumstances a model of consensus has been replaced by a model of dissensus.

In order to appreciate the full significance of such developments we must see that knowledge is also becoming a medium of cultural experience: we are experiencing social reality more and more through cognitive frameworks. This is what is meant by the term 'knowledge society', a term which I think is more pertinent than the expression 'information society' (with its too narrowly instrumentalist view of knowledge). As a leading proponent of the thesis of the 'knowledge society', Gernot Böhme (1997, p. 461), puts it: 'Human society as a cultural community consists essentially in the fact that produced knowledge does not remain individual but through symbolization and rule formation is made intersubjectively available permanently; that is, knowledge becomes cultural capital.' In the resulting confluence of culture and knowledge, the politics of identity are released. Therefore we must ask again the question concerning the relationship between democracy and knowledge: can the new discursive spaces be captured for democracy?

When we pose the question like this the challenge of democratic politics is inseparable from the cultural politics of knowledge. It has been widely recognized in recent times that democracy is becoming more and more cultural. In human rights, for instance, the question of cultural rights has changed our understanding of universalistic morality; the cultural question has also entered the agenda in relation to the media and in feminism it has been central for a long time; in the nature or nurture debate and in environmental concerns, cultural identity and politics are inseparable. This idea has been central to the writings of Touraine and Melucci, in particular, and recent developments in 'social postmodernism' (Nicholson and Seidman, 1995).

I think the general point that emerges from this is that democracy is becoming more and more drawn into cultural issues at precisely the same time that knowledge is becoming a key cultural dimension (Trend, 1997). What cuts across knowledge and democracy is the dimension of contestability in the ability to define the boundaries of experience. Thus, in the knowledge society we see a great increase in its discursive capacity, manifest in everyday life as well as in professional and political domains. In terms of the fundamental question underlying the idea of modernity, the clash between the struggle for autonomy and the reality of fragmentation, integration and differentiation, we can now see how the cultural and social projects of modernity are mediated in the politics of knowledge, bringing together the discourses of creativity, reflexivity and discursivity. The implications for the problem of mediation can be seen to lie in what might be called discursive institutionalization, the discursive regulation of power by a reflexively constituted and self-regulating society of creative citizens. The public is of the utmost importance in this since it observes the different competing frames and through public opinion (i.e. the evaluation and selection of one frame as against another) exerts pressure on the competing and conflicting actors and hence sends the discursive mediation and eventually institutionalization in a particular direction.[4] Discursive democracy remains unintelligible with reference only to the autonomy and creativity of social actors. The role of the public in resonating in relation to communicated ideas and in selecting from the variety generated and thus stabilizing a particular cross-section of knowledge (i.e. a cultural frame, form, model or code) is absolutely crucial.

The 'new obscurity', which Jürgen Habermas (1989b) detected in the late modern condition, and which has suffered a loss in the culture of certainty as a result of a weakening in political ideology, is to be explained precisely by the disengaging of discourse from agency. Leon Mahew, in a path-breaking work *The New Public* (1997), writes of the emergence of a 'new public', which has replaced the modern public of the Enlightenment, which was, supposedly, based on free discussion. Instead, the new public, he argues, is a realm of conflict and debate, albeit one in which rhetoric and persuasion rather than argument play a central role. The public engages in contesting and creating meaning, and it may be the case that social integration in advanced societies will become more and more shaped by the dynamics of public discourse, which, as Piet Strydom (1999b) argues, has become a domain of a new kind of contingency. Conceiving of the public as a domain of communication and experience, in which social knowledge and democracy are discursively constructed, may provide social theory with a new range of possibilities for theorizing the social.

# Notes

## Introduction

1   It may be noted that the theory of modernity coincided with the re-
    vival of civil society, both concepts reflecting a reorientation in the
    conceptualization of modern society towards reflexivity. See Friese
    and Wagner (1999), Outhwaite (1999) and Szakloczai (1998).
2   This is undoubtedly related to the recognition of the autonomy of
    culture in the social sciences since the 1960s, as is evidenced in the re-
    flexive turn induced by Kuhn (1970), Berger and Luckmann ([1966]
    1984), and Habermas ([1968] 1978), for instance.
3   This Enlightenment idea of critique was also central to the work of
    Pierre Bayle ([1667] 1965).
4   The references in the text include, in cases where I have considered it
    relevant, the original year of publication. This date is given in square
    brackets.
5   See Rundel (1987) for a discussion of the social and political thought of
    Kant, Hegel and Marx. See also Delanty (1999).
6   See Honneth (1995a) on the concept of recognition.
7   The best account of this is McCarthy (1996) and Swidler (1986). See
    also Archer (1988), Holland and Quinn (1991), Münch and Smelser
    (1992) and Swidler (1995). On constructivism more generally, see
    Delanty (1997c).
8   See the debate on social integration and system integration in Giddens
    (1984), Habermas ([1981] 1984) and Lockwood (1964), summarized by
    Mouzelis (1997).
9   The importance of a cognitive approach has been stated by Eyerman
    and Jamison (1991) and was an important dimension to the early work
    of Alain Touraine, who emphasized the role of cultural models and
    models of knowledge (see Chapter 5). I am grateful to Piet Strydom for

further clarification on this development. See Strydom (1999a, 1999b) and Chapter 2.

10 This is one of Habermas's principal arguments. See Habermas (1990).

11 In this context, one of the central challenges for social theory is the question of democratic institutionalization.

## Chapter 1  Defining Modernity

1 For further discussion of the sociology of modernity see Wagner (1994). See also Friese and Wagner (1999), Haferkamp and Smelser (1992), Kumar (1995), Rengger (1995) and Santos (1995).

2 See Horowitz and Manley (1994 ).

3 Blumenberg's book was written as a critique of Karl Löwith's *Meaning in History* [1949]. This debate revolves around the question whether the modern world-view is a secularized version of Christendom or a radical break from it.

4 England was to an extent an exception in this context. As a result of the English Revolution of 1688–9 it was parliamentary sovereignty which triumphed over both popular sovereignty and monarchical sovereignty.

5 Held (1996, p. 149) makes the important qualification that autonomy per se was more specific to the liberal tradition than to either the Marxist tradition or the republican tradition associated with Rousseau, which emphasizes more democratic participation than questions pertaining to individual autonomy.

6 On the question of social order in social theory, see Wrong (1994).

7 In my view Toulmin makes the mistake of equating the idea of the cosmopolis with what he calls 'the hidden agenda' of modernity.

8 See O'Mahony and Delanty (1998) for an empirical analysis of this.

9 From the point of view of a theory of modernity there is the interesting question whether the communist system collapsed as a result of its internal structural contradictions or as a result of the assertion of autonomy. See Castells (1998). See also Lefort (1986).

10 This is also the case with the revolutions in Eastern Europe in 1989/90 which may be regarded as the last of the modern revolutions.

11 According to Arno Mayer, many modern revolutions were in fact restorations. This is particularly the case with the English Revolution of 1688–9.

12 See Derrida (1992) and Delanty (1998a, 1998b).

13 This notion of discursivity is central to Foucault and Habermas. See Chapters 3 and 4. See also Eyerman and Jamison (1991) who use the concept of cognitive praxis to express this.

14 There is a considerable body of literature in Marxist historical sociology on the idea of the transition from feudalism to capitalism, for instance Holton (1985) and Hilton (1978) .

15 On time, see Adam (1990, 1995).

## Chapter 2    The Limits of Modernity

1   On Western Marxism, see Anderson (1976), Jameson (1971) and Jay (1984).
2   See Frisby (1984) for an excellent account of Simmel's social theory.
3   From a different perspective, Reinhart Koselleck ([1959] 1988) took up the theme of modernity as a crisis-ridden discourse. Koselleck's argument, in one of the classic studies on the European Enlightenment and its consequences, was that modernity became a utopian discourse and therefore a hypocritical and politically useless world-view because it saw itself excluded from politics.
4   The concept of de-differentiation has been proposed by Crook et al. (1992: 68–74) and Lash (1990: 11–12).
5   The concept of interpenetration is suggested by Münch (1990).
6   Though Castells does not acknowledge it, the notion of the 'net' was first elaborated by Simmel.
7   Simmel was the exception here in that he was more concerned to relate differentiation to fragmentation, albeit within the contours of the modern.
8   This is certainly the case as far as the European Union is concerned. According to critics such as Milward (1992), Milward et al. (1993), European integration was a project aimed at enhancing, not undermining, the state. For a discussion, see Delanty (1997d).
9   It is believed that 30 per cent of the occupational structure in the OECD is accounted for by informational labour (Webster, 1997, p. 74).
10  Postfordism is a contested concept. For some debates, see Webster (1995, pp. 147–62).
11  On postmaterialism, see Abramson and Inglehart (1995) and Inglehart (1977). See also Pahl (1995).
12  See Alexander and Colomy (1990) for a wide-ranging application of neo-functionalism.
13  See Chapter 6 for further discussion on Alexander's approach.
14  For a similar position, see Robert Wuthnow (1989), who proposes the idea of 'discursive communities' to capture the sense by which social actors arise along with the production of cultural ideologies and gain control over new social spaces: discursive communities are cultural producers who challenge power by articulating new ideologies. The importance of his approach is that it shows how social actors are constituted in the opening of discursive spaces in society.
15  On social learning, see also Miller (1986).
16  See Haas (1992) on the idea of epistemic community.
17  I have explored this in Delanty (1998b).
18  This position can be contrasted to the institutional approach of Robert Merton (1949).
19  I am grateful to Piet Strydom for alerting me to some of the recent literature.
20  It must be remarked, however, that his recent theoretical work suggests a more radicalized conception of reflexivity which is projected

back as far as Pascal (Bourdieu, 1997). See the symposium on Bourdieu's *Pascalian Mediations* in *European Journal of Social Theory,* 1999, especially Heilbron (1999).

## Chapter 3   Discourse and Democracy

1   On theories of democracy, see Held (1996).
2   See Dryzek (1990) for a fuller account of discursive democracy.
3   For a similar view on democracy and complexity, see Peters (1993) and Zolo (1992).
4   The cognitive question is also central to his theory of science ([1968] 1978), but it is noteworthy that in his early work there can be no reconciliation with nature, which is conceptualized as external to subjectivity.
5   Parts of the following analysis are adapted from Delanty (1997b).
6   This concept of civil society as a network of communicative links can be compared to Castells's (1996, 1997, 1998) theory of the network society.
7   I have argued elsewhere that his concept of constitutional patriotism, developed in the context of a critique of German national identity, is highly pertinent to European integration and societies, where the nation-state has failed to provide a model of integration (Delanty, 1996c).
8   See Habermas's debate with Grimm (Habermas, 1998).
9   I have explored this more fully in Delanty (1997b).
10   For a discussion of the relationship between modernity and the nonwestern world, see Arnason (1997).
11   See for example Dallmayr (1996).
12   See also Burns and Ueberhorst (1988) and Trend (1997).
13   It is to be noted that Habermas never revised his earlier notion of the cognitive ([1968] 1978). In this earlier work cognitive interests – or interests in knowledge – were defined entirely in relation to the sciences.

## Chapter 4   The Rise of Postmodernism

1   For an extensive critique of postmodernism see Habermas (1987b) and O'Neill (1995). See also Harvey (1990), Smart (1992) and Turner (1990).
2   Derrida's (1993, 1997) later works do make some concessions to social theory. See Critchley (1998) and O'Neill (1999).
3   For a more detailed outline of the origins of poststructuralism, see Delanty (1997c, ch. 5).
4   It is evident, however, that the question of opposition became more pronounced in his latter writings.
5   On the Foucault–Habermas debate, see Kelly (1994).
6   For one of the best surveys, see Anderson (1998).
7   The book was commissioned by the government of Quebec as a 'report on knowledge'.
8   On his importance, see Rojek and Turner (1993).

9  A more extreme version of this kind of postmodernism is the theory of the coming of the cyborg. Part human and part machine, the cyborg epitomizes the end of the individual as the logical outcome of the end of the social.

10  An exception to this approach is Gianni Vattimo (1988, 1992), whose thought is very close to Baudrillard, but for whom emancipation is still a real possibility. This is also the case with Jameson (1991), who is closer to Western Marxism.

11  For a critical discussion, see Kalyvas (1999), who attempts to rescue Castoriadis from Habermas's infamous dismissal and argues for a politics of autonomy as opposed to recognition, since this ultimately entails a retreat into communitarianism and a loss of the critical impetus. See also Honneth's reply (1999).

12  For a critique, see Joas (1998), Kellner (1998) and Outhwaite (1999).

## Chapter 5   The Return of Agency

1  For some general accounts of NSMs see Buechler (1995), Dalton and Kuechler (1990), Eyerman and Jamison (1991), Jackall and Vidich (1995), Klandermans et al. (1988), Larrana et al. (1994), Morris and McClurg (1992), Tarrow (1995) and Castells (1997).

2  Touraine's concept of historicity can be compared to Castoriadis's notion of the imaginary, which apparently was an important influence on Touraine.

3  See the symposium on Touraine in the *European Journal of Social Theory* (vol. 1, no. 2, 1998) and Touraine's own contribution (Touraine, 1998b).

4  It is evident that Touraine still attaches importance to the workers' movement, even though it is no longer the central movement today (Touraine, Wieviorka and Dubet, [1966] 1987).

5  Melucci goes beyond resource mobilization theory in that he sees grievances and a pre-existing social problem as one aspect of the building of a social movement. In his analysis a collective identity is an independent dimension and grievances do not explain collective action. In other words, Melucci operates with a stronger concept of constructiveness: objective situations do not exist; they are constructed by social actors (1989, pp. 192–3).

## Chapter 6   Reflexive Modernization

1  As I argue later in this chapter, I disagree with Alexander and Smith's (1996) exaggerated claim that the success of the book is due to its theological discourse of salvation and apocalypse prophecy.

2  This perspective on temporal structures is more developed in Luhmann's (1993) theory of risk.

3  Hans Jonas (1984, 1994) has argued that the overriding need at the start of the twenty-first century is for a global ethic of responsibility capable of addressing technology. See also Apel on collective responsibility (1978, 1991, 1992).

4   The attempt to reconcile realism and constructivism, it may be noted in passing, has been the subject of Randall Collins's major work on global intellectual change (1998, especially pp. 858–81).
5   This also has far-reaching consequences for a theory of institutionalization, though this is something Beck does not explore. The issue now becomes how latent forms of reflexivity are transferred into institutional practices (Beck, 1996a, pp. 180–1).
6   This is formally developed in *The Constitution of Society* (1984), but these ideas are also present in some of his early work – see Giddens (1976). See Held and Thompson (1989).
7   With the publication of *The Third Way* (Giddens, 1998), the radical impetus is weakened, with a stronger emphasis on the institutional dimension.
8   See Strydom's (1999a) critique of Lash.
9   For a more elaborated account of this position, see Lash and Urry (1994).
10  See also Alexander (1998). See also Chapter 2.
11  See also Alexander (1992).
12  For a more detailed critique of Alexander and Smith, see Strydom (1997).

## Conclusion

1   Due to limitations of space I have not considered the work of Bourdieu and Luhmann who are clearly crucial figures in the reconceptualization of modernity.
2   It is important to say that these processes have separate trajectories: the information revolution coincided with the worldwide crisis of capitalism and statism in the early 1970s and the rise of the new social movements around feminism, environmentalism and human rights. The interaction of these levels led to the emergence of the information society.
3   I not wish to enter into a debate on Castells here beyond remarking that he uses the term 'information' in many different ways, as a result of which there is a fundamental lack of clarity on the causal power of information. See Webster (1997) and the symposium on *The Information Age* in the *European Journal of Social Theory*, 2, 4, 1999.
4   I wish to acknowledge Piet Strydom for this formulation. For a more extensive account, see Strydom (1999b).

# Bibliography

Abramson, P. and Inglehart, R. 1995: *Value Change in Global Perspective*. Michigan University Press: Ann Arbor.

Adam, B. 1990: *Time and Social Theory*. Cambridge: Polity.

Adam, B. 1995: *Timewatch: The Social Analysis of Time*. Cambridge: Polity.

Adorno, T. 1973: *Negative Dialectics*. London: Routledge and Kegan Paul.

Adorno, T. 1984: *Aesthetic Theory*. London: Routledge and Kegan Paul.

Adorno, T. and Horkheimer, M. [1947] 1979: *Dialectic of Enlightenment*. London: Verso.

Ahmed, A. 1992: *Postmodernism and Islam: Predicament and Promise*. London: Routledge.

Al-Azmeh, Z. 1993: *Islams and Modernities*. London: Verso.

Albrow, M. 1996: *The Global Age: State and Society Beyond Modernity*. Cambridge: Polity.

Alexander, J. 1992: 'The Promise of a Cultural Sociology'. In R. Münch and N. Smelser (eds), *Theory of Culture*. Berkeley: University of California Press.

Alexander, J. 1995: *Fin-de-Siècle Social Theory: Relativism, Reduction and the Problem of Reason*. London: Verso.

Alexander, J. 1996: 'Critical Reflections on "Reflexive Modernization" ', *Theory, Culture and Society*, 13, 4, 133–8.

Alexander, J. 1998: *Neofunctionalism and After*. Oxford: Blackwell.

Alexander, J. and Colomy, P. (eds) 1990: *Differentiation Theory and Social Change: Historical and Comparative Approaches*. New York: Columbia University Press.

Alexander, J. and Smith, P. 1996: 'Social Science and Salvation: Risk as Mythological Discourse', *Zeitschrift für Soziologie*, 25, 4, 251–62.

Allen Roberson, B. 1988: 'The Islamic Belief System'. In R. Little and S. Smith (eds), *Belief Systems and International Relations*. Oxford: Blackwell.

Anderson, B. 1983: *Imagined Communities*. London: Verso.

Anderson, P. 1974: *Lineages of the Absolute State*. London: Verso.

Anderson, P. 1976: *Considerations on Western Marxism*. London: Verso.

Anderson, P. 1998: *Origins of Postmodernity*. London: Verso.

Apel, K.-O. 1978: *Diskurs und Verantwortung: Das Problem des Übergangs zur postkonventiontellen Moral*. Frankfurt: Suhrkamp.

Apel, K.-O. 1991: 'A Planetary Macroethics for Humankind: The Need, the Apparent Difficulty, and the Eventual Possibility'. In E. Deutsch (ed.), *Culture and Modernity: East–West Philosophical Perspectives*. Honolulu: University of Hawaii Press.

Apel, K.-O. 1992: 'The Ecological Crisis as a Problem for Discourse Ethics'. In A. Ofsti (ed.), *Ecology and Ethics*. A. Trondheim: Nordland Akademi for Kunst og Vitenskap.

Archer, M. 1988: *Culture and Agency: the Place of Culture in Social Theory*. Cambridge: Cambridge University Press.

Archibugi, D. and Held, D. (eds) 1995: *Cosmopolitan Politics: An Agenda for a New World Order*. Cambridge: Polity.

Arendt, H. 1958: *The Human Condition*. Chicago: University of Chicago Press.

Arnason, J. 1997: *Social Theory and Japanese Experience: The Dual Civilization*. London: Kegan Paul International.

Arnold, M. [1869/1875] 1960: *Culture and Anarchy*. Cambridge: Cambridge University Press.

Aronowitz, S. and Cutler, J. (eds) 1998: *Post-Work*. London: Routledge.

Axford, B. 1995: *The Global System: Economics, Politics and Culture*. Cambridge: Polity.

Barber, B. 1996: *Jihad vs McWorld*. New York: Ballatine.

Barthes, R. 1973: *Mythologies*. London: Granada.

Baudrillard, J. 1980: 'The Implosion of Meaning in the Media and The Implosion of the Social in the Masses'. In K. Woodward (ed.), *The Myths of Information: Technology and Postindustrial Culture*. London: Routledge and Kegan Paul.

Baudrillard, J. 1983: *In the Shadow of the Silent Majorities . . . or The End of the Social and Other Essays*. New York: Semiotext(e).

Bauman, Z. 1973: *Culture as Praxis*. London: Routledge.

Bauman, Z. 1987: *Legislators and Interpreters: On Modernity, Postmodernity and Intellectuals*. Cambridge: Polity.

Bauman, Z. 1989: *Modernity and the Holocaust*. Cambridge: Polity.

Bauman, Z. 1991: *Modernity and Ambivalence*. Cambridge: Polity.

Bauman, Z. 1992: *Intimations of Postmodernity*. London: Routledge.

Bauman, Z. 1993: *Postmodern Ethics*. Oxford: Blackwell.

Bauman, Z. 1995: *Life in Fragments: Essays in Postmodern Morality*. Oxford: Blackwell.

Bauman, Z. 1996: 'Morality in the Age of Contingency'. In P. Heelas, S. Lash and P. Morris (eds), *Detraditionalization*. Cambridge: Polity.

Bauman, Z. 1997: *Postmodernity and its Discontents*. Cambridge: Polity.

Bayle, P. [1667] 1965: *Historical and Critical Dictionary: Selections*. Indianapolis: Bobbs-Merrill.

Beck, U. 1992a: *Risk Society: Towards a New Modernity*. London: Sage.

Beck, U. 1992b: 'From Industrial Society to the Risk Society'. In M. Featherstone (ed.), *Cultural Theory and Cultural Change*. London: Sage.

Beck, U. 1994: 'The Reinvention of Politics: Towards a Theory of Reflexive Modernization'. In U. Beck, A. Giddens and S. Lash, *Reflexive Modernization*. Cambridge: Polity.

Beck, U. 1995a: *Ecological Politics in an Age of Risk*. Cambridge: Polity.

Beck, U. 1995b: *Ecological Enlightenment*. New Jersey: Humanities Press.

Beck, U. 1996a: *The Reinvention of Politics: Rethinking Modernity in the Global Social Order*. Cambridge: Polity.

Beck, U. 1996b: 'Risk Society and the Provident State'. In S. Lash, B. Szerszynski and B. Wynne (eds), *Risk, Environment and Modernity*. London: Sage.

Beck, U. 1996c: 'World Risk Society as Cosmopolitan Society?', *Theory, Culture and Society*, 13, 4, 1–32.

Beck, U. and Beck-Gernsheim, E. [1990] 1994: *The Normal Chaos of Love*. Cambridge: Polity.

Beck, U., Giddens, A. and Lash, S. 1994: *Reflexive Modernization*. Cambridge: Polity.

Bell, D. 1960: *The End of Ideology: On the Exhaustion of Political Ideas in the Fifties*. New York: Free Press.

Bell, D. 1979: *The Cultural Contradictions of Capitalism*. London: Heinemann.

Berger, P. and Luckmann, T. [1966] 1984: *The Social Construction of Reality*. Harmondsworth: London.

Berman, M. 1982: *All that is Solid Melts into Air: The Experience of Modernity*. London: New Left Books.

Berry, C. 1997: *Social Theory and the Scottish Enlightenment*. Edinburgh: Edinburgh University Press.

Beyer, P. 1994: *Religion and Globalization*. London: Sage.

Bloggs, C. 1993: *Intellectuals and the Crisis of Modernity*. New York: State University of New York Press.

Blumenberg, H. [1966] 1983: *The Legitimacy of the Modern Age*. Cambridge, MA: MIT Press.

Böhme, G. 1997: 'The Structures and Prospects of Knowledge Society', *Social Science Information*, 36, 3, 447–68.

Böhme, G. and Stehr, N. (eds) 1986: *The Knowledge Society*. Dordrecht: Reidel.

Bourdieu, P. 1984: *Distinction: A Social Critique of the Judgement of Taste*. London: Routledge and Kegan Paul.

Bourdieu, P. 1990a: *The Logic of Practice*. Cambridge: Polity.

Bourdieu, P. 1997: *Méditations pascaliennes*. Paris: Editions du Seuil.

Bourdieu, P. and Wacquant, L. 1992: *An Invitation to Reflexive Sociology*. Cambridge: Polity.

Buechler, S. 1995: 'New Social Movement Theories', *The Sociological Quarterly*, 36, 3, 441–64.

Burns, T. 1999: 'The Evolution of Parliaments and Societies in Europe: Challenges and Prospects,' *European Journal of Social Theory*, 2, 3, 167–94.

Burns, T. and Ueberhorst, R. 1988: *Creative Democracy*. New York: Praeger.

Bürger, P. 1984: *Theory of the Avant-Garde*. Manchester: Manchester University Press.

Calhoun, C. 1995: *Critical Theory of Society*. Oxford: Blackwell.

Calhoun, C. (ed.) 1993: *Habermas and the Public Sphere*. Cambridge, MA: MIT Press.

Calinescu, M. 1987: *Five Faces of Modernity*. Durham: Duke University Press.

Castells, M. 1996: *The Information Age*, vol. 1: *The Rise of the Network Society*. Oxford: Blackwell.

Castells, M. 1997: *The Information Age*, vol. 2: *The Power of Identity*. Oxford: Blackwell.

Castells, M. 1998: *The Information Age*, vol. 3: *End of Millennium*. Oxford: Blackwell.

Castoriadis, C. [1975] 1987: *The Imaginary Institution of Society*. Cambridge: Polity Press.

Castoriadis, C. 1994: 'The Radical Imaginary and the Social Imaginary'. In G. Robinson and J. Rundell (eds), *Rethinking Imagination*. London: Routledge.

Castoriadis, C. 1997: *World in Fragments: Writings on Politics, Society, Psychoanalysis, and the Imagination*. Stanford: Stanford University Press.

Cohen, I. 1996: 'Theories of Action and Praxis'. In B. Turner (ed.), *The Blackwell Companion to Social Theory*. Oxford: Blackwell.

Cohen, J. and Arato, A. 1992: *Civil Society and Political Theory*. Cambridge, MA: MIT Press.

Collins, R. 1998: *The Sociology of Philosophies: A Global Theory of Intellectual Change*. Cambridge, MA: Harvard University Press.

Critchley, S. 1998: 'The Other's Decision in Me (What are the Politics of Friendship?)', *European Journal of Social Theory*, 1, 2, 259–79.

Crook, S., Pakulski, J. and Waters, M. 1992: *Postmodernization: Change in Advanced Society*. London: Sage.

Dallmayr, F. 1996: *Beyond Orientalism: Essays on Cross-Cultural Encounter*. New York: State University of New York Press.

Dalton, R. and Kuechler, M. (eds) 1990: *Challenging the Political Order: New Social and Political Movements in Western Democracies*. Oxford: Oxford University Press.

Delanty, G. 1995a: *Inventing Europe: Idea, Identity, Reality*. London: Macmillan.

Delanty, G. 1995b: 'The Limits and Possibility of a European Identity: A Critique of Cultural Essentialism', *Philosophy and Social Criticism*, 21, 4, 15–36.

Delanty, G. 1996a: 'The Frontier and Identities of Exclusion in European History', *History of European Ideas*, 22, 2, 93–103.

Delanty, G. 1996b. 'The Resonance of Mitteleurope: A Habsburg Myth or Antipolitics?', *Theory, Culture and Society*, 13, 4, 93–108.

Delanty, G. 1996c. 'Habermas and Postnational Identity: Theoretical Perspectives on the Conflict in Northern Ireland', *Irish Political Studies*, 11, 20–32.

Delanty, G. 1996d: 'Northern Ireland in a Europe of Regions', *Political Quarterly*, 67, 2, 127–34.

Delanty, G. 1997a: 'Models of Citizenship: Defining European Identity and Citizenship', *Citizenship Studies*, 1, 3, 285–303.

Delanty, G. 1997b: 'Habermas and Occidental Rationalism: Moral Learning, the Politics of Identity and the Cultural Limits of Ethical Universalism', *Sociological Theory*, 15, 1, 30–59.

Delanty, G. 1997c: *Social Science: Beyond Constructivism and Realism*. Buckingham: Open University Press.

Delanty, G. 1997d: 'Towards a Postnational Europe? The Future of Democracy and the Crisis of the Nation-State'. In P. Nemo (ed.), *The European Union and the Nation-State*. Paris: ESCP Press.

Delanty, G. 1997e: 'Beyond the Nation-State', *Sociological Research Online*, 1, 2, <http://socresonline.org.uk/socresonline/1/3/1.html>

Delanty, G. 1997f: 'Social Exclusion and the New Nationalism', *Innovation*, 10, 2, 127–43.

Delanty, G. 1998a: 'The Idea of the University in the Global Era: From Knowledge as an End to the End of Knowledge', *Social Epistemology*, 10, 1, 3–25.

Delanty, G. 1998b: 'Rethinking the University: The Autonomy, Contestation and Reflexivity of Knowledge', *Social Epistemology*, 10, 1, 103–13.

Delanty, G. 1998c: 'Biotechnology in the Risk Society'. In P. O' Mahony (ed.), *Nature, Risk and Responsibility: Discourses of Biotechnology*. London: Macmillan.

Delanty, G: 1998d: 'Reinventing Community and Citizenship in the Global Era: A Critique of the Communitarian Concept of Community'. In E. Christodoulidis (ed.), *Communitarianism and Citizenship*. Aldershot: Ashgate.

Delanty, G. 1998e: 'Redefining Political Culture in Europe Today: From Identity to the Politics of Identity'. In U. Hedtoft (ed.), *Political Symbols, Symbolic Politics: Europe Between Unity and Fragmentation*. Aldershot: Ashgate.

Delanty, G. 1999: 'The Foundations of Social Theory'. In B. Turner (ed.), *The Blackwell Companion to Social Theory*, 2nd revised edition. Oxford: Blackwell.

De Mey, M. 1982: *The Cognitive Paradigm*. Dordrecht: Reidel.

Derrida, J. 1977: *Of Grammatology*. Baltimore: Johns Hopkins University Press.

Derrida, J. 1978: *Writing and Difference*. London: Routledge and Kegan Paul.

Derrida, J. 1992: 'Mocholos; or, The Conflict of the Faculties'. In R. Rand (ed.), *Logomachia: The Conflict of the Faculties*. Lincoln: University of Nebraska Press.

Derrida, J. 1993: *Spectres of Marx*. London: Routledge.

Derrida, J. 1997: *The Politics of Friendship*. London: Verso.

de Vries, H. and Weber, S. (eds) 1997: *Violence, Identity and Self-Determination*. Stanford: Stanford University Press.

Dewey, J. 1927: *The Public and its Problems*. New York: Henry Holt.

Douglas, M. and Wildavsky, A. 1982: *Risk and Culture: An Essay on the Selection of Technical and Environmental Dangers*. Berkeley: University of California Press.

Dryzek, J. S. 1990: *Discursive Democracy: Politics, Policy and Political Science*. Cambridge: Cambridge University Press.

Dunn, J. (ed.) 1995: *Contemporary Crisis of the Nation-State*. Oxford: Blackwell.

Durkheim, E. [1912] 1915: *The Elementary Forms of The Religious Life*. London: Allen and Unwin.

Durkheim, E. 1975: *Suicide: A Study in Sociology*. London: Routledge and Kegan Paul.

Eder, K. 1985: *Geschichte als Lernprozess? Zur Pathogenese politischer Modernität in Deutschland.* Frankfurt: Surhkamp.

Eder, K. 1992: 'Contradictions and Social Evolution: A Theory of the Social Evolution of Modernity'. In H. Haferkamp and N. Smelser (eds), *Social Change and Modernity.* Berkeley: University of California Press.

Eder, K. 1996a: *The Social Construction of Nature.* London: Sage.

Eder, K. 1996b: 'The Institutionalization of Environmentalism: Ecological Discourse and the Second Transformation of the Public Sphere'. In S. Lash, B. Szerszynski and B. Wynne (eds), *Risk, Environment and Modernity.* London: Sage.

Eder, K. 1999: 'Societies Learn and Yet the World is Hard to Change', *European Journal of Social Theory*, 2, 2, 195–215.

Eisenstadt, S. N. 1992: 'A Reappraisal of Theories of Social Change and Modernization'. In H. Haferkamp and N. Smelser (eds), *Social Change and Modernity.* Berkeley: University of California Press.

Eisenstadt, S. N. 1998: 'The Construction of Collective Identity – Some Analytical and Comparative Indications', *European Journal of Social Theory*, 1, 2, 229–54.

Elias, N. 1978: *The Civilizing Process*, vol. 1: *The History of Manners.* New York: Pantheon.

Elias, N. 1982: *The Civilizing Process*, vol. 2: *State Formation and Civilization.* Oxford: Blackwell.

Elias, N. 1987: 'The Retreat of the Sociologists into the Present', *Theory, Culture and Society*, 4, 223–48.

Eriksson, B. 1993: 'The First Formulation of Sociology: A Discursive Innovation of the 18th Century', *European Journal of Sociology*, 34, 251–76.

Esposito, J. (ed.) 1983: *Voices of Resurgent Islam.* Oxford: Oxford University Press.

Eyerman, R. 1994: *Between Culture and Politcs: Intellectuals in Modern Society.* Cambridge: Polity.

Eyerman, R. and Jamison, A. 1991: *Social Movements: A Cognitive Approach.* Cambridge: Polity.

Featherstone, M., Lash, S. and Robertson, R. (eds) 1995: *Global Modernities.* London: Sage.

Foucault, M. [1966] 1970: *The Order of Things.* London: Tavistock.

Foucault, M. [1969] 1972: *The Archaeology of Knowledge.* London: Tavistock.

Foucault, M. 1977: *Language, Counter-Memory, Practice: Selected Essays and Interviews*, ed. D. Bouchard. Oxford: Blackwell.

Foucault, M. 1980a: *History of Sexuality*, vol. 1. London: Penguin.

Foucault, M. 1980b: *Power/Knowledge: Selected Interviews and Other Writings, 1972–1977*, ed. C. Gordon. New York: Pantheon Books.

Foucault, M. 1982: 'The Subject and Power'. In H. Dreffus and P. Rabinow (eds), *Michel Foucault: Beyond Structuralism and Hermeneutics.* Brighton: Harvester Press.

Fraser, N. 1995: 'Politics, Culture, and the Public Sphere: Toward a Postmodern Conception'. In L. Nicholson and S. Seidman (eds), *Social Postmodernism: Beyond Identity Politics.* Cambridge: Cambridge University Press.

200                                    *Bibliography*

Friese, H. and Wagner, P. 1999: 'Inescapability and Attainability in the Sociology of Modernity', *European Journal of Social Theory*, 2, 1, 27–44.
Frisby, D. 1984: *Georg Simmel*. London: Routledge.
Frisby, D. 1986: *Fragments of Modernity*. Cambridge, MA: MIT Press.
Fukuyama, F. 1992: *The End of History and the Last Man*. Harmondsworth: Penguin.
Fuller, S. 1984: 'The Cognitive Turn in Sociology', *Erkenntnis*, 74, 439–50.
Fuller, S. 1993: *Philosophy, Rhetoric, and the End of Knowledge*. Madison: University of Wisconsin Press.
Furlong, A. and Cartmel, F. 1997: *Young People and Social Change: Individualization and Risk in Late Modernity*. Buckingham: Open University Press.
Gellner, E. 1981: *Muslim Society*. Cambridge: Cambridge University Press.
Gibbons, M. et al. 1994: *The New Production of Knowledge*. London: Sage.
Giddens, A. 1976: *New Rules of Sociological Method*. London: Hutchinson.
Giddens, A. 1981: *A Contemporary Critique of Historical Materialism*, vol. 1: *Power, Property and the State*. London: Macmillan.
Giddens, A. 1984: *The Constitution of Society: Outline of a Theory of Structuration*. Cambridge: Polity.
Giddens, A. 1985: *A Contemporary Critique of Historical Materialism*, vol. 2: *The Nation-State and Violence*. Cambridge: Polity.
Giddens, A. 1990: *The Consequences of Modernity*. Cambridge: Polity.
Giddens, A. 1991: *Modernity and Self-Identity*. Cambridge: Polity.
Giddens, A. 1992: *The Transformation of Intimacy: Sexuality, Love and Eroticism in Modern Societies*. Cambridge: Polity.
Giddens, A. 1994a: *Beyond Left and Right: The Future of Radical Politics*. Cambridge: Polity.
Giddens, A. 1994b: 'Living in a Post-Traditional Society'. In U. Beck, A. Giddens and S. Lash, *Reflexive Modernization*. Cambridge: Polity.
Giddens, A. 1996: *In Defence of Sociology*. Cambridge: Polity.
Giddens, A. 1998: *The Third Way*. Cambridge: Polity.
Haas, P. (ed.) 1992: 'Epistemic Communities and International Policy Coordination', *International Organization*, 46, 1, 1–36.
Habermas, J. [1973] 1976: *Legitimation Crisis*. London: Heinemann.
Habermas, J. [1968] 1978: *Knowledge and Human Interests*. London: Heinemann.
Habermas, J. [1976] 1979: *Communication and the Evolution of Society*. London: Heinemann.
Habermas, J. 1981: 'Modernity and Postmodernity', *New German Critique*, 22, 3–14.
Habermas, J. [1981] 1984: *The Theory of Communicative Action*, vol. 1: *Reason and the Rationalization of Society*. London: Heinemann.
Habermas, J. 1985: 'Questions and Counter-Questions'. In R. Bernstein (ed.), *Habermas and Modernity*. Cambridge: Polity.
Habermas, J. [1981] 1987a: *The Theory of Communicative Action*, vol. 2: *Lifeworld and System: A Critique of Functionalist Reason*. Cambridge: Polity.
Habermas, J. 1987b: *The Philosophical Discourse of Modernity*. Cambridge: Polity.

Habermas, J. 1988: 'Law and Morality'. In S. M. McMurrin (ed.), *The Tanner Lectures VIII*. Cambridge: Cambridge University Press.

Habermas, J. [1962] 1989a: *The Structural Transformation of the Public Sphere*. Cambridge: Polity.

Habermas, J. 1989b: 'The New Obscurity'. In *The New Conservatism: Cultural Criticism and the Historians' Debate*. Cambridge, MA: MIT Press.

Habermas, J. 1990: *Moral Consciousness and Communicative Action*. Cambridge: Polity.

Habermas, J. 1991: 'What does Socialism Mean Today?'. In R. Blackburn (ed.), *After the Fall: The Failure of Communism and the Future of Socialism*. London: Verso.

Habermas, J. 1992a: *Autonomy and Solidarity*. In P. Dews (ed.), revised edition; interviews with Jürgen Habermas. London: Verso.

Habermas, J. 1992b. 'Citizenship and National Identity: Some Reflections on the Future of Europe', *Praxis International*, 12, 1, 1–19. Republished in Habermas (1996a).

Habermas, J. 1992c: *Postmetaphysical Thinking*. Cambridge: Polity.

Habermas, J. 1994. 'Europe's Second Chance'. In M. Pensky (ed.), *The Past as Future*. Cambridge: Polity.

Habermas, J. 1995: 'On the Internal Relationship Between Law and Democracy', *European Journal of Philosophy*, 3, 1, 12–20.

Habermas, J. [1992] 1996a: *Between Facts and Norms: Contributions to a Discourse Theory of Law and Democracy*. Cambridge: Polity.

Habermas, J. 1996b: 'An Interview with Jürgen Habermas'. Interviewed by M. Carleheden and R. Gabriels, *Theory, Culture and Society*, 13, 3, 1–17.

Habermas, J. 1998: *The Inclusion of the Other: Studies in Political Theory*. Cambridge: Polity.

Habermas, J. and Luhmann, N. 1971: *Theorie der Gesellschaft oder Sozialtechnologie*. Frankfurt: Suhrkamp.

Haferkamp, H. and Smelser, N. (eds) 1992: *Social Change and Modernity*. Berkeley: University of California Press.

Hall, J. (ed.) 1995: *Civil Society: Theory, History, Comparisons*. Cambridge: Polity.

Harvey, D. 1990: *The Condition of Postmodernity*. Cambridge: Polity.

Heilbron, J., Magnusson, C. and Wittrock, B. (eds) 1998: *The Rise of the Social Sciences and the Formation of Modernity*. Dordrecht: Kluwer.

Heilbron, J. 1999: 'Reflexivity and its Consequences', *European Journal of Social Theory*, 2, 3.

Held, D. 1996: *Models of Democracy*, 2nd edition. Cambridge: Polity.

Held, D. and Thompson, J. 1989: *Social Theory and Modern Societies: Anthony Giddens and his Critics*. Cambridge: Polity.

Hilton, R. (ed.) 1978: *The Transition from Feudalism to Capitalism*. London: Verso.

Hirst P. and Thompson, G. 1996: *Globalization in Question*. Cambridge: Polity.

Hobsbawm, E. and Ranger, T. (eds) 1983: *The Invention of Tradition*. Cambridge: Cambridge University Press.

Hohendahl, P. 1979: 'Critical Theory, Public Sphere and Culture: Jürgen Habermas and his Critics', *New German Critique*, 16, 89–118.

Holland, D. and Quinn, N. (eds) 1991: *Cultural Models in Language and Thought*. Cambridge: Cambridge University Press.

Holton, R. 1985: *The Transition from Feudalism to Capitalism*. London: Macmillan.

Honneth, A. 1991: *Critique of Power*. Cambridge, MA: MIT Press.

Honneth, A. 1995a: *The Struggle for Recognition*. Cambridge: Polity.

Honneth, A. 1995b: *The Fragmented World of The Social: Essays in Social and Political Philosophy*. New York: State University of New York Press.

Honneth, A. 1999: 'Reply to Kalyvas'. *European Journal of Social Theory*, 2, 3.

Horowitz, A. and Manley, T. (eds) 1994: *The Barbarism of Reason: Max Weber and the Twilight of Disenchantment*. Toronto: Toronto University Press.

Inglehart, R. 1977: *The Silent Revolution: Changing Values and Political Styles Among Western Publics*. Princeton: Princeton University Press.

Jackall, R. and Vidich, A. (eds) 1995: *Social Movements: Critiques, Concepts, Case-Studies*. London: Macmillan.

Jacobsen, D. 1997: *Right Across Borders: Immigration and the Decline of Citizenship*. Baltimore: Johns Hopkins University Press.

Jameson, F. 1971: *Marxism and Form*. New Haven: Princeton University Press.

Jameson, F. 1991: *Postmodernism. Or, The Cultural Logic of Late Capitalism*. London: Verso.

Janoski, T. 1998: *Citizenship and Civil Society*. Cambridge University Press.

Jay, M. 1984: *Marxism and Totality: The Adventures of a Concept from Luckás to Habermas*. Berkeley: California University Press.

Joas, H. 1998: 'Bauman in Germany', *Theory, Culture and Society*, 15, 1, 47–55.

Joas, H. 1996: *The Creativity of Action*. Cambridge: Polity.

Joas, H. 1998: 'The Meadian Heritage and the Postmodern Challenge', *European Journal of Social Theory*, 1, 1, 7–18.

Jonas, H. 1984: *The Imperative of Responsibility: In Search of an Ethics for the Technological Age*. Chicago: University of Chicago Press.

Jonas, H. 1994: 'Philosophy at the End of the Century: A Survey of its Past and Future', *Social Research*, 61, 4.

Kalyvas, A. 1999: 'Critical Theory at the Crossroads: Comments on Axel Honneth's Theory of Recognition', *European Journal of Social Theory*, 2, 2, 99–108.

Kant, I. [1798] 1978: *The Conflict of the Faculties*. New York: Abaris Books.

Kant, I. [1784] 1995: 'What is Enlightenment?' In I. Kramnick (ed.), *The Portable Enlightenment Reader*. Harmondsworth: Penguin.

Keane, J. (ed.) 1988a: *Civil Society and the State*. London: Verso.

Keane, J. 1988b: *Democracy and Civil Society*. London: Verso.

Kellner, D. 1998: 'Zygmunt Bauman's Postmodern Turn', *Theory, Culture and Society*, 15, 1, 73–86.

Kelly, M. (ed.) 1994: *Critique and Power: Recasting the Foucault/Habermas Debate*. Cambridge, MA: MIT Press.

Klandermans, B., Kriesi, H. and Tarrow, S. (eds) 1988: *From Structure to Action: Comparing Social Movement Research Across Cultures*. International Social Movement Research, vol. 1. Greenwich, CT: JAI Press.

Koselleck, R. [1959] 1988: *Critique and Crisis: Enlightenment and the Pathogenesis of Modern Society*. Oxford: Berg.

Kuhn, T. (1970): *The Structure of Scientic Knowledge*. 2nd edition. Chicago: Chicago University Press.

Kumar, K. 1995: *From Post-Industrial to Post-Modern Society*. Oxford: Blackwell.

Kurasawa, F. 1999: 'The Exotic Effect: Foucault and the Question of Cultural Other', *European Journal of Social Theory*, 2, 2, 147–65.

Landes, J. 1988: *Women and the Public Sphere in the Age of the French Revolution*. Ithaca: Cornell University Press.

Larrain, J. 1994: *Ideology and Cultural Identity: Modernity and the Third World Presence*. Cambridge: Polity.

Larrana, E., Johnson, H. and Gusfield, J. (eds) 1994: *New Social Movements: From Ideology to Identity*. Philadelphia: Temple University Press.

Lash, S. 1990: *Sociology of Postmodernism*. London: Routledge.

Lash, S. 1994: 'Reflexivity and its Doubles: Structure, Aesthetics, Community'. In U. Beck, A. Giddens and S. Lash, *Reflexive Modernization*. Cambridge: Polity.

Lash, S. and Friedman, J. (ed.) 1992: *Modernity and Identity*. Oxford: Blackwell.

Lash, S. and Urry, J. 1987: *The End of Organized Capitalism*. Cambridge: Polity.

Lash, S. and Urry, J. 1994: *Economies of Signs and Space*. London: Sage.

Lefort, C. 1986: *The Political Forms of Modern Society*. Cambridge: Polity.

Lepenies, W. 1988: *Between Literature and Science: The Rise of Sociology*. Cambridge: Cambridge University Press.

Lockwood, D. 1964: 'Social Integration and System Integration'. In G. Zollschan and W. Hirsch (eds), *Explorations in Social Change*. London: Routledge.

Luhmann, N. 1982: *The Differentiation of Societies*. New York: Columbia University Press.

Luhmann, N. 1990: *Political Theory and the Welfare State*. Berlin: Walter de Gruyter.

Luhmann, N. 1992: 'The Direction of Evolution'. In H. Haferkamp and N. Smelser (eds), *Social Change and Modernity*. Berkeley: University of California Press.

Luhmann, N. 1993: *Risk: A Sociological Theory*. New York: de Gruyter.

Luhmann, N. 1995: *Social Systems*. Stanford: Stanford University Press.

Luhmann, N. [1992] 1998: *Observations on Modernity*, Stanford: Stanford University Press.

Lury, C. 1993: *Cultural Rights*. London: Routledge.

Lyotard, J.-F. [1979] 1984: *The Postmodern Condition: A Report on Knowledge*. Manchester: Manchester University Press.

McCarthy, D. E. 1996: *Knowledge as Culture: The New Sociology of Knowledge*. London: Routledge.

Maffesoli, S. 1996: *The Time of the Tribes*. London: Sage.

Majone, G. 1996: *Regulating Europe*. London: Routledge.

Mannheim, K. [1929] 1936: *Ideology and Utopia*. London: Routledge and Kegan Paul.

Marcuse, H. 1964: *One Dimensional Man*. London: Routledge and Kegan Paul.

Mardin, S. 1995: 'Civil Society and Islam'. In J. Hall (ed.), *Civil Society: Theory, History, Comparison*. Cambridge: Polity.

Marshall, T. H. [1950] 1992: *Citizenship and Social Class*, ed. T. Bottomore. London: Pluto Press.

Mayer, A. 1981: *The Persistence of the Old Regime*. London: Croom Helm.

Mayhew, L. 1997: *The New Public: Professional Communication and the Means of Social Influence*. Cambridge: Cambridge University Press.

Mehmet, O. 1990: *Islamic Identity and Development: Studies of the Islamic Periphery*. London: Routledge.

Melucci, A. 1989: *Nomads of the Present: Social Movements and Individual Needs in Contemporary Society*. London: Hutchinson.

Melucci, A. 1996a: *Challenging Codes: Collective Action in the Information Age*. Cambridge: Cambridge University Press.

Melucci, A. 1996b: *The Playing Self: Person and Meaning in the Planetary Age*. Cambridge: Cambridge University Press.

Melucci, A. and Lyyra, T. 1997: 'Collective Action, Change, and Democracy: Do Social Movements Still Matter?' In M. Guigni et al. (eds), *How Social Movements Matter: Theoretical and Comparative Studies on the Consequences of Social Movements*. Minneapolis: University of Minnesota Press.

Merton, R. 1949: *Social Theory and Social Structure*. Glencoe: Free Press.

Meyrowitz, J. 1986: *No Sense of Place: The Impact of Electronic Media on Social Behaviour*. Oxford: Oxford University Press.

Midgley, M. 1989: *Wisdom, Information and Wisdom. What is Knowledge For?* London: Routledge.

Miller, M. 1986: *Kollektive Lernprozesse: Studien zur Grundlegung einer soziologischen Lerntheorie*. Frankfurt: Suhrkamp.

Milward, A. 1992: *The European Rescue of the Nation-State*. London: Routledge.

Milward, A. et al. 1993: *The Frontier of National Sovereignty*. London: Routledge.

Moore, B. 1978: *Injustice: The Social Bases of Obedience and Revolt*. London: Macmillan.

Morris, A. and McClurg, M. (eds) 1992: *Frontiers in Social Movement Theory*. New Haven: Yale University Press.

Moscovici, S. 1977: 'The Reenchantment of the World'. In Norman Birnbaum (ed.), *Beyond the Crisis*. Oxford: Oxford University Press.

Moscovici, S. 1993: *The Invention of Society*. Cambridge: Polity.

Mouzelis, N. 1997: 'Social and System Integration: Lockwood, Habermas, Giddens', *Sociology*, 31, 1, 111–19.

Münch, R. 1990: 'Differentiation, Rationalization, Interpenetration: The Emergence of Modern Society'. In J. Alexander and P. Colomy (eds), *Differentiation Theory and Social Change*. New York: Columbia University Press.

Münch, R. and Smelser, N. (eds) 1992: *Theory of Culture*. Berkeley: University of California Press.

Nicholson, L. and Seidman, S. (eds) 1995: *Social Postmodernism: Beyond Identity Politics*. Cambridge: Polity.

Nowotny, H. 1973: 'On the Feasibility of a Cognitive Approach to the Study of Science', *Zeitschrift für Soziologie*, 2, 3, 282–96.

Offe, C. 1985: *Disorganized Capitalism*. Cambridge: Polity.

O'Mahony, P. and Delanty, G. 1998: *Rethinking Irish History: Ideology, Identity and Nationalism*. London: Macmillan.

O'Neill, J. 1995: *The Poverty of Postmodernism*. London: Routledge.
O'Neill, J. 1999: 'What Gives (with Derrida)?', *European Journal of Social Theory*, 2, 2.
Ortega y Gasset, J. [1930] 1932: *The Revolt of the Masses*. New York: Norton.
Outhwaite, W. 1999: 'Myth of Modernity Method', *European Journal of Social Theory*, 2, 1, 5–25.
Pahl, R. 1995: *After Success: Fin-de-Siècle Anxiety and Identity*. Cambridge: Polity.
Peters, B. 1993: *Die Integration moderner Gesellschaften*. Frankfurt: Suhrkamp.
Piaget, J. 1970: *Genetic Epistemology*. New York: Columbia University Press.
Polanyi, K. [1944] 1980: *The Great Transformation*. New York: Octagon Books.
Rand, R. (ed.) 1992: *Logomachia: The Conflict of the Faculties*. Lincoln: University of Nebraska Press.
Rengger, N. 1995: *Political Theory, Modernity and Postmodernity*. Oxford: Blackwell.
Ricoeur, P. 1977: *The Rule of Metaphor*. Toronto: University of Toronto Press.
Robertson, R. 1992: *Globalization: Social Theory and Global Culture*. London: Sage.
Rojek, C. and Turner, B. (eds) 1993: *Forget Baudrillard?* London: Routledge.
Rorty, R. 1979: *Philosophy and the Mirror of Nature*. Oxford: Blackwell.
Rundel, J. 1987: *Origins of Modernity*. Cambridge: Polity.
Santos, B. S. 1995: *Toward a New Common Sense: Law, Science and Politcs in the Paradigmatic Transition*. London: Routledge.
Sassen, S. 1996: *Losing Control? Sovereignty in an Age of Globalization*. New York: Columbia University Press.
Sayyid, B. 1994: 'Sign O' Times: Kaffirs and Infidels Fighting the Ninth Crusade'. In E. Laclau (ed.), *The Making of Political Identities*. London: Verso.
Scheler, M. [1924] 1980: *Problems of a Sociology of Knowledge*. London: Routledge and Kegan Paul.
Seidman, S. 1998: *Contested Knowledges*, 2nd edition. Oxford: Blackwell.
Sennett, R. 1977: *The Fall of Public Man*. Cambridge: Cambridge University Press.
Shari'ati, A. 1980: *Marxism and Other Western Fallacies: An Islamic Critique*. Berkeley: Mizan Press.
Simmel, G. [1914] 1968: 'The Concept and Tragedy of Culture'. In *The Conflict in Modern Culture and Other Essays*. New York: Teachers College Press.
Simmel, G. [1918] 1971a: 'The Conflict in Modern Culture'. In *On Individuality and Social Forms*. Chicago: University of Chicago Press.
Simmel, G. [1903] 1971b: 'The Metropolis and Mental Life'. In *On Individuality and Social Forms*. Chicago: University of Chicago Press.
Simmel, G. [1907] 1978: *The Philosophy of Money*. London: Routledge and Kegan Paul.
Simons, J. 1995: *Foucault and the Political*. London: Routledge.
Smart, B. 1992: *Modern Conditions, Postmodern Controversies*. London: Routledge.
Somers, M. 1995: 'Narratives and Naturalizing Civil Society and Citizenship Theory', *Theory, Culture and Society*, 13, 3, 229–74.
Soysal, Y. N. 1994: *Limits of Citizenship: Migrants and Postnational Membership in Europe*. Chicago: University of Chicago Press.

Spengler, A. [1918] 1971: *The Decline of the West*. London: Allen and Unwin.

Stehr, N. 1992: *Knowledge Societies*. London: Sage.

Strydom, P. 1987: 'Collective Learning: Habermas's Concessions and Their Implications', *Philosophy and Social Criticism*, 13, 3, 265–81.

Strydom, P. 1992: 'The Ontogenetic Fallacy: The Immanent Critique of Habermas's Developmental Logical Theory of Evolution', *Theory, Culture and Society*, 9, 65–93.

Strydom, P. 1993: 'Sociocultural Evolution or the Social Evolution of Practical Reason?: Eder's Critique of Habermas', *Praxis International*, 13, 3, 304–22.

Strydom, P. 1997: 'Cultural Models in Social Theory: Alexander and Smith on "Risk Society"'. Unpublished ms.

Strydom, P. 1998: 'The Civilization of the Gene'. In P. O'Mahony (ed.), *Nature, Risk and Responsibility: Discourses of Biotechnology*. London: Macmilllan.

Strydom, P. 1999a: 'Hermeneutic Culturalism and its Double: A Key Problem in the Reflexive Modernization Debate', *European Journal of Social Theory*, 2, 1, 45–69.

Strydom, P. 1999b: 'Triple Contingency: The Theoretical Problem of the Public in Communication Societies', *Philosophy and Social Criticism*, 25, 2, 1–25.

Sugimoto, Y. and Arnason, J. (eds) 1990: *Japanese Encounters with Postmodernity*. London: Kegan Paul International.

Swidler, A. 1986: 'Culture in Action. Symbols and Strategies', *American Sociological Review*, 51, 273–86.

Swidler, A. 1995: 'The Cultural Analysis of Social Movements'. In H. Johnson and B. Klandermans (eds), *Social Movements and Culture*. London: UCL Press.

Szakloczai, A. 1998: 'Reflexive Historical Sociology', *European Journal of Sociology*, 1, 2, 209–27.

Sztompka, P. 1998: 'Trust, Distrust and Two Paradoxes of Democracy', *European Journal of Social Theory*, 1, 1, 19–32.

Tarrow, S. 1995: *Power in Movement: Social Movements, Collective Action and Politics*. Cambridge: Cambridge University Press.

Taylor, C. (ed.) 1994: *Multiculturalism: Examining the Politics of Recognition*. Princeton: Princeton University Press.

Therborn, G. 1995a: 'Routes to/through Modernity'. In M. Featherstone, S. Lash and R. Robertson (eds), *Global Modernities*. London: Sage.

Therborn, G. 1995b: *Beyond European Modernity*. London: Sage.

Thompson, E. P. 1968: *The Making of the English Working Class*. Harmondsworth: Penguin.

Thompson, J. B: 1995: *The Media and Modernity: A Social Theory of the Media*. Cambridge: Polity Press.

Tönnies, F. 1957: *Community and Society*. East Lansing, MI: Michigan University Press.

Toulmin, S. 1992: *Cosmopolis: The Hidden Agenda of Modernity*. Chicago: Chicago University Press.

Touraine, A. [1969] 1971a: *The May Movement: Revolt and Reform*. New York: Random House.

Touraine, A. [1969] 1971b: *Post-Industrial Society*. New York: Random House.
Touraine, A. [1973] 1977: *The Self-Production of Society*. Chicago: Chicago University Press.
Touraine, A. [1978] 1981: *The Voice and the Eye: An Analysis of Social Movements*. Cambridge: Cambridge University Press.
Touraine, A. 1985: 'An Introduction to the Study of Social Movements', *Social Research*, 52, 749–87.
Touraine, A. [1984] 1988: *Return of the Actor: Social Theory in Post-Industrial Society*. Minneapolis: University of Minnesota Press.
Touraine, A. 1992a: 'Two Interpretations of Contemporary Social Change'. In H. Haferkamp and N. Smelser (eds), *Social Change and Modernity*. Berkeley: University of California Press.
Touraine, A. 1992b: 'Beyond Social Movements', *Theory, Culture and Society*, 9, 125–45.
Touraine, A. 1994: 'European Countries in a Post-National Era'. In C. Rootes and H. Davis (eds), *Social Change and Political Transformation*. London: UCL Press.
Touraine, A. [1992] 1995a: *Critique of Modernity*. Oxford: Blackwell.
Touraine, A. 1995b: 'Democracy: From a Politics of Citizenship to a Politics of Recognition'. In L. Maheu (eds), *Social Movements and Social Classes*. London: Sage.
Touraine, A. [1994] 1997: *What is Democracy?* Oxford: Westview Press.
Touraine, A. 1998a: 'Sociology without Society', *Current Sociology*, 46, 2, 119–43.
Touraine, A. 1998b: 'Can We Live Together Equal and Different?', *European Journal of Social Theory*, 1, 2, 165–78.
Touraine, A., Dubet, F., Wieviorka, M. and Strzelecki, J. [1982] 1983: *Solidarity: The Analysis of a Social Movement: Poland, 1980–81*. Cambridge: Cambridge University Press.
Touraine, A., Wieviorka, M. and Dubet, F. [1966] 1987: *The Workers' Movement*. Cambridge: Cambridge University Press.
Trend, D. 1997: *Cultural Democracy*. New York: SUNY Press.
Turner, B. (ed.) 1990: *Theories of Modernity and Postmodernity*. London: Sage.
Turner, B. 1994: *Orientalism, Postmodernism and Globalism*. London: Routledge.
Turner, S. (ed.) 1996: *Social Theory and Sociology*. Oxford: Blackwell.
Varela, F., Thompson, E. and Rosch, E. 1997: *The Embodied Mind: Cognitive Science and Human Experience*. Cambridge, MA: MIT Press.
Vattimo, G. 1988: *The End of Modernity*. Cambridge: Polity.
Vattimo, G. 1992: *The Transparent Society*. Cambridge: Polity.
Wagner, P. 1994: *The Sociology of Modernity: Liberty and Discipline*. London: Sage.
Wallerstein, I. 1974: *The Modern World System I: Capitalist Agriculture and the Origins of the European World-Economy in the Sixteenth Century*. New York: Academic.
Wallerstein, I. 1979: *The Capitalist World-Economy*. Cambridge: Cambridge University Press.
Wallerstein, I. 1980: *The Modern World-System II: Mercantilism and the Consolidation of the World Economy, 1650–1750*. New York: Academic.

Wallerstein, I. 1984: *The Politics of the World-Economy: The States, the Movements and the Civilization*. Cambridge: Cambridge University Press.

Wallerstein, I. 1991: *Unthinking Social Science: The Limits of Nineteenth-Century Paradigms*. Cambridge: Polity.

Wallerstein, I. 1996: 'Three Ideologies or One? The Pseudo-battle of Modernity'. In S. Turner (ed.), *Social Theory and Sociology*. Oxford: Blackwell.

Wallerstein, I. et al. 1996: *Open the Social Science: Report of the Gulbenkian Commission on the Restructuring of the Social Sciences*. Stanford: Stanford University Press.

Waters, M. 1995: *Globalization*. London: Routledge.

Webster, F. 1995: *Theories of the Information Society*. London: Routledge.

Webster, F. 1997: 'Is this the Information Age? Towards a Critique of Manuel Castells', *The City*, December, 71–84.

Wrong, D. 1994: *The Problem of Order: What Unites and Divides Society?* Cambridge, MA: Harvard University Press.

Wuthnow, R. 1989: *Communities of Discourse: Ideology and Social Structure in the Reformation, the Enlightenment, and European Socialism*. Cambridge, MA: Harvard University Press.

Zolo, D. 1992. *Democracy and Complexity*. Cambridge: Polity.

# Index

Adorno, T.   10, 23, 85, 151, 171
Ahmed, A.   97
AIDS   58, 185
Al-Azmeh, Z.   8
Albrow, M.   52
Alexander, J.   61–3, 170–8
Allen Robertson, B.   96
Althusser, A.   124
American Revolution, the   7, 21, 38
Anderson, B.   27
Anderson, P.   31, 57
Apel, K.-O.   48
Arendt, H.   35, 36, 119
Arnason, J.   5, 70, 97
Arnold, M.   8
Aronowitz, S.   54
Axford, B.   52

Bacon, F.   22
Barber, B.   5, 55
Barthes, R.   102, 139
Baudelaire, C.   8, 111–12, 159
Bauman, Z.   115–20, 132, 180–1
Beck, U.   48, 58, 148–60, 167, 169–78, 180
Beck-Gernsheim, E.   153
Bell, D.   5, 8, 54, 125–6

Benjamin, W.   8, 171
Bentham, J.   105
Berger, P.   13, 67
Berman, M.   2
Berry, C.   31
Beyer, P.   55
Bloggs, C.   36
Blumenberg, H.   20
Böhme, G.   11, 13, 57, 185
Bourdieu, P.   2, 59, 68, 161–2, 173
BSE   58, 185
Bürger, P.   2
Burns, T.   53
Byron, Lord   22

Calhoun, C.   2, 80
Calinescu, M.   2
Cartmel, F.   59
Castells, M.   11, 14, 46, 51, 53, 57, 59, 71, 123, 183–4
Castoriadis, C.   5, 12, 64–5, 105
Chernobyl   149
Chicago School, the   8
Christendom   28
Clinton, W. J. (Bill)   53
Cohen, I.   67
Comte, A.   18
Cutler, J.   54

Delanty, G.   10–11, 31, 40, 48, 53,
    56–7, 59, 153, 184
De Mey, M.   67
Derrida, J.   40, 102–3.
Descartes, R.   22, 25
de Vries, H.   8
Dewey, J.   63–4
Douglas, M.   159
Dunn, J.   52
Durkheim, E.   18–19, 25, 35, 43, 51,
    62, 66, 176, 183

Eder, K.   61, 65–6
Eisenstadt, S. N.   8
Elias, N.   6, 28, 61, 119
Enlightenment, the   1, 7, 11, 18, 38,
    41, 59, 74, 89, 151–2, 179
Eriksson, B.   3, 31
Esposito, J.   96
Eyerman, R.   36, 67

Featherstone, M.   71
Ferguson, A.   31
Foucault, M.   102, 104–9, 132, 139,
    174
Frankfurt School, the   44, 45, 119,
    136, 171
Fraser, N.   80
First World War, the   43
French Revolution, the   7, 21, 38
Freud, S.   43, 44, 135
Frisby, D.   2
Fukuyama, F.   41
Fuller, S.   67
Furlong, A.   59

Garfinkel, H.   67
Gellner, E.   96
Germany   28
Gibbons, M.   57
Giddens, A.   9, 10, 148–9, 158,
    160–78, 180–1
Goethe, W.   22
Gulbenkian Commission,   48

Habermas, J.   5, 32, 35–6, 65, 68,
    73–110, 141–5, 153–6, 162, 169–70,
    180–1, 184, 186.

Hegel, G.   3–4, 20, 24, 179
Heidegger, M.   43
Heilbron, J.   7
Herder, J.   63
Hirst, P.   52
Hobbes, T.   23
Hobsbawm, E.   55
Hohendahl, P.   80
Holland, D.   67
Honneth, A.   45, 115
Horkheimer, M.   23, 85, 151
Humboldt, A. von   34

Iranian Revolution, the   106
Islam   96–7

Jacobsen, D.   53
James, W.   64
Jamison, A.   67
Joas, H.   11, 61, 63–5, 98, 100–1, 108
Joyce, J.   8

Kant, I.   3, 22, 32, 33, 34, 66, 83, 88
Koselleck, R.   43
Koran, the   96
Kurasawa, F.   106

Landes, J.   80
Larrain, J.   56
Lash, S.   51, 54, 170–3
Lévi-Strauss, C.   102
Locke, J.   23
Luckmann, T.   13, 67
Luhmann, N.   6, 51, 76–7, 109,
    132, 137, 139, 157, 165
Lury, C.   53
Lyotard, J.   104, 108–11, 132, 137
Lyyra, T.   145–6

McCarthy, D.   68
McLuhan, M.   112
Maffesoli, S.   46
Mahew, L.   186
Majone, G.   52
Mannheim, K.   12, 66
Marcuse, H.   45, 106
Mardin, S.   96
Marshall, T. H.   31

Marx, K.   2–4, 10, 18–20, 32, 35, 44, 51, 63, 75, 179
Marxism   10, 42, 54, 71, 82, 125, 180
Mayer, A.   31
Mead, G.   24, 35, 63–4
Mehmet, O.   96
Melucci, A.   123, 140–86
Meyrowitz, J.   56
Midgley, M.   184
Millar, J.   31
Montaigne, M. de   31, 35
Montesquieu, Baron de   24, 31, 35
Moore, B.   35
More, T.   30–1
Moscovici, S.   66

Nicholson, L.   113–14, 186
Nietzsche, F.   43–4, 64, 83, 135
Nowotny, H.   67

October Revolution, the   71, 182
Offe, C.   51
Ortega y Gasset, J.   43
Outhwaite, W.   2

Parsons, T.   18, 51, 62
Peirce, C.   64
Peters, B.   47, 50–1
Piaget, J.   67
Polanyi, K.   7

Ranger, T.   55
Reformation, the   18, 21, 38
Rengger, N.   2
Renaissance, the   18, 21, 29, 38
Ricoeur, P.   63, 103
Robertson, R.   52, 71
Rorty, R.   48
Rousseau, J.-J.   22–3, 88

Santos, B. S.   56
Sassen, S.   49, 52
Sayyid, B.   97
Scheler, M.   66
Schopenhauer, A.   64
scientific revolution, the   21, 33
Scottish Enlightenment, the   24, 31, 35

Second World War, the   29, 41
Seidman, S.   113–14, 186
Sennett, R.   35–6
Simmel, G.   6, 8, 35, 43, 64, 163
Simons, J.   106
Smith, A.   32
social Darwinism   29
Soviet Union   41
Soysal, Y.   53
Spencer, H.   18
Spengler, O.   43
Stehr, N.   13, 57, 156
Strydom, P.   9, 14, 48, 65, 67, 68–9, 187
Sugimoto, Y.   97
Szakloczai, A.   2
Sztompka, P.   169

Tarrow, S.   36, 145
Taylor, C.   8, 173
Thompson, E. P.   35
Thompson, G.   52
Tilly, C.   143
Tönnies, F.   6, 56, 173
Toulmin, S.   2, 27
Touraine, A.   3, 5, 123–41, 144, 146, 180, 182, 186
Trend, D.   186
Turner, B. S.   8, 56
Turner, S.   2

University of Berlin, the   34
Urry, J.   51, 54

Varela, F.   67
Vico, G.   20

Wacquant, L.   2
Wagner, P.   5, 7
Wallerstein, I.   48, 56, 70
Weber, M.,   6, 8, 18–19, 25, 32, 44, 51, 55, 83, 179
Weber, S.   8
Wildavsky, A.   159
Wuthnow, R.   36

Zolo, D.   51